PT
405
.Z34
1984

     Zammito, John H., 1948-
       The great debate : "Bolshevism" and
the literary left in Germany, 1917-
1930 / John H. Zammito. -- New York :
P. Lang, c1984.
       208 p. ; 23 cm.   (American
university studies. Series IX,
History ; vol. 4)
   Bibliography: p. 183-208.
   ISBN 0-8204-0074-2
    1. Authors, German--20th century--political
and social views. 2. German Literature--20th
century--History and criticism. 3. Communism
and literature. 4. Socialism and Literature.
5. Germany--Politics and government--1918-
1933. 6. Soviet Union--History--Revolution,

                       (continued)

       WaOE   83-49096//r85

The Great Debate

American University Studies

Series IX
History

Vol. 4

PETER LANG
New York · Berne · Frankfurt am Main

John H. Zammito

The Great Debate

'Bolshevism' and the Literary Left in Germany, 1917–1930

PETER LANG
New York · Berne · Frankfurt am Main

Library of Congress Cataloging in Publication Data

Zammito, John H., 1948–
The Great Debate.

(American University Studies. Series IX, History;
v. 4)
Includes bibliographical references.
1. Authors, German – 20th Century – Political and Social
Views. 2. German Literature – 20th Century – History and
Criticism. 3. Germany – Politics and Government – 1918–
1933. 4. Soviet Union – History – Revolution, 1917–1921.
5. Communism and Literature. 6. Socialism and Literature.
I. Title. II. Series.
PT405.Z34 1984   830'.9'358   83-49096
ISBN 0-8204-0074-2
ISSN 0740-0462

CIP-Kurztitelaufnahme der Deutschen Bibliothek

Zammito, John H.:
The Great Debate: 'Bolshevism' and the Literary
Left in Germany, 1917–1930 / John H. Zammito.
– New York; Frankfurt am Main; Berne:
Lang, 1984.
(American University Studies: Ser. 9,
History; Vol. 4)
ISBN 0-8204-0074-2

NE: American University Studies / 09

Printed by Lang Druck, Inc., Liebefeld/Berne (Switzerland)

TABLE OF CONTENTS

Acknowledgements 6

Introduction 7

I.   The Bolshevik Revolution and
      "Cultural Bolshevism" in Germany, 1917-1919 11

II.   Proletkult in Germany: The Left-Radical Debates
      Over the Relation of the Intellectual to the
      Proletariat, 1920-1924 57

III. The Writer and the Party: The Split Between the
      Negativists and the Communists, 1925-1930 81

IV.   The Left-Radical Controversy over Alfred Döblin's
      Wissen und Verändern! 113

V.   A New "Bolshevism"? — Brecht's Idiosyncratic
      Communism 139

Epilogue: The New Negativists and Brecht:
            The Case of Benjamin 169

Notes 183

ACKNOWLEDGMENTS

I wish gratefully to acknowledge grants from the Social Science Research Council, the German Academic Exchange Service and the Mabelle McLeod Lewis Memorial Foundation in support of this work. In addition I wish to thank the Historical Commission for Berlin and Brandenburg and the German Literary Archives in the Schiller National Museum, Marbach am Neckar, for their hospitality and assistance during my research. I thank my mentors Wolfgang Sauer, Martin Malia and Reinhard Bendix of the University of California at Berkeley for their encouragement in the project, and my colleague Robert Crunden of the University of Texas at Austin, who tried to salvage what there was of grace and substance in my early drafts. The faults that remain are entirely my own. For enduring the arduous genesis of this project without abandoning me, I dedicate this work to my wife.

John H. Zammito
Madrid, Spain
February 1984

INTRODUCTION

The left-wing intellectuals of the Weimar Republic enjoy a certain historical notoriety. Their role in the failure of the republic has been a matter of some controversy.[1] At the same time, the connection between their aesthetic and cultural innovations and their political impatience has drawn a good deal of attention.[2] While several historical interpreters have recognized divisions among these leftist writers, for the most part attention has focused on their confrontation with the fascist right or with the defenders of the existing republic.[3] Alternatively, historians seeking the origins of a "socialist literature" in Germany have evaluated this history in terms of the conformity of German writers of the Twenties to fixed party orthodoxies.[4] In this study an attempt will be made to follow and to formulate the most important debates *within* the radical left over the nature of their political commitment and over the relation of literature to politics.

In short, this is a study of the debate among committed left-radicals over the role and responsibility of the creative writer in society. The artist's social or political responsibility remains an unresolved issue to this day, particularly on the radical left, and has occasioned many new debates whose forms and arguments derive, often explicitly, from those this study will examine. The rift between Georg Lukacs and Bertolt Brecht in the Thirties and thereafter and, even more, the *interpretation* of their differences, is one such ongoing debate. Another revolves around the views articulated by the so-called "Frankfurt School," especially Adorno and Marcuse. One of the study's objectives is to show the historical background out of which these theoretical controversies arose. But even more, it aims to show how contingent the issues and the arguments are upon the historical context out of which they came to be formulated. The heart of this study is the inquiry into the term "Bolshevism" and its manifold and murky meanings in the German literary left of the Twenties. If the issue of the political responsibility of the creative writers was lifted high onto the plane of principle, it originated out of a very specific political crisis.

This historical investigation sets out from the realization that the First World War and its aftermath, the years of political collapse and revolution, constituted the decisive socio-political experience in German literary life. In and through the war crisis, the intellectual identity of the literary left crystallized into its decisive forms. The war, which harrowed the spirit of Expressionism and robbed it of many of its greatest voices, awakened the German avant-garde to political responsibility. Only then did a seriously "engaged Expressionism" emerge, centered around key literary journals like Franz Pfemfert's *Die Aktion*, René Schickele's *Die Weißen Blätter*, Wilhelm Herzog's *Das Forum*, Kurt Hiller's *Ziel-Jahrbücher* and Wieland Herzfelde's *Neue Jugend*. [5]

A turning point in this literary opposition came in 1917. The Russian Revolution and the intervention of the United States in the European war removed the last ideological rationalizations which could sustain "progressive" intellectual compliance with the German war effort. For some German literary intellectuals, the impact of the Russian Revolution went beyond this. It seemed to offer a possible world-historical meaning to the carnage. It suggested that the war had brought the old order to dissolution and opened an epoch of revolution leading to greater social justice. For others, the Bolshevik Revolution signalled an even greater catastrophe than the war itself, ushering in a red tyranny and compromising the socialist utopia. Thus, the Bolshevik Revolution exerted a profoundly disruptive impact on the literary left in Germany: with the introduction of the issue of "Bolshevism," the apparent solidarity of anti-war Expressionism was shattered. The experience of the German Revolution of 1918-1919 fell, for most of these intellectuals, under the rubric of this "Bolshevism," and the failure of that revolution fixed in them a permanent hostility to a republican government which used fear of Bolshevism as an instrument of political hegemony. The literary left tended to filter all subsequent political experiences during the republic through the paradigms fashioned during its birth pains.

Once the hopes of the revolution of 1918-1919 were dashed, the literary left struggled to develop a viable stance in opposition to the regime. Conflicting concerns for intellectual integrity and for political integrity, however, tended to polarize them into hostile camps. Some chose a purist, "idealist" withdrawal into strictly literary pursuits. Others opted for immediate political action as counterpart of spontaneously revolutionary masses. Still others could accept neither the established government nor the tactics or organizational strictures of the revolutionary parties, yet refused at the same time to withdraw from social criticism. They seemed reduced to a pure "negativism" – a term used by Kurt Tucholsky in 1919 to defend his viewpoint, and by Walter Benjamin in the early 1930s to condemn Tucholsky and other literary leftists for their failure to align more closely with the Communist Party.[6] At issue in all these stances was the idea of "Bolshevism."

"Bolshevism" as an orientation in the German literary left was an *image*, oftentimes accompanied by little real understanding of Russian affairs, which was grounded in the revolutionary situation of 1917-1920 with its soaring hopes and devastating reversals. The image intensified its grip on the literary left with the failure of the revolution, as it came increasingly to be seen as the only alternative left them in a darkening world. The course of this "Bolshevist" infatuation had three phases over the years 1917-1930. The first phase, Berlin Dada, lasted from 1917 to 1920, and was characterized by revolutionary rage, destructive to the point of nihilism, whose great slogan was the equation, "Dada is Bolshevism in Art." The second phase set in with the disintegration of Dada at the close of the revolutionary struggle in 1920. Disappointed in their own efforts and awed by Russian success, the literary left made a cult of the proletariat, a German *Proletkult*, in the years 1920-1923. After the last, artificially incited revolutionary tremors ceased in 1923, a new and problematic phase began, the "Bolshevization" of the German Communist Party, i.e. the imposition of a party bureaucracy created and managed by Moscow, together with the increasing repression of dissenting intellectual views within the party. Great innovations in Marxist theory growing out of the Central European revolutionary situation – the works of Lukacs and Korsch – came to be counteracted by the crippled conception of Marxism which grew out of Stalin's interpretation of Lenin and, more ominously, by the ruthless

9

enforcement of Stalinist policies.

As "Bolshevism" went through these phases, those who found themselves at odds both with the established government and with the orthodox Marxist opposition became more numerous and the controversy between them and those loyal to the party of the Comintern more pointed. The bulk of this study focuses on these culminating debates between "negativists" and hard-line party writers. While a Johannes R. Becher could accommodate himself fully to the Comintern and to the cultural influence of the "Bolshevik" writers organizations in the Soviet Union, more conflicted and complex responses came from two of the greatest writers of the literary left in Weimar Germany, Alfred Döblin and Bertolt Brecht. Their confrontation with "Bolshevism" in the later Twenties forms the climax of this work.

In documenting the arguments of such figures as George Grosz, Wieland Herzfelde, Johannes R. Becher, Alfred Döblin, Erwin Piscator and Bertolt Brecht, this study will follow the most important debates within the radical left, staying very close to the text and the context of the writers themselves in order to stress the historical concreteness of their concerns as well as how complicated their stances were. These Weimar debates should not be read as esoteric in-fighting among dilettante political writers but rather as paradigmatic controversies meriting close historical attention. In the Weimar years the meanings of intellectual integrity and political integrity were probed and their limits of compatibility tested and overrun. The Weimar literary left's obsession with social commitment and political relevance raised fundamental questions about the purpose of intellectual action as well as the situation and opportunity of an intellectual in society, matters which have lost none of their relevance today.

Chapter One

THE BOLSHEVIK REVOLUTION AND "CULTURAL BOLSHEVISM" IN GERMANY, 1917-1919

> If earlier [i.e., during the anti-war phase] one
> was labelled an ideologue or a utopian, now one
> is — because he struggles (not simply on ideal,
> but also on real-political grounds) for purity in
> political life, against shameful compromises
> with the bearers of the old regime — what is
> one called because of this? A Bolshevik...
> — W. Herzog, editorial in *Republik*,
>   January 6, 1919

The distinctive left-radicalism of the German Twenties derived from the experience of the revolutionary interlude in European politics from 1917 to 1920, and even more specifically, from the linked Russian and German Revolutions. Literary radicalism in Germany was caught up in "Bolshevism," yet the relation is anything but simple and direct. Often the epithet "Cultural Bolshevist" was thrust upon figures whose knowledge of or allegiance to the particular Bolshevik Revolution or the emergent Soviet state were quite limited. Nonetheless, "Bolshevism" — as *image* far more than reality — proved central in the literary left experience. In this chapter the relation between "Bolshevism" and the literary left in Weimar Germany will be traced out in three phases. First, how did the image of "Bolshevism" impact the German Revolution of 1918-1919? Second, how did the most notorious German left-radicals, the Berlin Dadaists, respond to this political experience? And finally, how did the entire literary left wrestle with the issues posed by the idea of "Bolshevism?" In answering these three questions, the context and conflicts which underlie the entire study come clearly to the fore.

The Image of "Bolshevism" and the German Revolution of 1918-1919

One of the most important developments in the historiography of the First World War might very well be the stress which has come to be placed on the *illusions* which animated its policy makers and participants.[1] That same attentiveness to illusions and images has its place in evaluating the nature of the revolutionary experience in Germany in 1918-1919. In particular, the illusions and images surrounding the key term "Bolshevism" seem to be critical in the dynamic of the German Revolution. "Bolshevism" did not necessarily signify — and usually lacked altogether — an accurate understanding of the realities of the Russian situation. Indeed, after November 1917 there tended to be a conflation of all Russian revolutionary developments with "Bolshevism." The soviets were taken to have been "Bolshevik" from the outset, with everything leading necessarily to the triumph of Lenin. Those who used the term "Bolshevism" most glibly in the Central European context of 1918-1919 came usually from the extreme right, stimulated by white-Russian emigres. They were part of a widespread Western reaction, almost hysterical, which regarded Bolshevism as an apocalyptic retribution for the "great" war.[2]

Even more significant for the concrete developments of the German Revolution of 1918-1919 was the image of "Bolshevism" which infused German socialism. Gerhard Bassler has observed: "The Germans learned from the Russians before November 1918 the methods, the symbols, and the forms of a revolution. They had had no revolution for seventy years; there would have certainly been no revolution had the Russian Revolution not preceded, and had shown them how to bring about peace, namely by way of a mass strike, by what form to bring it about — by way of the councils, and what symbols to use — the red flag and the socialist program."[3] While there is a good deal of truth to that, it remains that there was at least an equal measure of autochthonous rebelliousness in Central Europe. Of far greater importance here, however, is the large measure in which the image of "Bolshevism" *thwarted* the German Revolution. The spectre of Bolshevism so distorted political perception among German socialists that those who misunderstood the nature of the revolutionary movement – the extreme leftists and above all the right wing of the majority socialists – had the initiative in 1918-1919. The majority socialists used the argument of "Bolshevik excesses" to quell revolutionary unrest and to defend collaboration with bourgeois and conservative forces. At the same time, the extreme left indulged in the imagery of "Bolshevism" as a device to incite restiveness. This failure of vision among both majority socialists and left-radicals, addled by the red mirage of "Bolshevism," contributed mightily to their failures of political leadership and to the missed opportunity of the revolutionary situation.

The red mirage of "Bolshevism" played a decisive role in the politics of the Majority Social Democratic Party.[4] The events in Russia, above all the Bolshevik dissolution of the Constituent Assembly in January 1918 and the bloody civil war that followed, had hardened the ideological split between German and Russian Marxism into a clash of "democracy versus dictatorship." The "excesses" of Bolshevism violated the SPD's long-standing commitments to the democratic principles of parliament, universal suffrage and civil rights. All the accomodationist and reformist tendencies which emerged in the majority SPD both before and during the war now hardened into a closed-mindedness especially vis à vis their former comrades in the left-socialist parties. The SPD leadership could not believe in the threat of counter-revolution. The fear of economic collapse, of Entente intervention, of Bolshevik subversion and domestic chaos dominated its concern. From the SPD vantage, by 1918 most of the legitimate aspirations of the German working class had been achieved: a democratic republic based on universal suffrage with socialist parties in the governing cabinet, recognition of civil rights, collective bargaining and the eight hour day. The SPD's primary concern was to reconcile other strata of society to the achievements of October-November 1918, not to extend them. More comfortable with and proud of its coalition with the bourgeois parties of the October 1918 government and later of the Weimar Coalition than with the "Socialist Republic" and alliance with the USPD, the leadership of the SPD pressed for a National Assembly at the earliest opportunity,

so that this entity, with the participation of all parties, could reconstitute German politics.

The revolution and the council movement proved an inconven-
ience under such circumstances. The SPD party newspaper, *Vorwärts*, equated the German council movement with Bolshevism,
terrorism and dictatorship. Yet to describe the domestic conflicts
in terms of "Bolshevism" was willful distortion. In fact, the council
movement was in the main loyal to the SPD. As a creation of the
rank and file of the working class, however, it did run afoul of the
oligarchical traditions of the German socialist movement. The iron
law of oligarchy had so structured the mentality of the party bureaucracy that it found it inconceivable that such spontaneity could
exist. The workers on their own "did not constitute agents capable
of action."[5] They required the mediation of party and union organization. Hence the emergence of councils could only be explained
by a conspiracy hostile to established German socialism, in a word,
by "Bolshevism."

From the outset, the majority SPD leadership had striven to
forestall revolution in November 1918. Revolution before armistice,
it was felt, would link socialism too closely with defeat. This seems
quite plausible in view of the subsequent "stab-in-the-back" legend
which blamed "November criminals" on the home front for Germany's defeat. Yet such reservations had not kept the SPD from entering
the October government which initiated the armistice negotiations,
and it was already implicated in the collapse. Still, a good deal of
the political heat for defeat might have gone to the Hohenzollern
dynasty if it had remained in power. This consideration dovetailed
with the second basis for SPD opposition to revolution: they believed
monarchism was too entrenched in the masses for democracy to
develop in Germany under the form of a republic. In the words of
the SPD party chairman, Friedrich Ebert, "the German people is not
yet ready for a republic and must first be educated up to that level.
That could best happen under a democratic monarchy."[6]

As the revolution grew in force, however, the SPD found itself
compelled to adopt it or be overrun by it. With great tactical finesse
the SPD succeeded in coopting leadership in the revolution while it
preserved a maximum of continuity with the parliamentary majority

14

government of October. When it became apparent that the old government could not be saved, the last Imperial Chancellor, Prince Max von Baden, transfered the Chancellorship to Ebert. Such an action had no legally binding character, but it carried with it the provisional cooperation of the German bureaucracy and military. With this fictive transfer of power, the old regime abetted Ebert's desires for continuity. He prefered to understand his authority as deriving from this arrangement rather than accepting the sovereignty of the revolution. The administrative apparatus cooperated with Ebert personally, and through him with his party, but it reserved its loyalty for the old regime. In his turn, Ebert made it clear that the problems uppermost in his mind − peace, food supply, withdrawal of the front armies and demobilization economic planning − could not be tackled without the expert participation of the old bureaucracy.

The truce with the old regime extended even to the arch-foes of German socialism, the Junker officer corps and the magnates of heavy industry. The war economy had accustomed the SPD leadership to accommodations with these elites. It had also taught the latter how to deal with the "loyal opposition" in the working class. They understood and employed the only appropriate tactic left them after the collapse of the old regime: cooperation with the moderating influences in the revolting classes until such time as power could be recouped. The military elite moved most swiftly. The Hohenzollern dynasty gone, Ludendorff in exile, the new adjutant of the Supreme Military Command, General Groener, moved decisively.[7] On November 10, 1918, in a telephone conversation, Groener came to an accord with Ebert to fight the "Bolshevik menace" of revolution in Germany. Military units were sent to Berlin as early as December 1918 to support Ebert in quelling the rebellion. In early December these units became involved in an abortive *Putsch* in Ebert's favor but ostensibly without his knowledge or consent. On Christmas Eve 1918, units of these forces were sent to attack the rebellious People's Marine Division, garrisoned in the center of Berlin. That exercise proved a fiasco. Citizens of Berlin were able to mix with the troops and dissuade them from attacking. As a result of this, the army set about culling units from the front armies which could be relied upon for discipline and loyalty in the looming domestic conflicts: the *Freikorps.*

A few days after the Ebert-Groener agreement, in November 1918 Carl Legien, chairman of the socialist unions, came to an agreement with Hugo Stinnes, representing German industrialists, regarding the nature of industrial relations in the new republic.[8] The concrete concessions made by the industrialists were largely forfeit by virtue of the revolution itself. By contrast, the union concessions of private property rights put drastic restrictions on the economic policy of the new socialist government. As a result, big industry was eventually able to reestablish itself as "lord in its own house" and to rescind the bulk of concessions tactically surrendered in November 1918.[9] Together, the Ebert-Groener and Stinnes-Legien agreements stymied the German revolution of 1918-1919.

The revolution was defeated not only by conservative sabotage and SPD obstruction but by the inadequacies of those who fostered it, above all the USPD, the creation and the embodiment of the revolutionary interlude of 1917-1920.[10] The USPD emerged in spring 1917 as the umbrella organization for three distinct socialist factions: the *Sozialdemokratische Arbeitsgemeinschaft,* a group of dissident but moderate SPD Reichstag delegates, led by Hugo Haase and united by opposition to the war; the *Spartakus-Bund,* a loose confederation of revolutionary socialist intellectuals led by Rosa Luxemburg and Karl Liebknecht, who advocated internationalism of a Zimmerwald stripe; and the *Revolutionäre Obleute,* the radical shop-stewards organization of Berlin factory workers, led by Richard Müller and Ernst Däumig, opposed not only to the war effort but to the union oligarchy.[11]

The USPD as a party institution was the creation and the concern almost exclusively of the moderate wing derived from the *Sozialdemokratische Arbeitsgemeinschaft.* This wing provided the majority of the party's administrative leadership, parliamentary representation and political press. The dominant figures were Hugo Haase, Rudolf Hilferding and, as ideological mentor, Karl Kautsky. Ironically, the moderate wing's devotion to the party as an institution and commitment to unity at all costs, proved the downfall of its particular

16

political aspirations. The Spartacists and the Revolutionary Shop Stewards were in the USPD but not really of it, and their actions underminded the moderates. Both the Spartacists and the Revolutionary Shop Stewards had resolved by summer 1918 upon a revolutionary uprising. While the moderates were sympathetic, Haase, Hilferding and others in the leadership had deep reservations about the success of a revolution against the seemingly so firmly entrenched military and governmental elite. In addition, certain inherent difficulties in party organization – the principle of decentralization of command, the weakness of the party press, the geographical limitations of party strength to certain highly industrialized regions and cities – restricted the operative efficacy of the party and induced the leadership to confine its activities to legal protest in the Reichstag.

In the first days of November 1918, as rumors of sailors mutinies on the Baltic reached Berlin, Haase prevailed upon the leaders of the Revolutionary Shop Stewards, Müller and Däumig, to put off a planned uprising. Then he set off for Kiel to investigate first hand the sailors' mutiny. When the revolutionary movement swept into Berlin on November 9, 1918, consequently, it caught both the USPD leadership and the shop stewards by surprise. The crucial leadership of the revolutionary movement in the capital city was up for grabs, and in the jockeying of the night of November 9-10, it was the moderate SPD which acted most effectively.[12] By the morning of the 10th, it had secured the decisive support of the Berlin military garrisons. Arriving in Berlin that morning, Haase had to prevail upon the divergent groups in his party to accept a coalition government with the SPD. The move remained extremely unpopular among the Spartacists and the Revolutionary Shop Stewards, and they proceeded over the next two months to undermine the efficacy of the USPD delegates in the governing cabinet.

This left-radical wing within the USPD was also caught up in a mirage of "Bolshevism," albeit a positive one. Dominated by radical workers in big cities like Berlin with large-scale, high-technology industry, the Revolutionary Shop Stewards lacked sophistication in Marxist theory and organizational tactics beyond the plant level. They were inclined to follow reasoning by analogy to "Bolshevism." In the "confined revolutionary world" of Berlin they saw themselves the German analogue of the Petrograd Soviet.[13] The Berlin experience — the factory environment, the big-city radicalism, the excitement of capital city politics, and above all the *journées*, the days of great mass demonstrations — captivated their imagination. The council movement as they wished it to be seemed an irresistible revolutionary force.[14] The few intellectuals in their ranks, notably Ernst Däumig, assured them that the council model of revolution characterized not only the Russian Revolutions of 1905, February 1917 and October 1917, but also the Paris Commune and the entire span of Marxist revolution. In advocating "dictatorship of the proletariat" with explicit reference to Bolshevism, the Revolutionary Shop Stewards meant the political hegemony of the council movement as a *majority* revolution. They were convinced that the council movement in Germany embodied the political and social will of the vast majority of the German people. It did not so much represent dictatorship as an advance to true democracy.

Yet, in their fervor, the shop stewards failed to pay attention to the actual will of the council movement.[15] By opposing the idea of a National Assembly at least up through the First Councils Congress, by conducting a continual skirmish with the government coalition through the executive council of Berlin workers and soldiers councils, and by calling for a dictatorship of the councils beyond the political will of the councils themselves, the shop stewards movement managed to alienate the mass base in whom they wished to vest sovereignty. Even when what they proposed was in the best interest of the council movement, their vision remained too circumscribed by their local experience and too suspect beyond it, as the elections and the outcome of the First Councils Congress in December 1918 revealed. The preponderant majority in the Congress was won by the SPD.

If the Revolutionary Shop Stewards retained a minority of representation within the Councils Congress, the Spartacists failed even to get Luxemburg and Liebknecht elected to the Congress, for they had virtually no following in the rank and file of the council movement.[16] Despite their rhetoric of "all power to the workers and soldiers councils," the Spartacists remained predominantly an intellectual circle. When that circle was broadened at the close of 1918, the new elements which joined the Spartacists proved significantly different.[17] At the mass base, a number of previously apolitical workers and soldiers had become politicized by hunger and by war to such an extent that they drifted to the far left extreme of German socialism. Aware of a distant but momentous revolution in the east, they were enthusiastic for "Bolshevism," but for them it meant little more than "revolution now" — an image and a rallying cry for impulsive rebellion. This emergent mass base on the far left, insignificant compared with the SPD or USPD bases, and without organizational discipline, destabilized the politics of the disciplined radical left. Misled by the fanfare of left-extremist ideologists, these forces entered into a series of political misadventures which robbed them of their greatest leaders and of all prospect of political success.

It is important to note that the left-extremist proponents of "Bolshevism" often lacked any grounding in Marx and certainly grasped neither Leninist theories of organization nor the very complex trajectory of the two Russian revolutions of 1917.[18] These factions proved to be the targets of Lenin's subsequent polemic, *"Left-Wing" Communism: An Infantile Disorder* (April 1920). Yet at the close of 1918 these groups were able to intervene decisively in the politics of the German radical left. In November 1918 the left-extremist factions — the *Bremer Linken*, the Hamburg and Dresden circles and similar elements in Berlin — had constituted themselves the International Communists of Germany (IKD), and at the end of December 1918 they threatened to form a Communist Party of Germany with or without Spartacist participation.

In view of the weakness at the base, the Spartacist leaders, especially Luxemburg and the tactician Jogliches, did not wish to leave the USPD umbrella, although they had long since followed an independent line. Luxemburg realized there was a large leftist base in the USPD and with time she hoped to use it to win the entire party over to the Spartacist position. As a first step, she wanted a party congress of the USPD, where a forthright ideological discussion would clarify the political lines in the party. Two forces thwarted this effort. First, the moderate USPD leadership, above all Haase, wished to leave the situation of the party undefined in order to keep all possible elements, however divergent in goal or tactic, within the party fold. But second, a growing fascination with rebellion was emerging within the Spartacist leadership itself, with Liebknecht increasingly captivated by the revolutionary ardor of the extremists in Berlin. This made it difficult for Luxemburg to resist the IKD ultimatum and the call for immediate action, for she feared losing initiative to the far left. The Spartacists therefore joined in the December 1918-January 1919 founding congress of the Communist Party of Germany (KPD).

This proved a fatal capitulation. The founding congress was dominated by the left-fringe elements.[19] After doing the Spartacists the honor of electing them into leadership positions, they proceeded to reject the Spartacist program of participation in the elections for the National Assembly and to insist upon direct action and an immediate dictatorship of the councils. Their adamance on these points cost Luxemburg the collaboration of the Revolutionary Shop Stewards. They had negotiated with the KPD Congress regarding a merger, but rejected the platform of the new KPD as "putschist."

The momentum of events had moved out of the control of both Luxemburg and the shop steward leadership, however. Swayed by the unrealistic optimism of Karl Liebknecht of the Spartacists and Georg Ledebour of the left-wing USPD, a revolt broke out in Berlin in the first days of January 1919.[20] This so-called "Spartacist Uprising" was forced on Müller and Däumig. Though only a fringe of the left was responsible for the uprising, however, the entire left suffered defeat with it.

The SPD had assumed exclusive control of the government of the Republic in the aftermath of the Christmas Eve incident, for that had provoked the resignation of the USPD delegates in the cabinet. When the uprising broke out in January 1919, the SPD resorted to military force to suppress the Berlin dissidents. *Freikorps* units were brought it, despite the pleas from local trade union delegations and from moderates in the USPD to seek a negotiated settlement. The *Freikorps* units demonstrated ruthless efficiency in smashing the resistance of rebels occupying the *Vorwärts* publishing house and then subjugating the Berlin population to martial law. They sought out and executed Luxemburg and Liebknecht and imprisoned Ledebour. With that, the revolutionary impetus was shattered.

In the National Assembly elections of January 19, 1919, the socialists failed to win a majority. Part of the explanation of their defeat must be the bitterness and withdrawal of a substantial segment of the working class. In addition, over the interval November 1918 - January 1919, a pronounced change of heart — or perhaps recovery of nerve — had transpired in the bourgeois classes.[21] In November 1918 a progressive commitment had seemed forthcoming from the bourgeois parties. With the old authority removed, these parties felt especially responsible for an orderly resolution of pressing national difficulties, and served willingly in administrative posts under the direction of revolutionary bodies. In its major editorial statement, Germany's premier liberal-bourgeois newspaper, the *Frankfurter-Zeitung*, endorsed the new order and a "democracy of social justice."[22] This enthusiasm for the new order found its classic expression in the founding manifesto of the German Democratic Party (DDP), with its proposal to overcome class conflict and to cooperate with the socialists in building a new Germany. Especially with the SPD's clear affirmation of a National Assembly and hence of bourgeois participation in the new government, the middle classes recovered their nerve and accepted the Republic (provisionally) as a *fait accompli*. They even evinced a mild appreciation for the bloodlessness and efficiency of the revolution. Just as swiftly and more ominously, however, a parallel tendency emerged: the reassertion of narrow class interest. A manifestation of this tendency to consolidate on the basis of narrow class interest were the many *Bürgerräte* which sprang up in November 1918.

Middle class interest groups gathered as early as November 28, 1918, to call for greater emphasis on nationalism and more sustained resistance to socialization in the emergent liberal parties. Under the pressure of the immediately approaching National Assembly elections, these interest groups were able to intervene substantially in defining the platform and organization of the new party. In addition, old party functionaries who had been without influence in founding the new party, now proved indispensable for their organizational skills and election contacts. As a result, the nominees and the platform of the DDP reflected the viewpoint of the narrower class interests or the old fashioned political style of the more conservative elements.

The composition of the liberal party delegations to the National Assembly confimed the conservative trend of the politics of the previous months. Over two thirds of the DDP delegates and even more of the DVP delegates came from the elite — government officials, lawyers, academics and industrialists. Hardly reformist, their political orientation was rooted in the Wilhelmian order, and their attitudes toward a "democracy of social justice" were quite cool. The reluctant republicanism of one half of the liberal leadership was matched by the old-fashioned liberalism of the other half, with its paternalistic-idealistic resonances of the "Socialists of the Chair" and the "Parties of Dignitaries" of a bygone day. Toward the few "men of good will" who had founded the party and striven to ally with the new socialist government, this new leadership felt suspicious. Symptomatically, Theodor Heuß complained of these "leftists" in the party that they were "inwardly corroded by the metropolis."[23]

The *Vossische Zeitung* summed up the position of the bourgeois parties:

> In our view, the workers councils, in so far as
> they claim political rights, are an absolutely
> undemocratic set-up and *therefore must disappear*
> *as a political institution* as soon as the National
> Assembly has taken the reins into its hands; the
> same goes for the soldiers councils. *Agreement*
> *with this thesis on the social-democratic side*
> is the test of the presence of a true democratic
> spirit which rejects all class domination, in our
> view; here is the *indispensable premise.* (italics
> in original)[24]

The SPD leadership proved to everyone's satisfaction that it felt no warmer toward the council movement than did the bourgeois parties. The government took steps to accelerate the disbanding of the soldiers councils and the communal councils in January 1919.

As for the councils themselves, Philipp Scheidemann confided to an American journalist on February 25, 1919: "No member of the cabinet has any thought or ever had any thought to integrate the council system in any form, be it in the constitution, be it in administrative apparatus."[25]

22

The campaign against the council movement in Germany was buttressed by a mammoth anti-Bolshevik publicity campaign, aimed not only at alarming the German middle classes against a "Bolshevik analogy" at home, but at motivating Germany to participate in the Entente powers' anti-Bolshevik interventionism in Russia and thus winning support from the established bourgeois regimes in the West for the reassertion of bourgeois hegemony in Germany.[26] Taken together with the majoritiy socialist "betrayal" of the revolution, this bourgeois anti-Bolshevism provoked an unmitigated rage among the left-wing literary intellectuals, especially in Berlin, who found their last hope for some redeeming outcome to the horror of the war, a progressive revolution, dashed beyond retrieval. The result was an intentionally extreme and provocative affimation of "Bolshevism" — Berlin Dada.

Berlin Dada: The Origin of "Cultural Bolshevism"

Prior to the Great War, Marxism had not been a significant force in German avant-garde circles. They were far more taken with anarchism. But the war and the Russian Revolution changed all that. They introduced "Bolshevism" into the avant-garde. As with the political image of "Bolshevism" we have just considered, this term had little determinate basis in Russia or Leninist theories of revolution. It was less a political reality than an image, an intellectual vision which, moreover, represented a great deal which Lenin expressly disdained. The most notorious usage of the term in this way came with the Berlin Dada movement's proclamation that Dada was German Bolshevism.[27] The Dadaists claimed that Bolshevism, like Dada, aimed to dispell all lingering elements of the "swindle" of European bourgeois civilization. In drawing this equation, they created the context for the reactionary epithet "Cultural Bolshevism," and accentuated the dread of established European culture that Bolshevism and avant-garde modernism of the type represented by the Dada literati represented a new and fatal barbarism.

Perhaps the most important early advocate of "Bolshevism" in the Berlin avant-garde was Franz Pfemfert, heroic editor of the

Expressionist and antiwar journal, *Die Aktion*. [28] Pfemfert had established himself before the war as the avant-garde's leading editor, and also as a figure committed to the politicization of German literary life. His wartime opposition made *Die Aktion* the beacon to which young German intellectuals, appalled and outraged by the war, turned for guidance and eventually for self-expression. In the pages of his journal such leading left-wing figures as Franz Jung, Erwin Piscator and Carl Zuckmayer published their early work. [29] Around Pfemfert and his journal gathered the cream of the literary opposition. Hence his political influence was substantial.

The roots of Pfemfert's radicalization lay in his bitterness over the war's outbreak and especially the betrayal by the SPD and by a number of his literary colleagues in supporting the war effort. He could never forgive those who took the wrong stand in 1914. That left him few friends and fewer heroes. Among them, however, were two crucial ones: Rosa Luxemburg and Karl Liebknecht. Especially under the influence of the latter after spring 1918, Pfemfert began to orient his thought and his journal toward the new prospect opened by the Bolshevik Revolution.

Censorship circumscribed the explicitness with which Pfemfert could articulate his new viewpoint until the collapse of the old cabinet and the creation of a new government coalition in October 1918, in which, for the first time in German history, the Majority Social Democratic Party participated. Pfemfert lost no time in showing his colors − flaming red. [30] He called upon the public not to be misled. Scheidemann and company were still in the service of the old order. Their "conversion" to socialist democracy and peace could not be trusted. They were not worthy to lead the new Germany, because they had fatally compromised themselves in the war. As evidence Pfemfert reprinted the parliamentary record of the proceedings against Karl Liebknecht for treason during the war, in which the majority socialists repudiated Liebknecht's call for a peace of understanding.

The November Revolution revealed the full extent of Pfemfert's radicalization. On the sixteenth of November, *Die Aktion* greeted the revolution with a manifesto, "The Call of the Anti-Nationalist Socialist Party, German Branch," addressed to all revolutionary socialists in nations still dominated by capitalism.[31] It proclaimed, "German militarism has collapsed. The Revolution is on the march!" Essentially it warned against those in the German socialist camp who called for "unity" and meant thereby accommodation with the forces which had led Germany into the First World War. "Soldiers, workers, women of the Revolution, be not misled!" the manifesto advised; those who had supported the old regime in the war could not now be accepted as allies in the revolutionary struggle. The masses had to retain their purity. The "social patriots" had betrayed the proletariat into the hands of the militaristic-capitalist regime, and the international working class could not submit to their leadership. The key points of the manifesto were, then, its clear internationalism, its vehement rejection of cooperation with the "social patriots" and its revolutionary rhetoric.

Other aspects of the radicalism of the *Aktion-Kreis* and the so-called Antinational Socialist Party came in two further manifestos which followed the first immediately. "Comrades!" by Hans Siemsen, proclaimed the key sense of solidarity with Bolshevik Russia as "the only actual representative of the international proletariat and of the revolution."[32] Siemsen called upon German socialists and the proletariat everywhere to resist the Allied campaign against Soviet Russia. This stance in favor of Bolshevik Russia in November 1918 placed *Die Aktion* on the far left in the German political spectrum. In a third manifesto, which followed Siemsen's, Pfemfert set forth the final element in the left-radical program: total opposition to the National Assembly and to any accommodation with the bourgeois-democratic elements in Germany.[33]

In the next issue of *Die Aktion*, November 30, 1918, Pfemfert reiterated this last point with even greater vehemence in his editorial "National Assembly *is* Counter-Revolution."[34] He claimed the revolution was in danger since capitalists and warmongers had taken up a strategy to turn the revolution to their profit — the National Assembly. "They know that Karl Marx said 'A democratic republic is the best form of government for the exploiters.'" Against the National Assembly and "capitalist" democracy, Pfemfert called for "true" democracy, the "real, total dominion of the people" [*die wirkliche, restlose Herrschaft des Volkes*]. That meant the rule of

Workers-and-Soldiers-Councils. Pfemfert called for the dictatorship of the proletariat (*Herrschaft der Werktätigen*).

Pfemfert's "Bolshevism" was still predominantly *political*, and can be seen to parallel that of the Revolutionary Shop Stewards and the Spartacists of the left wing of the Independent Social Democratic Party. Far more extreme and boisterous was a circle of younger men, many of whom he had sponsored in one way or another during the war years, for whom "Bolshevism" signified a posture of all out rejection of the established order and a license for radical cultural provocation: the Berlin Dada movement.

Dada in Berlin almost from its origins took on a distinctly political tenor. The antics of Dada were still there, but the orientation and the intention had a more radical and even revolutionary cast than its Zurich prototype.[35] The figure who has emerged as the source of this political turn is Franz Jung. He remains, despite a recent flurry of critical interest, one of the most enigmatic figures in the Berlin avant-garde.[36] Born in Neisse, Silesia in 1888, he was the son of a watchmaker with lively intellectual interests, including a passion for Nietzsche. Jung proved an unstable student, bouncing from Leipzig to Breslau to Munich, picking up a wife and a child and travelling as far afield as St. Petersburg in the process. By 1913 he emerged as a key figure in the Munich Expressionist journal *Revolution*. A member of Erich Mühsam's anarchist *Gruppe Tat*, Jung also became associated with the maverick psychoanalyst Otto Groß. Then, in late 1913, Jung moved to Berlin and became associated with the *Aktion-Kreis* of Franz Pfemfert. Eventually Groß joined Jung in Berlin and togerther they established their own journal, *Die freie Straße*. Before this transpired, Jung had further misadventures, provided this time by the First World War. Drafted, Jung was sent without training to the Russian front. He deserted and managed to get all the way to Vienna before being arrested and shipped back to prison in Berlin. Awaiting trial for desertion, one day Jung found his jailer came to release him. He gathered up his various manuscripts and made his way back into the Berlin avant-garde.

Perhaps it was through this time in jail that Jung developed his contacts with the underworld of left-extremists and war-resistors;

in any event, by 1916, he was active in this underground.[37] With Claire Öhring, soon to be his second wife, he became involved in forging papers for the revolutionary underground.[38] At the time he worked as a business journalist, and his business offices became a communications center for the revolutionaries. On the other hand, Jung was not at all versed in Marxism. He was one of those "infantile left-extremists" of whom Lenin was soon to complain.[39] His enthusiasm for "Bolshevism" had the flavor of a caper, not the seriousness of social revolution, and Jung communicated this to the entire Dada movement in Berlin.

In his autobiography, George Grosz characterized Jung as a "man of force," a "clever adventurer who shrank from nothing."[40] In the context of 1917-1919, such a personality proved very influential. Grosz proved Jung's prime convert in political Dada. Moreover, Grosz was by far the most gifted artist to become involved.[41] His works of the period are the closest things to masterworks that Berlin Dada was capable of producing. Grosz proved amenable to Jung's politicization because the experience of the First World War had harrowed the artist profoundly. If before the war Grosz had been merely a self-indulgent cynic, his military experience turned him into a nihilistic misanthrope. In his autobiography, Grosz gave expression to the outrage the war experience instilled in him:

> I defended no ideals and no beliefs; I defended
> myself. Beliefs? Haha! In what? In German
> heavy industry, those big profiteers? In our
> glorious generals? In the beloved fatherland?
> At least I had the guts to say what so many were
> thinking. Only it wasn't really guts so much
> as madness. What I saw filled me with disgust
> and contempt for mankind.[42]

Letters to Robert Bell from the war years substantiate this retrospective representation of his feelings. He wrote in September 1915 that he wished for a socialist revolution in which William II and the crown prince would go to the slaughterhouse, only the socialists were as corrupt as the dynasty.[43]

27

Grosz's hatred and contempt were not reserved for the masters of war. In 1916 he wrote that it filled him with esthetic pleasure to think of all the Germans dying on the field of honor, because "to be German always means to be tasteless, stupid, ugly, fat and inelastic..."[44] Grosz believed Germans were "without spirit," incapable of "objectively observing what is really going on." This was the product of German education, indoctrination with "attributes of stupifying reaction like God, Fatherland, militarism...," which transformed the individual into a "herd and mass animal."[45]

Grosz's initial experience in the military was brief. He never saw action, but he saw enough of military discipline to know he hated it. On his way to the front he was afflicted with a sinus infection and hospitalized, February 1915. A few months later, on May 11, 1915, he was released from service on a medical discharge and he made his way back to Berlin.[46] Upon his return to Berlin Grosz became acquainted with a young poet named Wieland Herzfelde who had had a similarly brief experience in the ranks, receiving a dishonorable discharge over Christmas 1914. Herzfelde counted double, because he had a brother, the artist John Heartfield (Helmut Herzfeld). To show his disdain for German war propaganda, the latter changed his name and insisted upon speaking English. The three men formed an inseparable team with a major impact on the culture of the avant-garde.[47] In 1916 the Herzfelde brothers decided to found a new journal. With it they hoped to accomplish the two things closest to their hearts: make a clear statement against the war and promote the success of their discovery, Grosz.

The whole Berlin avant-garde was enthusiastic about a pacifist journal. There were few outlets of protest left. Wilhelm Herzog's *Das Forum* had been censored out of existence. René Schickele's *Die Weißen Blätter* had to emigrate to Zurich. And Pfemfert's *Die Aktion*, the only remaining internal forum for protest, had to play a coy game with censors, utilizing circuitous techniques in the marginal notes, *Ich schneide die Zeit aus*, to get across its anti-war message. The avant-garde wanted to try something more. The Herzfelde brothers proposed to do it.

The first issue of their journal, *Neue Jugend*, appeared in July 1916. Its frontispiece was a poem by J.R. Becher, "To Peace," the most militantly pacifist work to appear in the entire life of the new journal.[48] It seemed an entirely literary-artistic issue − except for the marginalia at the end. Above all, there was a programmatic postscript: "We throw over our earlier standpoint of being a purely *literary* journal of the newest tendency: *it is time for all intellectuals to confront united their greatest enemy!*" It was clear they meant the war.[49] The program went on to welcome *all* European artists and intellectuals to contribute to the journal.

Such effrontery could not last long. By 1917 both Grosz and Wieland Herzfelde were drafted once again and sent to the front. Grosz was recalled to active military service in January 1917. The result was a nervous breakdown. He was placed in a sanitarium for some time, then in April he was sent home to Stolp. Finally, on May 20, 1917, he was declared permanently unfit for duty, whereupon he returned to Berlin.[50] This second bout with the warlords left Grosz even bleaker of spirit than the first, and it can safely be assumed he stockpiled the seemingly infinite reserves of hatred he carried into the next years in these early months of 1917.

When Grosz returned to Berlin in late May 1917, the censors had already banned the monthly publication of *Neue Jugend*. But John Heartfield had not abandoned the venture. Following the advice of Franz Jung, Heartfield obtained a license to found a new publishing house, the Malik-Verlag. Under its auspices, he turned *Neue Jugend* into an even more experimental venture. On May 23, 1917, the first of two weekly issues of *Neue Jugend* appeared. It was a radical departure from the staid format of the monthly journal. It appeared as a fourpage newspaper in red and black ink. The title was printed in great red lettering. Red facing and titles, especially in the advertisements, gave the issue a striking appearance. This was complemented by experimental typesetting in which numerous type-faces were used. The interior pages, devoted to a single essay, were printed in very large, very bold Roman type. The front page titles were set in a variety of faces. Particularly innovative were the advertisements, most of them for *Neue Jugend* itself. Several of these ads announced the creation of an Advertising Consulting Agency (*Reklame-Beratung*) at the *Neue Jugend*, promising to "hold a special propaganda evening the middle of next month for advertising specialists."[51] All these innovations were the work of Heartfield.

Grosz had a hand in the second weekly issue, which appeared in June 1917. This issue, printed in three colors (red, green and black), proved even more experimental in its setting and format than the first. In his contribution, Grosz took an extremely provocative swipe at high Germanic *Kultur*:

> Admit it, now, don't you get the creeps in art salons?
>   in oil painting galleries?
> In the literary soirees?
> Dear reader! A good football player has a great deal
> of value even though he doesn't write poetry or paint
> or make music!
> Is there any question?
> Do you know Schiller and Goethe —? — yes!
> *But can you ride a bicycle?*[52]

The extremes of Berlin Dada in 1919 would merely amplify and extend the provocation of these lines. Perhaps this is the origin of the idea for that rarest and most outrageous of Berlin Dada publications, *Jedermann sein eigner Fußball*. Yet all this transpired in 1917 and there was no sign yet of Dada in Berlin.

To be sure, Hülsenbeck had returned to Berlin from Zurich by this time and contributed extensive articles to *Neue Jugend*, but these articles had more to do with ecstatic Expressionism than with Dada. Only later in 1917 did the elements of Dada converge in the German capital. Jung, Raoul Hausmann and the circle at *Die Freie Straße* adopted Hülsenbeck as a figurehead for their own provocations. Jung himself made contact with the Grosz circle through John Heartfield. Berlin Dada was launched by the end of 1917, but it only came to prominence after the outbreak of the German Revolution when Dada declared its allegiance to "Bolshevism."

Franz Jung introduced Grosz and the Herzfelde brothers to "Bolshevism." By the end of December 1918, Jung brought the circle at the Malik-Verlag into contact with that other circle of Berlin "Bolshevism" around Franz Pfemfert's *Die Aktion*. On the last day of 1918, Rosa Luxemburg and Karl Liebknecht formed the

Communist Party of Germany, and Luxemburg herself issued membership cards to Grosz and the Herzfeldes. They thereupon put their considerable propaganda talents at the service of the revolutionary cause and political Dada was born.

Political Dada found expression in a number of actions and publications each of which tried to oudo the rest in provocation. These provocations extended from January 1919 through 1920, but reached their maximal intensity in the months of early 1919, at the height of the revolution. For these months Harry Graf Kessler's diaries prove a valuable source. He first mentioned this circle after a visit by Wieland Herzfelde on January 18, 1919, three days after the arrest and murder of Luxemburg and Liebknecht put a brutal close to the so-called "Spartacist insurrection." Kessler noted in his diaries that Herzfelde "frankly admitted to being a Communist and supporter of the Spartakus League."[53] Herzfelde explained the uprising to Kessler as "a spontaneous flare-up organized on amateur lines." He denied any Russian connection and insisted that even the leaders of the Spartacists had been surprised by the revolt.

Herzfelde had come to discuss the establishment of a new little magazine. Kessler and he agreed on a cheap, newspaper-format periodical to appear at irregular intervals and to be sold on the street. The tenor of the journal would be set by the "younger writers and artists...imbued with the Spartacus-Bolshevist outlook," whom Herzfelde represented. Herzfelde claimed Grosz and all those associated with the Malik-Verlag for this outlook. A few days later Kessler saw Simon Guttmann, who affirmed that "the young intellectuals are almost without exception against the Government" and that it was "impossible to exaggerate their bitterness."[54]

Ten days after his first visit, Herzfelde returned to Kessler with the proofs for his first issue. It was Kessler who suggested that the title of one of Grosz's drawings, *Jedermann sein eigner Fußball* be used for the periodical itself. Kessler recorded in Herzfelde's own words the principal aim of the new journal: "to sling mud at everything that Germans have so far held dear."[55] Grosz was to provide the bulk of the ammunition. Kessler thought all this might "let in a little fresh air and smooth the way for fresh ideas." On February 5, 1919, Kessler visited Grosz's studio, where they discussed art

31

before Grosz's unfinished painting, *Germany — a Winter's Tale.* Grosz indicated that art for art's sake did not interest him at all. "Grosz argued that art as such is unnatural, a disease..." All this led Kessler to consider him "a Bolshevist in the guise of a painter" and to conclude that "intellectually his thought processes are in part rudimentary and easily demolished."[56] The young theater director, Erwin Piscator, who met Grosz during the uproar of the January disturbances, got a different impression from evening discussions "in the 'Grosz ministry.'" There Grosz "presided, letting loose a thunderblast of wit and irony against the political situation, against the social order and its types."[57] His passion fueled the entire circle.

Piscator was born in 1893, the same year as Grosz, and five years before Brecht, to a pastor's family in provincial Germany.[58] Like Grosz and others here considered, Piscator looked back upon his schooling with disgust. In his youth, because of the desire of his father to raise him according to "simple, peasant-patriarchal" notions and Christianity, Piscator spent several years in the *Volksschule* rather than the *Vorschule*. He eventually attended the higher schools, only to reject their "petit bourgeois" mentality and to turn, under the influence of Nietzsche and Wilde, to aestheticism and poetry.

Again like his age-peer, Grosz, the war was the decisive event in Piscator's development. He was studying theater at Munich when the war broke out. "Everyone around me volunteered. Not me."[59] The generation that went to war with "Goethe and Nietzsche in their knapsacks" revealed only that they had not learned to think before August 1914. The war, for Piscator, signalled the bankruptcy of German culture and society. When he was eventually drafted, Piscator accepted the war as inevitable fate. He landed on the front at Ypern. His only relief came from *Die Aktion*, which he read at the front, and to which he contributed both to give vent to his protest and to achieve some measure of clarity in his own values.[60] After two years in the lines, he was assigned to a theater unit for entertaining front-line soldiers. There he met Wieland Herzfelde. This fateful contact drew him, in January 1919, after *Zusammenbruch* and revolution "feverishly toward Berlin, the 'bastion of Bolshevism.'"[61] Once there he swiftly joined the ranks of Dada, the Malik-Verlag and the KPD.

32

Grosz and his circle worked on the new journal into the first weeks of February. The first and only issue appeared on February 15, 1919. The front page carried a photo-montage by Heartfield, with the leaders of the new government displayed on a Japanese fan with the question "who is the handsomest?" Grosz's caricatures dominated the issue, but it included poems by Walter Mehring and Wieland Herzfelde's essay "Nein, Karl Marx!", which he claimed to have written in 1917 for the weekly edition of *Neue Jugend*. In his own words, this essay was "an acknowledgement of Marx as I understood him then: as the Liebknecht of his century, abandoned by those for whom he fought."[62] Harry Kessler commented on the essay as "only a beginning" in which "a good deal is childish, but a fresh breeze blows..."[63]

Walter Mehring has described how the new journal was distributed. The Dadaists hired a horse-drawn carriage and a bugler-band in top hats and tails and set out from the Gedächtniskirche eastward, selling their journal as they went. They were hooted on the Kurfürstendamm, but as they moved eastward the reception grew more cordial. By the time the police caught up with them at Alexanderplatz, they had sold the entire edition. The police forbade all further publication of the journal.[64]

The Dadaist met to discuss their success and develop a second journal. Carl Einstein suggested a new title, *Die Pleite* (Bankruptcy). The authorities were sure to ban it as well, he argued, and think how ridiculous the government would look banning bankruptcy. The title was accepted.[65] On March 5, 1919, Herzfelde visited Kessler with the first issue of the new journal *Die Pleite*. Kessler thought the Grosz caricatures brillant, and praised the one of Ebert as monarch in an easy-chair as a "masterpiece." On the other hand he found the texts "terribly pedestrian." He felt distaste for the "collection of manifestos, yelps and solemn pronouncements." He prefered "wit and colorfulness." Yet the Herzfelde circle insisted on a more political and agitational line. They repudiated their earlier "flippancy."[66] The literary space of the first issue of *Die Pleite* was taken up primarily with a reprint of the "Invitation to the First Congress of the Communist International." In their own commentary, "Total Bankruptcy confronts you," the Dadaists blasted the SPD for betraying the revolution. Grosz's caricatures constituted the documentation for their charges. Erwin Piscator has written of the discussions behind this shift away from mere flippancy. In the Dada circle in Berlin, Piscator noted, there was a great deal of discussion about art, but always from the point of view of politics. "We determined that if this art were to have any value it could only serve as a means for class struggle."[67] They dedicated themselves consistently to organized struggle by the proletariat. Conquest of power, proletarian dictatorship, world revolution on the Russian model: that was their program. Piscator welcomed the shift from *Jedermann* to *Die Pleite*:

> Dada had gotten meaner. The old anarchistic
> attitude against the philistine bourgeoisie,
> the assault on art and other intellectual
> business, had sharpened and taken virtually
> the form of political struggle. *Jedermann*
> *sein eigner Fußball* had still been impertinent
> "*épater le bourgeois.*" *Die Pleite*...was already
> a gauntlet thrown down to bourgeois society.[68]

On March 9, 1919, four days after his visit to Kessler with the *Pleite* issue, Wieland Herzfelde was arrested by the Freikorps during the suppression of the second uprising in Berlin. Grosz, too, was to be arrested. The story goes that soldiers stormed into his studio and found Grosz and Mehring there. They confronted Grosz, asking if he were not the communist artist. Grosz, who had false papers, responded in broad American accent: "Nope! *Tue ich nicht kennen!* I'm a cartoonist!" The soldiers believed him and he got away.[69]

Several days later, on March 16, Kessler visited Grosz at his studio. Grosz, Kessler discovered, "now professed himself to be a Spartacist." Given "middle-class inertia," Grosz had committed himself to force. Seeing the Spartacist resistance to the *Freikorps* over the past two days had "converted him to a totally fresh outlook on the proletariat." The gist of this conversion was that "the artist and the intellectual must take a duly modest place."[70] This was the essence of the *Proletkult* conversion experience which the botched revolution induced in a segment of the Berlin avant-garde. Grosz was not alone. Wieland Herzfelde's experiences in prison camp accentuated his own radicalism. He was released on March 21, and drafted a sixteen page pamphlet, *Schutzhaft*, describing his experiences, which was published as issue two of *Die Pleite*. Herzfelde was extremely bitter, talking to Kessler of "lynching" and warning that should the rebels win they would "exterminate the middle class, one and all."[71] Kessler was genuinely shocked to hear of Herzfelde's treatment. He gathered together a number of associates to hear Herzfelde tell his story, and they agreed something should be done. The day after this meeting, Kessler went to Stresemann to "mobilize him for action against the atrocities."[72] But nothing was ever done.

Die Pleite became even more bitter. On March 23, John Heartfield visited Kessler and set forth the position of the circle.[73] No more poetry — not even by Däubler or Becher — would be accepted. They were not interested in art any more; they wanted to support the revolution. The Dadaists were enraged, and they declared war against the civilization which perpetrated the series of barbarities from August 1914 to March 1919. Art was a casualty of the conflict. As Hans Richter has noted in his memoirs, "the demand that art should be banished to the scrap heap turned into a battle, not against art as such, but against social conditions in Germany."[74] When, in April, new issues of *Die Pleite* appeared, street vendors were afraid to handle them. Herzfelde had to distribute four to five thousand copies directly in factories.[75]

At the end of 1919 another journal joined the ranks of Dada: *Der blutige Ernst*, which Carl Einstein and George Grosz converted, after three issues under a prior editor, into a key document of Dada. Some of Grosz's most famous drawings first appeared there. Meanwhile Dada had been busy at other escapades. The mad architect Baader had appeared at the opening of the Weimar National Assembly and showered it with pamphlets proclaiming himself "Oberdada, President of the Universe."[76] And, in Berlin, December 1918, as Ben Hecht has recorded, the Dadaists Grosz and Mehring organized and advertised all over Berlin the "First German Post-war Renaissance of the Arts. Admission 20 Gold Marks. Formal Dress Required."[77] Of course the audience filled with "Berlin's most distinguished citizens" in full regalia. They were treated to the great race between a sewing maching and a typewriter, which has gone down in the annals of Dada. Also performed: Grosz's niggerjig to the accompaniment of a man tuning a cello, and a "Pan-Germanic Poetry Contest" in which vagabonds were ushered on stage and proclaimed Germany's leading poets. They competed by reading poems simultaneously. This was followed by a "musical performance" in which single notes were carried on stage by girls in tights. The audience was outraged. Dada triumphed.

That was only the beginning of Walter Mehring's Dadaist cabaret. His first volume of cabaret lyrics, *Das politische Cabaret*, was full of provocations and political commentary which found their way into performances in 1918-1919 and thereafter as part of Dada. It is important to note that even Mehring, who would later express contempt for the Bolshevism of the Herzfelde brothers, should in these years have been one of its staunch defenders.[78] The style of the lyrics in *Das politische Cabaret* derived heavily from Mehring's constant parody of advertising slogans, billboards, posters and the language of the streets.[79] The poems were a jumble of blatantly satirical fragments and aphorisms, interspersed with short, acid commentary. In his *Dada Prologue 1919*, the introductory poem, Mehring summarized the thrust of the entire work, lashing out at the press, the National Assembly, the SPD, the *Rat der geistigen Arbeiter*, the *Freikorps*, William II, Hindenburg and Noske. Typical of the style of the poem is this excerpt:

> In Peace wrappers —
> Indispensable for National Assemblies and pogroms,
> For headaches, fear of Bolshevism, vomiting and press
> swindles:[80]

The key message of the Prologue and indeed of the whole volume was about the reaction against Bolshevism:

> The League for the Defense of German Culture
> Produces on 100,000 rotation presses
> Bolshevik gorillas with handgrenades —
> Ancestors of [the evolutionist] Häckel...[81]

This theme of fear of Bolshevism was the basis for the prose satire "In Silk Gloves," written in November 1918.[82] It was a lament by a

German bourgeois, now that the Kaiser was in Amerongen and the socialists were in control. "If only they'll let us keep our money," the bourgeois sighed. His nightmare was Bolshevism. "Alert! The Bolsheviks are coming!...In the name of God, intellectuals and workers, unite," he pleaded. "Save culture!" To which Mehring replied tersely: "Yeah, *your* culture, you scholars, artists and intellectuals!" He continued:

> When the whole Siegesallee is in smithereens,
> with all its (pseudo) Gothic, with its iron
> Hindenburg, with the scholars, intellectuals
> and mental laborers in silk gloves, when we
> finally emerge naked, without our historical
> figleaf, and Bolshevism is introduced...[83]

But then the bourgeois politely interrupted: "Pardon me, but you have your ideas mixed up. Bolshevism will not be introduced. Bolshevism is a catastrophe." Against this dread the hopes of revolution foundered in Germany.

Mehring went on in a series of poems to sketch the tragedy and travesty of the German Revolution — the "Celebration of Murder" among the German people in August 1914 and again in 1919. "Berlin," he wrote, "your dance-partner is death!" His poem by this title once again portrayed the bourgeois reaction to the revolution:

> In Berlin there's a big to-do —
> The prole is on a binge.
> In the north they're partying.
> They dance and they don't genuflect —
> A big shindig for the little people!
> Shame! In such serious times!
> The mob is completely out of hand.
> Workers, defend the Fatherland!
> > Every shot at Spartakus!
> > A masquerade by Noske!
> > For blood money a social mask
> > And maxim: today is *red*!
> > Thump the proletarian dead![84]

There were bitter poems about the *Freikorps*, the perverted judiciary, the monarchist revivalism (*"Wir wollen unsern Kaiser wieder..."*), and the press. The rage behind these cynical poems was the spirit of Berlin Dada, a seething nihilism which found its greatest expression in the drawings of George Grosz.

The Dada impulse, especially in its political form, generated in George Grosz a major burst of artistic productivity. His most famous drawings and his greatest oil paintings date from these years. In 1919, Grosz's drawings constituted the decisive force in the little magazines of political Dada. His covers for *Die Pleite* and *Der blutige Ernst* represent some of the most important work Grosz ever did. The cover for the first issue of *Die Pleite*, the drawing Kessler found so excellent, caricatured the saddlemaker Ebert as a monarch. In that issue, too, appeared the drawing *Spartacus on Trial – Who is the Villain?* The three figures at the judge's bench appear again in Grosz's political art: the general, the pastor and the bureaucrat, the representative types of the established political elite. They had to be deposed, the situation of the drawing reversed, if democracy were to win out in Germany. This wish Grosz set to paper in a later drawing for *Der blutige Ernst: How the State Court Must Appear!*

The most powerful of all the drawings for *Die Pleite* was published in issue three, April 1919, after the brutal suppression of the March uprising. It is perhaps the most gruesome statement, but also the most effective. Tucholsky recognized it as the most powerful propaganda piece of the period. A Freikorps officer holds a champagne glass high in one hand. In the other, the officer holds a bloody sword. All around him lie hacked bodies and gore. "Prost, Noske!" the title goes, "The Proletariat is Disarmed." The drawing reappeared under a slightly different title in *Das Gesicht der herrschenden Klasse* with even greater horror: a baby skewered on the officer's sword. In the same issue, April 1919, there appeared another drawing by Grosz which could serve as the artistic counterpart to Brecht's famous *Legend of the Dead Soldier*. A medical examination group determines that a skeleton is fit for military duty. Both Grosz and Brecht were stimulated by the complaint *"They're digging up the dead,"* concerning conscription practices in the final phase of the war. But there is no substance to the suggestion – apparently from Herzfelde — that Brecht drew his idea from the Grosz drawing.[85]

In 1920 the Malik-Verlag issued a new limited edition portfolio of Grosz drawings entitled *Gott mit uns*.[86] It contained nine lithographs on the theme of German politics. One drawing in this group was that of the fit-for-service skeleton, now entitled *The Faith Healer*. The whole story of the Revolution was contained in another drawing of this portfolio: *The Communists Fall — And the Exchange Rate Rises*. Equally powerful is the drawing *Pimps of Death* which shows three German generals as pimps for prostitutes with skulls for faces. Another drawing, *Full Democracy*, shows three prisoners in chains, dominated by an enormous, grinning soldier with whip in hand and cigar in mouth.

This development culminated in the classical locus of Grosz's political art, *Das Gesicht der herrschenden Klasse* (1921).[87] In these fifty-five political drawings Grosz impaled the ruling class of Germany. The volume contained all the drawings from *Die Pleite, Der blutige Ernst* and *Gott mit uns*. By merely leafing through *Das Gesicht der herrschenden Klasse*, it becomes apparent how much hatred seethed in Grosz and how hated he became in turn. The government brought him and Herzfelde to trial for the first time in 1920 on a charge of impugning the army, for the portfolio *Gott mit uns*.[88] It would not be the last time. In exile, Grosz joked about the threats uttered by generals, and noted the ferocity with which the Nazis destroyed all trace of his work in Germany as their first act in the "cleaning of the temple of art."[89]

Das Gesicht der herrschenden Klasse is a sociological analysis of the early Republic at least as fully wrought as the editorials of the *Weltbühne*. The overriding image it presents is of the persistence in power of entrenched German elites, above all the military and the capitalists. The opening drawing expresses the theme clearly. A German general struts forward. Around him soldiers present arms. In the background, rebels are herded into prison or put before the firing squad. Several bourgeois gentlemen cry hurrah. The title of the piece: *Return to Order*. The next pages present Ebert and Noske as betrayers of the revolution. The fourth drawing, preliminary to Groß's masterly oil painting *Pillars of Society* (1925), shows the unregenerate pre-war elite rejoicing at the victory God granted them over the revolution.

One of the most bitter and bizarre drawings of the volume, a new work, was *Vox populi vox dei* which shows men turned into animals proclaiming their political allegiance. "Man is not good, but rather a beast!" Grosz wrote as the introduction to a solo-exhibit in Hannover in 1922. Here was the documentation. This drawing seems clearly a response to the election of 1920 in which the middle class and conservative parties scored a clear victory over the left. The hope expressed in the drawing *How the State Court Ought to Appear* has grown more and more forelorn (note: in place of "*müß-te*" in *Der blutige Ernst*, the title now reads "*sollte*" — already a diminution of hope) as it is overwhelmed by the "vampires of humanity," the generals who are the "pimps of Death." Class injustice is underscored in juxtaposed drawings such as *Where Dividends Come From — Where they go*, which shows miners working to premature death on one side, and glutted capitalists, their tables overflowing with delicacies, on the other. A similar juxtaposition within the framework of a single drawing was *The Communist Fall — And the Exchange Rates Rise*, first published in *Der blutige Ernst*. Two bloated gentlemen sit conversing over dinner while in the background soldiers kill the last Communist rebels.

A collage of newspaper advertisements for leisure entertainment, superimposed upon which a fat and smug gentleman is coddled by a whore, bears the bitter title *Labor and Do not Despair!* More of Grosz's hideous capitalists appear in *The Toads of Property*, great sums of money under their thumbs, glaring at the misery of the proletariat with arrogant satisfaction. As another drawing has it: "These people *can* work, they just don't want to." It was said in reference to a crippled war veteran.

The themes of *Das Gesicht der herrschenden Klasse* are summarized in the oil painting of 1917-1919, *Germany — A Winter's Tale*, which dominated the 1920 Dada Messe. The three figures of German authoritarianism — officer, clergyman and bureaucrat — serve as the basis upon which the entire edifice of German philistinism rests. Above and behind them in tones of ochre, umber and black, an angular metropolitan jungle rises up, the colors suggesting bluntly what Grosz wrote about the world of his *Dedicated to Oskar Panizza*: "Think, wherever you go, it smells of shit."[90] In the center of the painting sits the archetypal philistine, the Herr Schulze of the Dadaists, knife and fork in hand, a napkin tucked into his collar. Before him are the symbols of his station, his plate of meat and potatoes, his dividend coupon, his glass of beer, his cigar and his *Lokal-Anzeiger* (the daily newspaper of the *völkisch*-royalist August Scherl publishing house, edited by the rabid reactionary Hussong). In the city behind him the invariable whore hustles about her business. A sailor strides along and, behind him, blending into the bleakness, a man pushes a wheelbarrow with a child's coffin and a cross. *Germany, A Winter's Tale* — a thoroughgoing indictment to match Heine's nineteenth-century polemic. At the bottom left, in black silhouette, Grosz's hard profile glares upon the scene.

"Bolshevism" and Political Responsibility: The Avant-Garde Dilemma

If Pfemfert and the Dadaists embraced "Bolshevism," others in the avant-garde repudiated it just as swiftly. One of the most prominent figures in this repudiation was the editor of another great anti-war Expressionist journal, René Schickele of *Die Weißen Blätter*.[91] For Schickele, the Bolsheviks represented the "cossacks of socialism," imbued with the same militarism and violence as the warmongers. Red praetorians, he feared, would merely displace white. "I am a socialist," he wrote. "But if I were persuaded that socialism could be realized only by Bolshevik methods, I — and not I alone — would renounce its realization."[92] This dread of Bolshevism was, indeed, more widely shared, for example by writers for *Die Weltbühne* like Siegfried Jacobsohn, Willy Wolfradt and Kurt Tucholsky.[93] And yet all of these figures were in favor of a democratic revolution in Germany, and almost all of them were enthusiastic for what seemed to be taking place in November 1918.

Artistic and literary intellectuals demonstrated their identification with the upheaval in the swift formation of numerous organizations: the *Novembergruppe* and *Arbeitsrat für Kunst* among visual artists, and especially the *Rat der geistigen Arbeiter*, the council

41

of mental workers, founded by Kurt Hiller on the very day of the November Revolution.[94] Hiller produced a manifesto at this first meeting which proposed a parallel intellectual council should rule along with the workers and soldiers councils of the revolution. In the first days of the revolution, many intellectuals of diverse viewpoints joined Hiller's *Rat*.[95] *Die Weltbühne*, for example, set out in November 1918 with an explicit repudiation of dictatorship of the proletariat and an identification with the Expressionist utopianism of Hiller's council.[96] But by December 1918, the intellectual megalomania proved too much for Siegfried Jacobsohn and he repudiated this affiliation.[97] By late 1918 most, and by spring 1919 almost all of the intellectuals who had at first been attracted to Hiller's group had broken away. The solidarity so easily found in the glow of utopian expectation had shattered in the harrowing course of the revolution. It is illuminating to follow the reflections of those on both sides of this rift, those who repudiated "Bolshevism" and those who found themselves "Bolshevists" *faute de mieux*.

René Schickele will serve as an apt representative of the first position. This Alsatian writer had distinguished himself early on not only as a leading Expressionist poet and editor, but as a figure committed to literary activism. His difficult position in the war years had only shown the force of his integrity, and *Die Weißen Blätter* became one of the most influential literary and anti-war journals in Central Europe. As its editor, Schickele devoted a great deal of his concern to the question of intellectual responsibility in the face of war and politics.

In August 1918, Schickele published a long meditation on the question of intellectuals, the war and politics, "The Convention of the Intellectuals."[98] In this essay Schickele proposed to analyze the four possible positions of intellectuals "in all lands" under the conditions of the war. In the first group, to which he himself adhered, were those who found it irreconcilable to be an intellectual and to contribute in any way to the continuation of the war. In the second group were those intellectuals who served as the ideologists of this or that party and who followed whither it led. The third group consisted of "utopians and revolutionaries" who, in the name of an ideal, had begun actively working for a particular state and its particular interests — Bolshevik Russia. Schickele castigated the "revolutionary opportunism" of "those opposed to the state on principle who, out of tactical considerations, struggle for a specific state."[99] That seemed less honest than the "socialist opportunism" involved in "the idea of 'defending one's country.'" A fourth group, to which Schickele claimed he used to belong, resembled the third except that in place of a particular state it set up a cultural ideal as its rallying point. This group judged every party and action tactically on the basis of "whether they supported or hindered the realization of a democtratic Europe." This ideal of the "good European," Schickele now felt, produced not only "tactical disorientation" but a confusion of principles and then of instinct. Tactical alliances with those who did not share their ultimate values led intellectuals into fatal compromises, for ultimately no new solidarity could be based on negatives, on shared opposition, but only on a positive program.

The basis for affiliation had to be the principle "that force cease *categorically*." Some might affirm this ideal, claiming they fought the war out precisely to bring an end to violence, but that was the fatal compromise, Schickele went on. Once violence entered the equation, even to put an end to violence, the result could only be the perpetuation of violence. Society could not be changed by force. All the changes that society required were real, but they presupposed a change of heart in men first, as against the Jacobin conviction that if society were forcibly changed the individuals would change accordingly. The threat of onsetting reaction was no warrant for counterviolence: "You want to prevent it by force and you know that to do so the dictatorship of the proletariat will have to be perpetuated." Red praetorians would replace the others, but the rule of force would remain. Schickele concluded: "I hope for a revolution against bestiality and that cannot be a revolution which combats bestiality with bestiality. Whoever would emerge victorious, it would still be bestiality."[100]

Schickele envisioned two bleak futures: a perpetual dictatorship of red praetorians, a rule of force with colors reversed, or, on the other hand, a flight into banality. He spelled out this second alternative as: "an *after us the deluge* which would betake itself shamelessly to the dance-hall...the triumph of the dance leg over all the consequences one would expect to follow from what has happened."[101] Schickele claimed to fear the rise of cynicism, but it seems that he also feared the masses and social upheaval, a posture which reinforced his dread of the "red praetorians" and the dictatorship of the proletariat on the one hand, and his insistence on a "convention of intellectuals," an intellectual elite *au dessus de la mêlée* on the other.

Two forces worked upon him to reinforce these attitudes: the reactionary tenor of German public opinion and the unfolding Russian Revolution, as sensationalized by the German-language press. With deep antipathy, the German press harped on the treason of the pacifists and the megalomania of the intellectuals as these were embodied above all in *Die Weißen Blätter*. That same press provided jaundiced accounts of the Bolshevik Revolution and civil war in Russia. As a result, Schickele lost his sense of political efficacy and became far more concerned to preserve what he viewed as the essential and endangered ideals of European intellectual culture.

Schickele's long essay, "Revolution, Bolshevism and the Ideal," (December 1918), chronicles his state of mind from November 9 till mid December. Schickele described the ninth of November in Berlin with euphoria: "the new world has begun." In the ruins of the aftermath of war, a universal solidarity had the potential to remake the entire world.[102] There had come an interval of liberation in which all could be set right if socialism were only instituted: "In four weeks the socialization of production must have been begun — or economy, civilization and culture will be submerged in group warfare."[103] At the outset, Schickele pleaded for the established classes to embrace socialism as the "only order of society worthy of mankind." Yet the hostile images of socialism he rejected — "the invention of envious rabbis," "the swarm of red cutthroats," and "the ressentiment of a class" — were still too vivid, not just in the established classes but in himself. Disillusionment swiftly replaced euphoria: "In ten hours we could have set up the free city. Yesterday. If they had only let us."[104]

The idea that somehow a "they" had intervened to forstall the coming of utopia in November 1918 calls for critical comment.

Certainly if one considers the actions of Schickele from the moment the old regime collapsed it becomes apparent that Schickele's idealism lays him open to criticisms both from a pragmatic and from a radically committed perspective. His main concern in the initial moments of revolution was to preempt a "Bolshevik analogy." In his mind, the faces of Radek, Lenin and Zinoview – faces he remembered from Zurich – loomed ominously on the German horizon. "Put the thought of the Russian example off till tomorrow," he cautioned. Ebert and Haase did not have the same reactionary force behind them which worked behind Kerensky and Martov in Russia. "Wir sind keine Russen..."[105] Schickele demanded that socialists take an active role in the new order, for hesitation would open the way to the Spartacists.

As the euphoria of November 9 faded, there opened up deep cleavages of orientation not only between Schickele and Pfemfert, but between Schickele and his own close associate from Zurich, Ludwig Rubiner. The idea Rubiner had embraced and which set him so totally apart from Schickele, was dictatorship of the proletariat. For Schickele, this meant "a preference for the whip," a willingness to trade one dictatorship for another.[106] The dictatorship of the proletariat along Bolshevik lines was "not a transition but a persistent condition," a "terror." For Schickele the essential point was that an order instituted by force by a minority would require perpetuation by force. He insisted that he was not defending the militarists, and that he subscribed totally to the Bolshevik demands for peace without annexations and national self-determination. But, Schickele argued, the Bolsheviks, even in their very rhetoric, were infected with the same cult of violence and warfare as the warlords and militarists, "Militarism and imperialism had only to change their colors."

Schickele sought to document this with reference to Leninist tactics in Bolshevik Russia, quoting from Lenin's *The Immediate Task of the Soviet Government.* The Bolsheviks had no faith, no love, he charged. They were haters, the "praetorians of the proletariat in its mass madness, the cossacks of socialism." For Schickele there was no question that Bolshevism was a greater danger than capitalism. Capitalism was an error which democracy could cure, but

45

"the dictatorship of the proletariat, as the Bolsheviks have interpreted and exercised it, is counterrevolution within the party of the proletarian ideal."[107] Against this, Schickele held up Peguy's program for a "republic of mind," in which inhumanity was intolerable, no matter for what end. This led to Schickele's own credo: "I am a socialist, but if I were persuaded that socialism could be realized only by Bolshevik methods, I — and not I alone — would renounce its realization."[108] The only acceptable way to realize the ideal was to change men's hearts. Despite the prospects of failure, intellectuals could not withdraw into a cloister; they had to teach their message in the world.

> We intellectuals have no choice. We know and we have said
> for a long time that a spiritual development never can de-
> pend on a victory at arms, no matter on which side... We
> have just one task, and it remains ours under all
> circumstances: to see to it that the ideal — if
> only in a hundred, if only in ten people — not be
> lost to memory.[109]

Schickele realized how this cut him off from all sides. For the trade-unionists and practitioners of "Realpolitik" he seemed a fool; for the red praetorians he was a harmless but also a useless dreamer, a poet. Yet he felt this was the intellectual condition and it could not be evaded. Schickele stood forth as an eloquent and passionate defender of intellectual integrity and of a critical, detached intelligentsia unwilling to enter into compromises either with the fatal "pragmatists" of right socialism or with the murderous "praetorians" of Bolshevism.

Yet there remained a profound weakness in Schickele's stance. His purism undermined his political efficacy. His dread of the left underestimated — albeit unwittingly — the consolidation of counter-revolutionary forces. If Schickele urged that intellectual integrity could not be preserved by adopting the politics of the Bolshevik Revolution, Wilhelm Herzog counterposed the argument that political integrity could not be preserved by remaining in the utopian idealism of Activism. Nor was Herzog a man insensitive to intellectual integrity. Herzog subsumes Schickele in the course of his devel-

46

opment and drives us to confront a dilemma from which no left-wing intellectual would emerge unscathed.

In the aftermath of the November Revolution, *Das Forum* and Herzog spoke forth after three years of censorship. In the first issue of the journal, revived under a new publisher headquartered in Potsdam and Berlin, Herzog addressed an open letter to Romain Rolland calling for an "international of intellectuals." While he and Rolland negotiated, Henri Barbusse created the *Clarté* movement, which embodied most of their ideas.[110] Meanwhile Herzog took on the responsibility of editing *Republik*, a newspaper of the left-wing Independent Social Democratic Party of Germany. His editorials for that newspaper, reprinted in *Das Forum*, document his experience of the revolution and its aftermath in January and March 1919 and his turn to "Bolshevism."

Herzog's first editorial, "The Spiritual Type of the Revolutionary," appeared on December 18, 1918 in *Republik*. In the editorial he was concerned to secure the victory of the revolution against the forces which worked to undermine it: generals still in command, pseudo-democrats, the diplomatic corps, and the "Walter Rathenau socialists" of big business. To do this socialist unity was required, he argued, but not the compromise of all principle to accommodate a reticent bourgeoisie. There had to be solidarity about the goal and the ideal: world revolution for humanity and socialism, and "integration into the Western democracies."[111] Herzog put as his first priority association with Western democracy: not Wilson or Lenin, but Wilson and Lenin, a revolutionary socialism oriented towards a new and humane post-war order. He believed the only ideological forces which could sustain it lay in the ideological vistas of democracy of these two emergent world leaders. He denied emphatically the "Bolshevist" argument that Wilson was merely an agent of American capitalist interests.

Through December 1918, Herzog was optimistic about the future and about a new, humane post-war order. In his second editorial, written January 6, 1919, in the midst of the so-called "Spartacist Uprising," that optimism was dashed. He noted bitterly that the German people had opted for war again: now it was to be civil war. Those who had opposed the first war and had sought to prevent its recurrence by reorganizing society after its collapse now became the targets of renewed hostility. They were condemned as "Bolshevists" by the "liberal" press and the "moderate socialists," to say nothing of the right.[112] So-called "socialists" manipulated circumstances to ostracize and assault their brethren committed to social reconstruction, claiming the "red menace" so alarmed the Entente that any reorganization, indeed even the mere existence of workers-and-soldiers councils, would provoke armed intervention.[113] The propaganda of center and right held that Wilson and the others would deal only with a National Assembly, a parliament on the old lines, not with the new revolutionary government.

A third editorial appeared on January 9, obsessed with one overriding fact: "innocent people are being arbitrarily and senselessly murdered by machine guns on the streets of Berlin."[114] It was clear that the people of Germany had not learned that the question of a just social order could not be resolved by force: "All dictatorship — whether that of Ebert-Scheidemann or that of Liebknecht — can only be sporadic; it is reprehensible, inimical to man, and ripe for decay..."[115]

The bitter realization of this infused Herzog's next editorial, published January 15, 1919, a long and grim reckoning with the German political conundrum. Entitled "August 1914 — January 1919," the point of the essay was clear in its title: the progressive voice in Germany was libelled and shouted down at each critical juncture. In the war, those Germans who saw with Wilson that it was a world catastrophe, rather than an expression of national destiny and glory, were damned as traitors or unrealistic utopians. And then, "in 1919 they call us Bolsheviks, friends of the Spartacists, defenders of plunderers and murderers. Because we believe that Germany can find itself once more in a respected and proud place among the nations of the world only through a purification of our entire public life."[116]

The intellectuals who dared cry out against injustice were placed will-nilly in the camp of "left extremists" and "Bolsheviks." They were damned, Herzog went on, because they dared to condemn the corrupt old regime pepetuated by the disgraceful compromises of so-called "socialists." In the end, Herzog came to a gloomy diagnosis of Germany's political dilemna: "Let us be just, even to the last moment. The people did not want it any other way, and does not want it different even today."[117] They were not mature enough for the revolution. Their ideas, their instincts, had been perverted by decades of political miseducation dating from 1871, the "triumph of militarism." The German people "cheered when war broke out. And they remained happy in their frenzy of power until the collapse." And the same thing was happening in the civil war.

Herzog asserted his opposition to the realization of any idea by force and proclaimed the mission of the intellectual in the ideological crossfire to be "to see the things as they are." He went on: "I am not for Spartacus and I am not for Ebert-Scheidemann. I am for the truth. And therefore I must fight lies wherever I find them."[118] Left-wing intellectuals could not make peace with the Republic, because the Republic betrayed all the ideals for which progressive German intellectuals had to stand. Political integrity required these intellectuals to reject the "democrats" of the propaganda press and the "pragmatists" of the political order. Yet they did not necessarily subscribe, as Herzog definitely did not, to the cult of left-extremism of which they were accused under the rubric of "Bolshevism."

On the eighteenth of January, Herzog's despair was almost total: "What is the use of words? One stands helpless before the sea of lies." All the ideals, all the hopes which he and others had advocated through the war and into the revolution, were now dashed. "It was a fateful error to believe that this revolution — which was no revolution but rather a sailor's mutiny — could have caused an upheaval in the spiritual and ethical perspective of the German people."[119] Two ideologies were in conflict, that of the "Realpolitiker," with their worship of power and contempt for spirit, and that of the believers in Leonhard Frank's words, "Der Mensch ist gut." And there could be no doubt which of these two visions the German people preferred. The German people did not want to hear the truth, that they had to rid themselves of their guilty leaders. They did not recognize the absolute incompatibility of these men with the moral order of the new post-war world. Instead they consented to the liquidation of the few men in Germany who aspired to social justice. The real guilt for January 1919 lay with the leaders of the SPD, whose compromise with the old regime allowed its bureaucracy and its military organization systematically to destroy the revolution and the prospect for a new Germany. Daily this regime became more hypocritical, more "Ullsteinized" in Herzog's words. Daily it paraded the idea of "democracy" while it entered into cabals with the generals of the old regime. Yet Herzog would not abandon his idealism altogether. After all, utopians and idealists like Wilson had brought the war to an end, and there was no reason to give up hope in the ultimate triumph of right. The intellectuals had to press on: "Therefore, illumination of and affiliation with international democracy, international socialism, and first and most essentially, international spirit."[120]

The position of Herzog in January 1919, then, was exactly that posture of the intellectual in defense of the ideal which Schickele propounded in his essay on the Revolution and Bolshevism. But just by taking this stance, the intellectual was *considered* a "Bolshevik." Shickele's insistence that a rule of force was irreconcilable with intellectual integrity here meets the other and bitter truth of Weimar Germany: confronted by an enemy without scruples, for whom force was the first recourse, *political* integrity demanded of the intellectual drastic measures versus that enemy and a regime which actively abetted it.

After all the murder and mayhem perpetrated in the name of democracy by the SPD regime, Herzog could no longer abide its pretensions and came explicitly to the side of the radicals. As long as capitalism was maintained, he argued, the assassin of a Jaurès would always walk away free, the agents of hate would have free rein. That was "democracy!" And people dreaded the dictatorship of the proletariat? When that dictatorship was in reality "the transition to true democracy: a corridor made dangerous by the resistance of the still ruling feudalism and of the bourgeoisie."[121] When "privilege continues to assault right," when "atavistic powers still assault reason and justice," the intellectual had to take up arms, Herzog insisted. Political integrity in Germany required commitment to revolution, the dictatorship of the proletariat, even violent revolution, for only through violent revolution could the vicious and powerful resistance of the old order be overcome. For Herzog it was manifest that the pacifistic non-violence and intellectual elitism of Schickele failed to live up to the realities of Germany's political situation. He became the advocate of Bolshevism.

The issue came to a head in an exchange of view with Friedrich Förster, the courageous academic pacifist of the war years. Förster wrote *Das Forum*: "For some time I have noted in a string of German intellectuals, who during the war virtuously withstood the ruling psychosis, a growing sympathy towards Bolshevism."[122] This alarmed Förster, though he fully comprehended the disillusionment these intellectuals felt regarding the *"Kultur"* which had instigated the war and all its brutality. Förster recognized that the strength of Bolshevism was its criticism of this murderous hypocrisy in European culture, but he felt it utterly insufficient as a solution to the problem it decried in the social, economic and cultural domains. Above all, he charged, it had no "spiritual principle," indeed, it was the opposite of Christianity, an insistence on "fraternity without fraternal love." This resulted in the worst excesses of authoritarianism, bureaucratic control and dehumanization. The writings of the Bolsheviks were full of "cold hatred;" their authors "abstract theorecticians or heartless fanatics." Finally, Förster argued, Germany was not Russia, and the German people were too mature for dictatorship.

Herzog replied in his introduction to Förster's letter. Carefully he praised Förster's courage during the war, but then he went over to the attack: "bourgeois idealism is played out; it is dead."[123] Bolshevism was not just a critique, it was a faith, a commitment. Herzog did not want to ignore the errors of the Bolsheviks, but he suggested that the recalcitrance of the bourgeoisie in reality made all hope of persuasion or enlightenment, much less of true solidarity with the oppressed futile. Many, he claimed, "have finally learned – taught by the German events – how necessarily the red terror had to follow on the white." If, indeed, the writings of the Bolsheviks were "cool and matter-of-fact," this was because warm, humane rhetoric had been used to mislead a whole civilization into carnage and all the great ideals had been "prostituted, day in and day out," to thwart the just aspirations of the hungry masses. It was not enough, Herzog went on, to proclaim brotherhood; one had to realize it:

> The intellectual principle of revolutionary socialism is fulfillment. The highest law: overcoming the exploitation of man by man. Hence struggle against bourgeois "*Kultur*," against European civilization, capitalist democracy... If we put aside all legends, conscious lies and misrepresentations, without accepting the many errors, false and dangerous methods of Bolshevism, it emerges that the constitution striven for by the Bolsheviks is the first earnest effort at the realization of socialism. [124]

Intellectual scruple — and intellectual autonomy — were luxuries which the German situation of 1918-1919 did not allow, Herzog concluded. It was a moment when politics simply overran the domain of intellectual and cultural values. To preserve intellectual purity would have meant to sacrifice altogether one's political integrity. To preserve one's political integrity, one would be forced to submit to the epithets "Bolshevist" or "Cultural Bolshevist" and one would have to come to the stern realization that the brutality of the forces of reaction in Germany necessitated countermeasures in kind, that hatred and violence were essential even if they outraged the delicate ideals of pacifist utopianism. There were moments, Herzog maintained, when the intellectual's ultimate values had to become besmirched with the mud of real life if they were ever to have a hope of human realization.

Such a position was asserted as well in the bitter essay "Democracy, Revolution, Bolshevism" published by Walther Rilla in his journal *Die Erde* in November 1919.[125] After an initial idealism which brought him to join Hiller's *Rat der geistigen Arbeiter*, Rilla became disillusioned and radicalized by the course of the revolution. A year after its outbreak, Rilla charged that one of the factors leading to its failure was that "progressive" intellectuals had been so taken up with "idealism" that they had repudiated violence. Such idealism was nothing short of irresponsibility in a revolution, he charged, and it allowed the emergence of a "bourgeois class dictatorship." The only viable alternative had been and continued to be "Bolshevism," the "dictatorship of the workers." The intellecutals were not leaders in their revolution, indeed they had not even proven reliable allies.

This position was taken by another of the most prominent left-wing Activists, Ludwig Rubiner, in his 1919 essay, "Renewal."[126] Rubiner, whose background is obscure but who by 1920, the year of his death, was one of the most respected of the "Bolshevist" literati around Pfemfert's *Die Aktion*, argued that the idea of the intellectual as leader had interfered with the revolutionary movement. The masses rebelled spontaneously, Rubiner believed. "Who leads this mass action? The workers. The proletariat," he wrote. Addressing himself to his colleagues, Rubiner concluded: "You cannot teach it, you can bring it no wisdom from on high...You can only work with it." It seemed that many on the literary left favored this idea of spontaneous revolution, for it suited their own individualistic-anarchistic rebelliousness as well. In the revolutionary situation it seemed easy to affirm an equally spontaneous solidarity between the masses and the radical intelligentsia. The problem seemed one of ideology, not organization, and the solution seemed simply to be increased agitation under the rubric "Bolshevism."

By 1919, however, it was becoming apparent at least to the astute that the revolutionary situation was coming to a close. In the wake of the botched revolution, their sense of political integrity required of them an unequivocal rejection of the regime, yet they were too realistic to expect its swift overthrowal. They wished to be revolutionary, but they despaired of winning. Yet this sobriety radicalized them; it did not reconcile them to the political compromise of 1919-1920. The left literati grew bitter and cynical, but they never ceased to protest. Militarism, authoritarianism, and monopoly capitalism, especially in the alliance these had formed during the Great War, drew their sustained enmity. For them, the use of military force in domestic affairs, the course of judicial actions, economic policy and institutional administration in the years after 1919 suggested that in many ways the political world of Weimar Germany seemed all too similar to that of Imperial Germany. Yet to oppose this system was to place oneself in a desperate situation, which Wilhelm Herzog spelled out: "Because one struggles (not simply on ideal, but also on real-political grounds) for purity in political life, against shameful compromises with the bearers of the old regime — what is one called because of this? A Bolshevik."[127] By the majority socialists and all the elements to their right these left literati were deemed "Cultural Bolsheviks." For themselves they could establish only a minimal identity: they saw themselves compelled to a general *negativism*.

Kurt Tucholsky's essay, "We Negativists," published March 1919, gave paradigmatic expression to this state of mind.[128] In it, Tucholsky rejected the criticisms voiced in several quarters that the *Weltbühne* circle did nothing but criticize and found nothing positive about the German situation. For Tucholsky, that was simply the truth of the situation. There was indeed nothing to affirm. He condemned the so-called German Revolution already in March 1919 as a mere *Zusammenbruch*, a collapse of authority, and he labelled the German bourgeoisie the most antidemocratic and banal in defending its self-interest of all such classes in Europe. He blasted the SPD as the party which had betrayed all progressive aspirations in Germany by its compromises. It had betrayed not only the socialist revolution, but even the "democratic revolution."[129] Tucholsky concluded by 1919 that there remained only one choice: rejecting the entirety of Germany's political order. "We know only one thing: that we must sweep away with an iron broom all that is rotten in Germany."[130]

A classic expression of this bitter animus of Negativism came in Alfred Döblin's essay of May 1920, "The German Masquerade." Tucholsky greeted the piece as a masterpiece of "Negativist" criticism. Döblin wrote:

> And then there was a Republic...One didn't know
> what to make of it...Five minutes before the thing
> was set up, the country was monarchist. Monarchist
> to the bone... It is one of the most important
> tasks of the Republic not to rub the monarchists
> wrong, especially if they are military. For...
> the Republic was brought into the Holy Roman Empire
> by a wise man from abroad. He didn't say what to
> do with it; it was a Republic without directions
> for use. The military could smash it up, and then
> what would one have left?[131]

54

A Republic whose greatest responsibility was to be inoffensive to monarchists: German democracy seemed merely dictatorship in masquerade. Everywhere the war had produced bitterness and dissension. The front-line soldiers felt disgust with the homeland to which they returned. The working class fragmented into futile little sects. Germany was not ready for a Republic in 1918. In the aftermath of the Kapp-Putsch of March 1920, Döblin dispensed with revolutionary anticipation and settled in for a guerilla war of words. "Weakness," he wrote despairingly, "thy name is democracy."

What had the November Revolution actually accomplished? Döblin asked. It had not created a republic, democracy and civilian rule. It had only created the possibility for these things. They had yet to be wrung out in political struggle. Yet the anachronism and recalcitrance was not limited to the upper classes; along with them even parts of the working class remained eagerly monarchist.

Döblin tried to place the historical responsibility for the political failure of 1918-1919 on the political regression of the bourgeoisie in the Second Reich. Their abdication of politics in favor of economic success contributed to the "feudalization" of life in the late 19th century, despite significant social and industrial development. After this sell-out, Döblin argued, the bourgeoisie lost its capacity for leadership: "liberalism long ago ceased to be an intellectual power in Germany."[132] The socialists were correct to feel contempt for bourgeois ideology, especially in light of the "thoughtless products of fear" which had emerged from that quarter since the November Revolution. In Germany in 1919 the bourgeois parties persisted in rationalizing their special interests and raved in terror about the rising new barbarism and threat to civilization in the proletarian movement. This intransigence of the bourgeoisie stimulated revolutionary radicalism. "Bolshevism grows not because of hunger and unemployment but because of the obstinate, shortsighted, self-serving bourgeoisie." The idea of a dictatorship of the proletariat came of the "desperate and committed conviction" that "the bourgeois will not understand that he should cooperate in building a just society."[133]

55

Chapter Two

PROLETKULT IN GERMANY:
THE LEFT-RADICAL DEBATES OVER THE RELATION
OF THE INTELLECTUAL TO THE PROLETARIAT.
1920 – 1924

Does intellect pollute?
— F. Pfemfert, *Die Aktion*
(1923)

By the end of January 1919, the situation for the council movement became actuely critical. The events of the last months had
changed the mood of the working class, tilting the workers to the left,
to a more class-oriented politics.[1] Yet the organizational and attitudinal
extent of the recent radicalization was by no means clear, nor, more
crucially, was its potential for a revolutionary overthrow of the
established government. The idea of a general strike throughout
industrialized Germany remained the last and the best hope for the
radicals after the military defeat of January 1919. The radicals
developed plans to coordinate a national general strike with a second
Workers and Soldiers Councils Congress to reverse the direction of
revolutionary events, disband the National Assembly and remove the
SPD government.

In February 1919 the government turned from its forcible dismantling of all local radical governments and council organizations
to the issue of factory councils, codetermination rights and socialization of industry. When the government reneged on an agreement
made in January for the socialization of the iron and coal works of
the Ruhr, this provoked a violent strike wave in that district.[2] The
radicals tried to seize the opportunity. Communal councils called
upon the *Zentralrat* in Berlin to convene a Second Councils Congress.
Meanwhile strikes were hastily organized in Thuringia. The *Zentralrat* procrastinated, however, on the instructions of the SPD govern-

ment. Similarly, the SPD faction on the executive council of workers and soldiers councils in Berlin stymied efforts to launch the strike movement in the capital until March 3. Thus the hoped-for national coordination of the strike movement was botched.

Stringing out the strikes, the government could concentrate military force on each location and crush resistance. This happened first in the Ruhr, where it was abetted by internal divisiveness among the rebels. In Thuringia, the SPD delegates to the National Assembly in Weimar negotiated with the strike leaders and promised to anchor the council system in the constitution and to proceed with socialization.[3] These concessions mollified a part of the strike movement and military force suppressed the rest. Then the *Freikorps* closed in on the Berlin strike movement. A particularly bloody interlude of this last action was the assault on the Lichtenberg district of the city after a false rumor was spread of working-class massacres of police officials. By mid March 1919, the workers movement had been suppressed.

By the end of spring 1919, all radical leftist regimes in Germany had been destroyed, including the ephemeral Munich Soviet. The *Freikorps* had become the decisive coercive force in Germany. The denouement of the revolution came over the balance of 1919. At the end of June, the SPD Party Congress endorsed a proposal for the institutionalization of factory councils which in effect reduced them to consultation committees. At the Trade Union Congress which followed shortly thereafter, Carl Legien defeated Richard Müller's radical factory council faction. In July 1919, the SPD withdrew from the Berlin executive council of workers and soldiers councils and in November, security forces disbanded the rump executive council. A Factory Council Law was promulgated in January 1920, the merest shadow of council aspirations. Frustrated Berlin workers marked the date the law took effect, January 12, 1920, with a large demonstration. The crowd grew unruly and advanced toward the Reichstag. With perfect consistency, the government called in armed units and a bloody massacre closed the books on the council movement.

In March 1920 the final act of the revolutionary tragedy was played out. In accordance with the terms of the Treaty of Versailles, the Allies demanded in that month that the Weimar government demobilize a substantial number of its *Freikorps* units. Openly contemptuous of the government ever since its acceptance of the Versailles Treaty, the *Freikorps* units responded to the government's efforts to disband them by marching on the capital city of Berlin.[4] The government turned to the regular army for protection, but the General staff refused to intervene.[5] Government officials had to flee ignominiously to Stuttgart to escape the rebellious *Freikorps* forces. These units took control of the capital and set up a new government headed by a Prussian official named Kapp. This so-called Kapp-Lüttwitz Putsch marked the moment of conservative reassertion of force. It went too far, however. Fearful that the Allies might intervene in Germany, most of the bureaucracy and even some party leaders and industrialists decided to withhold support from the new regime. Meanwhile the trade union leadership finally recognized the danger on the right and declared a general strike against the Kapp regime. Within a matter of days, the *Putsch* collapsed. A new opportunity for major political reform, this time sponsored by the trade union establishment, seemed at hand, but nothing came of it.

If the Kapp-Lüttwitz Putsch had gone too far, it nonetheless reflected a decisive rightward shift in the political constellation of Germany. This was confirmed in the general elections of May 1920, which drove the Weimar Coalition and especially the SPD out of office.[6] The middle classes, outraged over the terms of Versailles, abandoned the DDP for anti-republican parties of the right. The working class, angered by the SPD employment of force against the proletarian left, shifted its support to radical leftist parties. The SPD's share of the ballot fell from 38.6 percent in January 1919 to 21.6 percent in May 1920. It was a stinging political defeat, and it also represented the close of the revolutionary interlude.

German Proletkult

Glum pessimism seeped into the young intellectual rebels in Berlin after the March 1919 uprising. In April 1919, Simon Guttmann visited Count Kessler and they talked about the Spartacists. Guttmann admitted they hadn't the leaders to take over the government, but held out the hope that they would be ready in six months. In May 1919, however, Wieland Herzfelde seemed more pessimistic. In describing a KPD meeting for Kessler, he contrasted the "obviously hysterical" German Communists to the adeptness and control of Bolshevik observers. By August 1919, Kessler reported, Herzfelde was "depressed" and believed that "the revolution is probably over. A month later, total despair: "He does not think that any revolutionary events are in prospect at all, and according to his information the Berlin workers are determined not to let themselves be provoked into any."[7] Despite this pessimism, the immediate circle around Grosz did not disintegrate. Instead, it grew more tightknit and militant. Grosz's work stood as the cornerstone of their edifice, the Malik-Verlag. He, the Herzfeldes, Erwin Piscator and Franz Jung devoted themselves to "proletarian-revolutionary" art with redoubled fervor.

The massive disillusionment in the left-wing avant-garde occasioned by the political events of 1919-1920, culminating in the Kapp-Putsch, produced a fascination for all things "Bolshevik." In 1917, Russian Communism had been, even for the Bolsheviks, only the anticipation, at the periphery, of a world revolution whose center would be in industrial Europe. Afflicted by civil war, Allied intervention and economic collapse, the struggling Bolsheviks looked to European socialism for rescue and trusted in its strength. By 1920, the situation seemed totally reversed. Russian Communism had won the civil war, defeated the Allied intervention and begun to press its military advantage in a border war with Poland. Despair over domestic revolution and awe before Russian Bolshevik success stimulated in the German left-radicals a great interest in Soviet affairs.[8]

An informed appreciation of Soviet Russia was restricted to a very narrow circle in the years through 1921. There were only four main interpreters for the German left: Alfons Paquet, Arthur Holitscher, Franz Jung and Alfons Goldschmidt.[9] The circle was so small because it was so difficult to travel to the Soviet Union until the Civil War and interventionist blockade were over, i.e., until 1921. Of the four men who served in the crucial hiatus, not one was an orthodox party member in Germany. Holitscher and Goldschmidt were "fellow travellers" and Paquet was even more "bourgeois." Only Jung

60

was deeply involved in the extreme left parties, but his allegiance was to the factional German Communist Workers Party, and he found little favor with Lenin, to whom he represented everything "infantile" about left-extremism. Yet Jung played a major role in creating the idea of Soviet Russian culture in the German literary left.[10]

Jung reached this literary left via what was the major vehicle for "Bolshervism" in the early Twenties, the Herzfelde brothers' publishing firm, the Malik-Verlag.[11] When the firm took over the journal *Der Gegner* in December 1919, it became a "Bolshevist" organ, and Franz Jung made the key statement, "Asia as the Bearer of World Revolution," which proclaimed Russian soviets the only successful socialist revolutionary model.[12] His contributions both to journals and in book form had a major impact on the leftist literati. The Malik-Verlag, in addition, generated massive amounts of pro-Bolshevik material.

In 1920 this literature was supplemented by a new and sustained enthusiasm for Bolshevik Russia on the part of other literary journals, spearheaded by the new journal *Das Tagebuch*, edited by Stefan Großmann. Speaking for himself in 1919, before the journal was established, Großmann already indicated his preference for a turn eastward, away from France and toward the new Russia.[13] In one of the first issues of his new journal, Großmann's sentiments were echoed by his associate, Thomas Wehrlin, in "A Look Eastward."[14] *Das Tagebuch* serialized Alfons Paquet's reports on the Soviet Union in its first issues, as well as reports from Colin Ross on the first days of the Russian Revolution.[15] Großmann himself, in "The Radek Type," commented on the sophistication and talent of the Russian leadership and diplomatic corps.[16] Alfons Goldschmidt's reports on his visit to Moscow in 1920 were also carried in the first year of *Das Tagebuch*, as were a series of articles by Bertrand Russell on the Bolshevik Revolution.[17] In *Das Forum*, starting in 1920, Wilhelm Herzog, too, strenthened his commentary on Bolshevik Russia. In March he penned the editorial "Truth About Soviet Russia!" and printed a series of articles related to the Soviet Union: material by Lenin and Lunacharsky and documentation on conditions in Soviet Russia.[18]

Anatoly Lunacharsky's writings on Proletkult received wide publicity in Germany during 1919, primarily through the *Aktion-Kreis* around Pfemfert. Before the war, and even during it, Lunacharsky had written on German cultural history and participated in European literary discussions. He was known and respected as an intellectual. When Lenin appointed him to the Commissariat fo Enlightenment, the Bolshevik culture ministry, German intellectuals came to view him as the official spokesman of Bolshevik cultural aspirations. His speeches and writings were translated and "discussed thoroughly."[19] Meanwhile the cofounder of Proletkult, Bogdanov, had a similar impact. His books, *Art and the Proletariat* and *Scholarship and the Working Class*, appeared in 1919 and 1920 respectively, and in the latter year, *Die Aktion* published his key essay, "What is Proletarian Literature?"[20] Thus, by 1920, all the classic statements of the theory of Proletkult were available to and read by the German literary left.

The crucial document was the translation of Lunacharsky's essay "Proletarian Culture," composed in 1917 in connection with the founding of the Proletkult movement during the Russian Revolution. The piece appeared in Ludwig Rubiner's widely read anthology of social protest, *Community* (1919). In his essay, Lunacharsky argued that since culture was determined by class, Bolshevik Russia required a new, proletarian culture. In capitalist society, the proletariat as a class had been not only economically but culturally impoverished. It lived off the scraps of "bourgeois culture" and was even cut off from the older traditions of rural popular culture.

> But just this circumstance that the proletariat
> is the obverse side of the captalist medallion,
> jus this placement in the industrial city, in
> the world market and in scientific technology,
> just its orginally perfect integration without
> arbitrariness, and its discipline, had to become
> the driving force of its subsequent enormous
> development.[21]

For Lunacharsky, the proletariat was a "*Kultur*klasse," because it existed as the product of a highly sophisticated technical-industrial structure. It was only "artificially estranged" from art and science, though its behavior moved inherently along rational and aesthetic lines and was intrinsically responsive to them. Of course, the sudden realization of proletarian cultural consciousness led to excesses — a desire to throw over the whole of "bourgeois culture" — but this was either out of a Spartan concern to deal first with essentials or out of a romantic faith that the new energies would swiftly create a whole new culture out of the ruins of the old. Lunacharsky made one final, crucial distinction: between "socialist culture" and "proletarian culture." Socialist culture represented a future state in which a generally human culture, beyond all class divisions, would have emerged. By contrast, proletarian culture was an explicitly class cluture, militantly striving to win power for its class in order to create a socialist society. It was unjust to demand of the proletariat a socialist culture until it had successfully built a socialist society. Proletarian culture meant revolutionary criticism of "bourgeois civilization" on the lines of Marxist theory, and collective organization via the party, economic associations and increasingly, cultural associations, in order to achieve proletarian revolution.

In response to Lunacharsky and Bogdanov, a German Proletkult movement began to develop, finding support in the circles around Pfemfert's *Die Aktion* and at the Malik-Verlag. The figure who did most to advance this German Proletkult was Wieland Herzfelde, editor of the Malik-Verlag. His experience in a Freikorps prison camp in March 1919 had forged him into an indelible Communist. Though many of his comrades sooner or later abandoned the party, Herzfelde and his brother remained steadfast Communists throughout their long careers. Over the course of 1920-1921, in *Der Gegner*, Herzfelde issued his own position statement, "Society, Artists and Communism."[22] The essay asserted that art was class-bound, and that the only measure for the value of art was its relation to the proletariat. This was the principle on which Herzfelde built his publishing firm. It made absolutely no difference to him, he commented in the Malik-Verlag's first catalogue, published in May, 1922, if the conservatives bemoaned the decline of "art" into "mere journalism" or propaganda. Art for art's sake was over. Indeed, literature could not even keep pace with the tempo of change in modern life. The only purpose for art in the modern order, he concluded, was to support proletarian revolution.

In his position statement of 1920-21 Herzfelde launched into a sustained attack on "mass culture." There were those, he wrote, who claimed there was a separate culture of the little man, the popularity of which was attested by its mass distribution. But these detective novels, wild-west stories, sentimental romances and pornographic pulps were not authentically art at all. All this was merely industrial production. It had no proletarian character for all that since instead of stimulating class consciousness it concentrated on distraction. The escapism of these cheap novels, occultist and pious religious journals and plain pornography might be attractive to the "little man," but not to the true proletarian, he argued.

At the other extreme from this manipulative material developed by the industrialists of culture, stood so-called "pure art" — high culture, the fare of a narrow stratum of society, the upper classes. Herzfelde contended that "high culture" had a strong preference for complexity since it simultaneously heightened art's rarity, and hence its exchange value, while it absolved the upper class public from having to understand and to accept responsibility for its content. The artists themselves tended toward obscurity in an age of height-ened class conflict. In some measure this was an effort to cater to the public, whose perspective was determined by the ruling class. But there were other reasons why literature and art seemed so far removed from reality, so thoroughly unpolitical and unrevolutionary, Herzfelde continued. In the first place, most artists came from the middle classes. They were not born proletarians. Second, the econo-mic sitatuion of an artist in society made him totally vulnerable to the whim of the public or, as its surrogate, the publisher. Beyond this there were deeper reasons. Intrinsic to the nature of artistic production was an individual isolation which carried with it anarch-istic and elitist propensities. Herzfelde conceded this independence could bring with it the chance for critical perspective, but he argued even this perspective would remain merely individual, for the artist did not have any wider solidarity inherent in his productive situation. Each artist had to find his own personal path to the proletariat, to

64

Communism. Most would fail to pierce through all the obstacles and would continue willfully or inadvertently to propagate the ideological values of the ruling class.

Art was propaganda, Herzfelde concluded. The only question was whether one recognized this and chose the message, the ideology one wished to propound. The problem in Germany and the reason for the failure of the revolution, Herzfelde believed, was that no cultural alternative to the bourgeois ideology had been created – in contrast to the situation in pre-revolutionary Russia. Hence the great need in Germany for a proletarian art which could prepare the masses for successful revolution.

Herzfelde resolved to promote this cultural transformation both by publishing German Proletkult writers like Franz Jung and by providing a forum for the defense of Bolshevik Russia. The Malik-Verlag stepped up its pro-Bolshevik publishing in 1920-1921. During these years of famine and chaos in Russia, the Malik-Verlag became a cornerstone of the *Internationale Arbeiterhilfe* (IAH), the Communist propaganda operation led by Willi Münzenberg, directed to procuring support and relief for the Soviet Union in the West.[23]

The most uncompromising formulations of Proletkult orientation in German literary-artistic circles came from the so-called *Rote Gruppe*, an alliance of committed Communist writers and artists led by George Grosz and Erwin Piscator and associated with the Malik-Verlag.[24] Grosz set forth his views on art and proletarian culture in a short statement, *In Place of a Biography*, dated August 16, 1920. He claimed "Contemporary art is dependent upon the bourgeois class and dies with it."[25] Art and culture, just like religion, constituted ideological swindles for the oppressed classes. Yet artists continued to indulge in the fancy of their mysterious and sacred calling. He lashed out at the self-satisfied artists who saw themselves as aesthetic revolutionaries, who thought they were rejecting bourgeois society but who in reality served it by their "creative indifference" to social questions. Art should be a weapon, Grosz concluded.

In November 1920, he continued along this line with a new essay. His claim was: "Art today is an absolutely secondary matter."[26] All that really mattered was whether one stood for or against the exploiters. Those artists who thought they could continue to work for religious-metaphysical ideas were deluding themselves. They should go to workers' meetings and see those who really changed the world. They had finally to come up to date. "A time will come in which the artist will no longer be that bohemian, fungous anarchist, but rather a bright, healthy worker in the collective community." But this would only come when the working masses created a new order. Till then art would remain the diversion of the upper classes.

Similarly, Erwin Piscator rejected the avant-garde's elitism in favor of political agitation among the proletarian masses. He had no interest in artistic experimentalism, in "artistic revolution." For him, "in all questions of style the decisive question must be: will this be useful to the vast circle of the proletarian public? or will it bore them or infect and confuse them with bourgeois ideas?" Piscator did not reject out of hand "the new technical and stylistic possibilities of the most recent epoch in art," but these could only be employed if they exerted the correct influence. For Dada he had faint praise: its destruction of the swindle of bourgeois culture took a step in the right direction, but in so far as it remained a provocative harlequinade it did not attain the stature of art for the class struggle. "*Revolutionary* art can only emerge out of the spirit of the revolutionary proletariat..." He demanded that contemporary artists abandon elitist postures of intellectual individualism to subordinate themselves and their personal expression to the masses, speaking in plain language all could understand. In a manifesto he spelled out his program as follows: "simplicity in expression and construction; clear, unambigous influence on the sensibility of the working-class public; subordination of every artistic intention to the revolutionary goal; conscious emphasis and propagation of the idea of class struggle."[27]

An even more extreme advocate of German Proletkult wrote for Pfemfert's *Die Aktion*: F.W. Seiwert proclaimed, "Never can enough 'culture' be destroyed for the sake of culture. Never can enough 'works of art' be destroyed for the sake of art!"[28] All great cultural breakthroughs had the courage to destroy the idols of an earlier age. "Smash the images of the idols! In the name of proletarian culture!" Seiwert insisted that the only thing immortal about works of art, even those of a Beethoven or a Rembrandt, was the human urge to self-expression, and this urge in every age had to break out of the fixtures and strictures of past and obsolete forms. Seiwert's cultural argument sought to assimilate modernism to the postures of Proletkult. His 1920 essay, "Construction of Proletarian Culture," articulated the essential points of his radical program for German Proletkult: "The progressive realization of the communist idea means the same thing as the destruction of the present concept of art."[29] The "awe for bourgeois culture" had to be broken. There existed no connection between bourgeois and proletarian culture. "There is an end, here is a new beginning. Between there is chaos. We have to will the chaos! We must go through the chaos!" What the chaos Seiwert meant to affirm consisted in, he was blunt enough in expressing: "The contemporary art business must be annihilated, for it is the product of capitalism and a pillar of the bourgeoisie."

The theoretical and the practical thrust of German *Proletkult* was to expose the class basis of culture, to break the domination of bourgeois cultural values over the proletariat by helping it to its own cultural class-consciousness, and to break the established notions of art and intellectuality which kept the artist from commitment to the proletariat. There was an explicitly revolutionary commitment on the part of these artists and intellectuals who embraced *Proletkult*, but they were not proletarians, and the problem of reconciling the artist and intellectual with the proletariat remained. German *Proletkult* was the outcome of the disillusionment of left-wing German intellectuals over the failure of the revolution. It sought to support the proletarian revolution and to demonstrate solidarity with the working class, but there was unmistakable in the movement as well a sharp anti-intellectualism which boded ill for the intellectual integrity of the leftist avant-garde when confronted with the pressures of an increasingly authoritarian German Communist Party in the Twenties.

The Intellectual and the Proletariat: The Proletkult Debate

The strongly anti-intellectual rage behind the German Proletkult movement was manifest already in 1919 in the postures of Ludwig

Rubiner and Walther Rilla. The hatred for high culture among the Berlin Dadaists easily assimilated to this political outrage, so that in Proletkult this anti-intellectualism continued unabated. It found its explicit formulation in left radical journals like *Prolet* or the now factional *Die Aktion.* Yet an inescapable dilemma remained, for those propounding the anti-intellectualism were themselves intellectuals, and in the measure that they reinforced inherent proletarian suspicion into active hostility towards the intellectuals they undercut their own position as much as that of those they criticized. Hence in the same pages which carried the most bitter anti-intellectual diatribes there were ambivalent moments when intellectuals reminded themselves and their readers that not every intellectual had betrayed the revolution and not every proletarian remained loyal to it.

The height of proletarian resentment of the intellectuals came in 1919 in the journal *Prolet.* In an essay entitled "The Proletariat and the Bourgeois Intellectuals," Otto Steinicke insisted that proletarian orientations had nothing to do with idealism.[30] Their behavior was the objective and hence spontaneous response to their social condition. "Boundless fraternizing we consign to capitalistic publishers." Proletarianism had nothing to do with sentimental humanitarianism, and the proletariat was not interested in intellectuals of such sympathies. Similarly Heinz Lindemann wrote, in "Proletariat and Intellectual," that the proletariat obtained its consciousness directly from its social condition and through this condition was in a better position to discern proper tactics than any intellectuals whose education and practice made them servants of the ruling class.[31] Even those who drifted over to the proletariat were too full of idealistic and fantastic notions to be of service to the cause. All these figures represented, Lindemann asserted, was the "social disintegration of the bourgeois intelligentsia."

Such diatribes drew the protest of a longstanding intellectual radical, Erich Mühsam.[32] He charged the advocates of Proletkult anti-intellectualism with the worst kind of doctrinaire myopia. How were they defining their terms, he wondered, so that they could assert that proper conduct followed necessarily from social context? Did they not recognize that Ebert, who had betrayed the socialist

68

revolution, was a worker, while Luxemburg, Liebknecht, Marx and Lenin, who were its greatest leaders, were all intellectuals? Yet, having protested this much, Mühsam, too, blasted the pretentions of "intellectual workers" who presumed to "rule" for the rest of society. He went on to argue that in a true socialist order the distinction between intellectuals and workers would cease to be significant.

Yet the Proletkult current of anti-intellectualism swept past Mühsam's distinctions. In *Die Aktion*, Kurt Offenburg published an essay, "Intellectual and Proletariat," in which spontaneous revolutionary consciousness in the proletariat came to be arrayed against the intellectuals' elitism. Offenburg argued that in a modern socialist revolution, there was no place for individual leaders, for the proletarian revolution was a mass movement, a collective event. Moreover, intellectuals both in Russia and in Germany had proven unreliable allies in the real revolutionary crisis. He concluded: "To the workers alone — feeling themselves a united mass through their class consciousness, struggling for liberation after generations of the same suffering and the same aspiration — the first ranks of leadership must always be given, for these experiences weigh more than all theoretical knowledge."[33]

Leftist writers agonized over the role that remained for them if they affirmed this viewpoint. They had to define a role for themselves which did not fall back into the elitism and betrayal of the past, yet did not end in their utter self-abnegation. As Franz Pfemfert commented with real pathos, "Does intellect pollute?"[34] Just because one was an intellectual, was he automatically disqualified from participation in the revolutionary movement? Had the proletariat shown such decisively clear class consciousness? Indeed, many Marxist intellectuals observed, Pfemfert among them, the proletariat had not shown an appropriate class consciousness. The absence of these subjective conditions had led to the failure of the German revolution. It was not entirely the proletariat's fault, of course. Workers had been subjected to an all-too-effective ideological indoctrination by the ruling class and its intellectual servants. That was the shame of bourgeois intellectuals, yet it should also be recognized as the opportunity for socialist intellectuals. They had as their task the debunking of bourgeois culture and liberating the minds of the proletariat, so that it could become more rationally and effectively revolutionary.

The assessment of the failure of class consciousness in the proletariat during the revolution fostered two radically disparate intellectual impulses. The first was a theoretical examination of the nature and role of proletarian class consciousness in Marxist theory, which resulted in the great theoretical renewal of Marxism in Georg Lukacs' *History and Class Consciousness* and Karl Korsch's *Marxism and Philosophy*, both published in Berlin in 1923.[35] At the same time, the assessment reenforced the Leninist conclusion that proletarian class consciousness without the intervention of a directive vanguard party would lapse into trade unionism.[36] While the latter posture failed to do justice to the revolutionary mass impulse behind the council movement, the failure of that movement and the success of the Bolshevik seizure of power lent it a good deal of plausibility. Lenin felt justified in the aftermath of the failed Central European revolution to insist on the reorganization of the European parties on the lines of his vanguard party.

In addition to this first impetus toward a new sociological and organizational grasp of the proletariat, committed left-radicals felt compelled to formulate a theory of intellectual purpose. Two important formulations of this sort emerged in the mid-Twenties from the German literary left. The first was Friedrich Wolf's "Art is a Weapon!" — written in 1924 but not published until 1928.[37] Wolf, a playwright, began his essay with references to Zola in the Dreyfus Affair and to Tolstoy's criticism of the Tsarist war with Japan, then dwelt at length on German literary involvement in the Reformation and the Peasant Wars. He insisted that the artist had always been called upon to be the conscience of his times, and his art had to serve as a weapon for social justice. "At the great turning points, since ideas wish to realize themselves, at these high points of human history, worldviews become 'politics,' the writer becomes in his highest intensification a seer, an admonisher, a prophet!" This did not remove the artist from the immediate into some domain of timeless wisdom. "There is only one point of eternity within our grasp: the present." Artists who became so caught up in the timeless

70

that they did not see what was happening around them, Wolf went on, did not really live. For too long German art appeared merely a luxury, a matter for personal cultivation, but the times were too turbulent for that. Art had to become a weapon.

The second key statement appeared in 1925: an essay by Grosz and Herzfelde entitled "Art is in Danger."[38] It set forth their view definitively. "No time has been more hostile to art than today, and it is true for the average man of today when it is said that he could live without art."[39] The overriding reality of the new age was technological development. It set the cultural horizon of the masses in all the great cities of the world. Art used to satisfy a need for news and information in the masses, a "living hunger for images," as Grosz put it. But now that need was far more effectively serviced by the mass media, photography and film, with their collective form both of production and reception.

Artists at first tried to adapt to the technological transformation. Thus Futurism, with its accentuation of "simultaneity, movement, rhythm," tried to embrace the technical. But that frenzied enthusiasm was inappropriate. "In so far as one spoke of dynamism, one soon came to see that this dynamism found its most immediate expression in dry engineering drawings."[40] This was the insight of the Constructivists. "They want matter-of-factness; they want to work to satisfy actual needs." But in the measure that they remained artists they had not followed their logic through to the end. Constructivism led logically to the displacement of the artist by the engineer, the "real shaper of our age." Only in Russia, where technological principles were still novel, could art have an educational and progressive function by celebrating functionalism. In the West, technology was completely familiar to the average man. If all art meant was the recognition of the technological, the outcome of development led to an inevitable conclusion: "liquidation of art."[41]

Yet the artist resisted. He clung to his self-conception as creator of eternal values, clung to the hope that no matter how scorned or ignored today, in the future men would understand and appreciate his work. Artists, Grosz observed, "can never be more deeply wounded than by doubting that their work serves progress."[42] The avant-garde artist conceived himself as gifted to foretell the shape of things to come, to attain solidarity with a future society to make up for his estrangement from his contemporaries. But only if men changed would their reception of that art be possible, Grosz asserted. The real issue was how to realize the alternative social world. This was the insight of Dada, he believed. The world was not run by ideas or ideals, Dada recognized, and "it was perfect madness to believe that spirit or any intellectuals ruled the world." Dadaists recognized the irrelevance of art, that there were more important issues at hand than art. "They said... there is still shooting, there is still profiteering, there is still starvation, there are still lies — what does all art matter?"[43] The artist was merely deceiving himself in taking his avant-garde stance at its face value. There would never be a reconciliation of art, which remained the business and the play of the ruling classes, with a regenerated social order in the future unless the social order were really overturned, unless, as a part of a whole movement, the artist threw himself into the struggle and helped it to success.

It was not enough to be an artistic revolutionary, to make formal experiments. The modern artist was confronted with two choices, neither of which left room for "pure art." He could serve technology or he could serve politics. The autonomy of art and culture, the pride of the tradition, had been annihilated by modern social organization.

> Either as an engineer, architect or commercial artist he enters the ranks of the army which develops industrial forces and exploits the world (an army still unfortunately organized on feudal lines), or as the spokesman and critic of the revolutionary idea and of its followers he joins the army of the oppressed which struggles for its rightful share of the goods of the world, for a rational social organization of life.[44]

Technological subordination or political service: these were the alternatives facing the artist-intellectual in the twentieth century, Grosz concluded.

72

Ironically, however, these two alternatives collapsed rapidly into one — the challenge of technocracy. The seeming alternative of artistic intellectual activism and liberation in Grosz's notion of following the revolutionary idea and serving the oppressed came swiftly to be foreclosed by the Stalinist bureaucratization of the left. The choices of the left by the later Twenties reduced to technocratic subordination, as instruments either of technological production processes ruthlessly rationalized for their own ends or of bureaucratic political parties just as ruthlessly organized to preserve their own power. In that context, Grosz himself would be driven from the camp of the Bolshevists to that of the Negativists.[45] Many of the most prominent "Bolshevists" proved ideological victims of Stalinist "Bolshevization."

"Bolshevization" of the Party and German Left-Radical Response

From service as a mere image to the creation of a real model for cultural action, Soviet influence on the German literary left grew substantially from 1919 to 1923. Finally, the Russian Bolsheviks began to intervene directly, as cultural and organizational politics within the Soviet Union spilled over into the German cultural scene, and even more, as the Comintern exerted its authority over the German Communist Party. The interpenetration of Soviet cultural and political influence in German leftist affairs would become salient by mid-decade.

From the Bolshevik vantage both Futurism and Proletkult within the Soviet Union had carried their artistic revolution too far by 1920. Two aspects of their programs alienated Lenin and even the more sympathetic Lunacharsky: their demand for the destruction of the "bourgeois heritage" and their demand for cultural hegemony for their particular faction.[46] Lenin found neither demand acceptable. For one thing, he had no appetite for aesthetic modernism. As he put it:

> Why must we bow down to the new as though
> to a god whom we must obey simply because

he is new?...We are good revolutionists, but
nevertheless we feel obliged for some reason
to prove that we also stand "at the height of
contemporary culture." I however make bold to
declare myself a "barbarian." I am unable to
consider the productions of expressionism,
futurism, cubism, and other isms, the highest
manifestations of artistic genius. I do not
understand them. I experience no joy from them.[47]

He argued with young art students in the studios who expressed
disdain for traditional literature and enthusiasm for Mayakovsky
and modernism, urging them to return to Pushkin and Nekrasov.
When the actress Gzovskaya did a dramatic reading from Mayakovsky,
Lenin asked her to work on Pushkin as well. He expressed vehement
objections to the government publication of Mayakovsky's *The 150
Millions*, the most "Bolshevist" of his works, complaining to Gorky
that Futurism was not Bolshevism but "hooliganism."

Lenin thought Futurism esoteric and silly. Proletkult was an
entirely different matter, for it threatened to create an independent
mass base and it was led by his unregenerate opponent Bogdanov.
By 1920 its ranks had swollen to a dangerous level and it was making
gestures of independence not only toward the Commissariat of
Enlightenment but toward the Party itself. That proved too much
for Lenin and he intervened personally to break up the movement.
That turn figures into a wider policy shift away from left-extremism
and the excesses of "war communism" toward the New Economic
Policy (NEP). The implementation of NEP broke the Proletkult
momentum in Russia. As Alexander Kaun noted, "in 1922 the
number of proletkult units fell from three hundred to twenty and
in 1924 to seven."[48]

The German Communists simply followed the path broken by
Lenin in his attack not only on German Proletkult but on avant-
gardism altogether. The German Proletkult movement became
embroiled in controversy as part of the institutional conflict between
the KPD and the splinter factions on the extreme left. The left-
extremism which Lenin berated in the spring of 1920 as "infantile"
had indeed found its strongest following among the literary leftists,

both within the party and in the penumbra of its sympathizers and rivals.

By 1920 in fact, many advocates of Proletkult in Germany found themselves sharply out of sympathy with Lenin for all their reverence for the proletariat and for Russia's proletarian revolution. By late 1919, these left-radicals formed so unruly an element in the KPD that its leader, Paul Levi, engineered a confrontation which forced them to withdraw.[49] The Berlin *Aktion-Kreis* around Pfemfert left the party at that time. So did Franz Jung.[50] In the spring of 1920, these left-radical intellectuals formed the core of the new Communist Workers Party of Germany (KAPD). Its orientation was emphatically revolutionary, affirming total opposition to the parliamentary and accommodationist politics of other leftist organizations. Within its umbrella were leftists of a variety of stripes, from outright anarchists to anarcho-syndicalists to adherents of Pannekoek and Gortner or Luxemburg. One thing united them: a sharp hostility towards the party centrism and internal discipline exercised by Levi but associated with, and defended by Lenin.

The publication of *"Left-Wing" Communism: An Infantile Disorder* by Lenin in the spring of 1920 was a slap in the face to these left-radicals and a stream of sharply anti-Leninist polemics, drawing on the authority of Luxemburg but embracing a set of theoretical postures which covered the gamut of the left, began to appear in Germany. Lenin's concern to restore organizational order and political effectiveness to the European revolutionary movement through the famous "21 Conditions" imposed by the Comintern, while not primarily aimed at closing off theoretical debate, provoked further recriminations on the radical left.[51] Even greater criticism greeted his pragmatic adoption of the New Economic Policy in 1922. But the most important provocation of anti-Leninist, anti-Bolshevik sentiment in the radical left was the intervention of the Comintern in March 1921 to provoke an ill-conceived and disastrous uprising in Central Germany.[52] The action was taken while Paul Levi was away, and he responded with a public attack on Comintern interference. For this he lost his party position, and when he left, many of the intellectuals of the party followed him. This included the cream of the former USPD leftists, led by Ernst

Däumig. Even Clara Zetkin felt it necessary to resign her party office, though not her party membership, in protest.

Intellectual anti-Leninism by 1922 was a considerable force on the left. Leninism became associated not only with authoritarian centralism in party organization but with opportunism in political tactics. Yet Lenin remained the great symbol of successful revolution, and even the most critical of these leftists had to find some place for Lenin in their positive conception of Marxism. The disintegration of other radical organizations in the aftermath of the failed revolution, however, made the position of the KPD far more important on the radical left, and made the question of orthodoxy under the Comintern an issue of weight for leftists of all stripes. Even the most enthusiastic "Bolshevists" in Berlin had maintained a substantial intellectual independence from the Russian party and its leadership and dogma. Now, however, it seemed only the KPD remained as the institutional locus of left opposition.

Thus, the moment in the mid-Twenties when the Communist International really enforced a "Bolshevization" of German Communism was full of historical irony. In this "Bolshevization" process, the self-proclaimed "Bolshevist" intellectuals became a prefered target of attack. "Bolshevization" aimed to eliminate the influence of the "Spartacist" Marxism of Rosa Luxemburg as well as the new "Praxis" Marxism of Georg Lukacs and Karl Korsch.[53] The intervention of the Comintern in the German Communist Party after 1923 aimed to bring into rigid conformity with Moscow not simply the political and organizational practice of the KPD but also, if not primarily, its theoretical vision. As against the brilliantly innovative and philosophically profound "Praxis" Marxism of Lukacs and Korsch, it enforced Stalin's wooden dogmatization of Lenin.

The struggle between the Stalinizing Comintern and the "deviationists" of theoretical Marxism was not in the least remote from the intellectual circles hitherto examined. Indeed, Lukacs's classic work was published by Wieland Herzfelde's Malik-Verlag in 1923, while Korsch worked and wrote in Berlin and came later in the Twenties to tutor two of the most important avant-garde leaders, Alfred Döblin and Bertolt Brecht, in Marxist theory.[54] More generally, it was in the Berlin literary and intellectual circles that the new

"Praxis" Marxism had its most sympathetic reception, as it was in those circles that other left-radical traditions, from anarchism to Luxemburgism, survived the failed revolution. Yet Lukacs and Korsch considered themselves Leninists when they wrote the works for which the "Bolshevizing" Comintern would condemn them. In this complex web of ironies, for the Russians the "Praxis" Marxists seemed too influenced by the anti-Leninist German environment to be trusted, and they bore the brunt of the ideological "Bolshevization" campaign, an explicitly anti-intellectual one.

The campaign was launched in March 1924. Its origins lay in the struggle between Stalin and Trotsky. Trotsky, through his ally of the moment, Radek, seemed to have too much influence on the European parties. These "intellectuals" had to be put in their place by the organization men led by Stalin and his ally, Zinoviev, director of the Comintern. To lessen "deviationist" influence, Zinoviev brought pressure on the German Communist Party to alter its leadership. His goal was to encourage a faction around Maslow and Fischer to seize control of the KPD from the existing leadership presumed friendly to Radek.[55] Zinoviev sent two letters to the German party. The first went to Maslow and Fischer, promising Comintern support for the "left," but warning that it did not extend to the "ultra-left" intellectuals in the party like Arthur Rosenberg and Karl Korsch. The point of this warning was made explicit in a second letter sent virtually simultaneously to the "workers" Thälmann and Schlecht, urging them to support the "left" seizure of power in the party but at the same time to be on guard against intellectuals. The line of the Comintern was clear: engineering a split between the proletarian and the intellectual elements in the KPD along a characteristic fault line in the history of German socialism.

When Zinoviev's two letters were read to the April 1924 KPD Congress, they caused great unrest.[56] The party was unwilling to have this polarization introduced into its life, and Arthur Rosenberg bluntly charged Zinoviev and the Comintern with trying to split the party leadership from its base, thus endangering the revolutionary movement in Germany. The unity displayed by the "left" in its seizure of control in April 1924 thwarted Zinoviev's first move, but the sensitivity of the issue was plain for all to see, and Zinoviev returned to the attack from a position of greater strength in June 1924 at the Fifth Congress of the Comintern in Moscow. Zinoviev's remarks before the Congress were primarily directed to the German situation, critical of the ousted party leadership, but also critical of the "ultra-left" intellectuals still within the party.[57] Explicitly he attacked the new theoretical works of Lukacs and Korsch, disparaging them as "professors" who still had to "learn" Marxism. At the same time, the Russian ideological community and its German epigoni launched a barrage of disparaging criticism against Lukacs and Korsch. This attack was part of a larger assault on theory as such, aimed to discredit the intellectual theorist Trotsky by emphasizing the superiority of practical Leninism — the organizational control now in the hands of Stalin. Lenin had died in January 1924, and during the first half of that year in Russia his thought had been canonized into sacred writ largely on Stalinist lines.

The resistance of the KPD leadership in April turned into acceptance in June, and the new KPD leaders began to turn against the "ultra-left" in accordance with the Comintern line. While some of these intellectual "deviationists" were willing to abandon their positions and conform — most notably Georg Lukacs — others maintained their theoretical independence, even at the cost of expulsion. Thus Karl Korsch emerged, after being personally reprimanded by Zinoviev in Moscow in 1924, as one of the leaders of overt opposition to the "Bolshevization" program.[58] His position became sharply anti-Soviet, though not yet anti-Leninist. By 1926 he was expelled from the party and his anti-Soviet posture became even more sharply defined. The party, on the other hand, became more and more docile in its "Leninism." The somewhat independent "left" leadership of Maslow and Fischer was eased out in 1925 and replaced by party hacks led by Thälmann, and the "Bolshevization" process culminated in general with the replacement of ideological leaders of independent stature by apparatchiks, together with the promulgation and enforcement of a dogmatic "Leninist" orthodoxy. In the words of Hermann Weber, "by its ideological struggle against Trotskyism and Luxemburgism, the KPD adopted clearly and conclusively the position of an apparent Leninism which would swiftly prove itself to be Stalinism."[59]

Thus, the significant feature of the "Bolshevization" process of the mid Twenties was its anti-intellectualism and the permanent rupture it provoked in the Marxist camp. By its heavy-handed intervention the Comintern forced the realization that "Praxis" Marxism was indeed incompatible with what Leninism had become, and it led to the split of Western European from Soviet Marxism. In Germany, as in Russia, party bureaucrats won out over intellectuals. The bitter question which remained was how intellectual integrity could be reconciled with the new Bolshevik-Stalinist Marxism. Karl Korsch, for one, insisted it could not. That was to prove a very important position within the Berlin avant-garde, for Korsch articulated a militant Marxism which felt itself called upon to deny Bolshevism; in a word, Korsch represented Negativism. In his powerful statement of 1930, "The Present State of the Problem of Marxism and Philosophy," he commented: "There are many indications that despite secondary, transient or trivial conflicts, the real division on all major and decisive questions is between the old Marxist orthodoxy of Kautsky allied to the new Russian or 'Leninist' orthodoxy on the one side, and all critical and progressive theoretical tendencies in the proletarian movement today on the other side."[60] This would be the foundation of Negativist resistance to full "Bolshevization."

Chapter Three

THE WRITER AND THE PARTY: THE SPLIT BETWEEN NEGATIVISTS AND COMMUNISTS, 1925 – 1930

> You say: a writer who perceives the
> situation must carry on the struggle
> where the political forces are stored:
> in the Communist Party... We say: a
> writer must carry on the struggle where
> he can develop his strength: in *inde-*
> *pendence...*
> — G. Pohl, "On the Role of the
> Creative Writer" (1929)

From the outset, committed "Bolsheviks" like Wieland Herzfel-de, Willi Münzenberg and Johannes R. Becher had insisted that political responsibility required the complete subordination of art to political struggle. Until late into the Twenties, however, they studiously avoided imposing party affiliation as a criterion for participation in their campaigns and publications. They welcomed the support of unattached left-radicals. This strategy paid off well in the campaigns of the *Internationale Arbeiterhilfe*; it supplied Communist journals and propaganda campaigns with the considerable talents of figures like Tucholsky and Brecht; and it provided broader support for Becher and other Communist writers against state censorship and trials for sedition. It proved crucial as well for the success of the Piscator theater collective. In short, Communist intellectuals were never so successful in their actions as when they collaborated with the sympathetic but unattached left avant-garde.

The solidarity of the unattached left with the Communist writers reached its height in the mid-Twenties. It found expression in the campaign to defend Piscator's political theater and in the formation of the *Gruppe 1925*. What bound the unattached leftists to the Communists was *Tendenz* — specifically, political criticism of the bour-geois-capitalist republic and its cultural order. Yet by the late Twenties the bond between committed Communists and the critical negativists of the avant-garde dissolved, because the KPD intellectuals demanded *Parteilichkeit*, full subordination to the directives of the Party, and for many Negativists, that entailed too great a *sacrificium intellectualis*.

The impetus to stress *Parteilichkeit* emanated not from the KPD leadership but from Soviet Russia. Johannes R. Becher and a few other German party writers had come into contact with the "prole-tarian-revolutionary" writers organizations of Russia, the RAPP (Russian Association of Proletarian Writers) and its international arm, the IVRS (International Association of Revolutionary Writers).[1] These Soviet organizations were waging an intense political-cultural campaign within the Soviet Union which they wished to extend into German party life as well: the struggle for ideological purity over intellectual competence. RAPP engineered a polemical campaign along the ideological line of "red" versus "expert," attacking the so-called "fellow travellers," bourgeois intellectuals whose social origins or personal independence made their political purity suspect. The struggle for hegemony led by the RAPP and its journal, *On Guard*, was, to be blunt, a Stalinization of literary life. The RAPP launched a vehement attack against the residual Futurist impulses centered in the LEF (Left Front in the Arts) around Mayakovsky and Tretyakov, as well as against the major Soviet journal for literature, *Red Virgin Soil*, and its editor Voronsky. Most of the Communist "purists" of *On Guard* were literary hacks, writers substantially inferior in talent who sought by the orthodoxy and militancy of their ideological posture to secure their own positions. Ironically, most of these defenders of "proletarian culture" were themselves intellectuals. RAPP succeeded in drawing the Soviet Communist Party into literary disputes, becoming by the late Twenties an agency for the enforce-ment of the party line in literature, only itself to be liquidated in 1932 when literary Stalinization found its fulfillment in the Zhda-nov-Radek campaign for "socialist realism."

This RAPP and its international arm, IVRS, adopted and promo-ted what it saw as a parallel "proletarian-revolutionary" impulse in

82

Becher and his circle. When Becher travelled to the Soviet Union in 1927, he delivered an enthusiastic report on the progress of "Proletarian-Revolutionary Literature in Germany."[2] It was agreed to finance a German organization parallel to the Soviet one, with its primary object the cooptation or exclusion of unattached leftist intellectuals in Germany. In all this, the role of the German party was relatively passive.[3] The party hierarchy, in fact, had a far more ambivalent attitude on the whole question of cultural policy. For this there were several reasons. In the first place, the party concerned itself primarily with securing a mass base in competition with its hated rival, the SPD. Cultural politics, in this context, was secondary, and shrewd tacticians could and did argue that intellectual critiques of the SPD from outside the KPD would be ideologically more useful in the larger social conflict for the working class. Second, the party leadership was concerned to exert discipline within the party especially against the "ultra-left," those "infantile" left-extremist intellectuals out of step with the Comintern line. But the dissidents in this sphere had for some time tended to be the very advocates of intellectual intervention, hence their program was viewed with suspicion. Third, and of no small significance, those KPD leaders who took interest in cultural affairs tended to share with Lenin a pronounced preference for classical humanism, whether Pushkin or Schiller. At most they appreciated Maxim Gorky or the Gerhart Hauptmann of *Die Weber*. All the internal disputes in the avant-garde seemed to the party leaders incomprehensible and "bourgeois-decadent."

While of intellectuals within the party it demanded discipline and compliance with the party line, towards the "fellow-travellers" the KPD proved consistently mild. It remained more interested in the political cooperation of artistic intellectuals as "opinion leaders" for the public than in controlling their doctrinal orthodoxy. So long as these writers showed political sympathy for the party, the proletariat and the USSR, the party saw no need to attack them. That impetus came from the Bolshevist intellectuals themselves.

Against the disillusionments of the failed revolution and the abandonment by the moderates, the Bolshevists in the Berlin avant-garde took solace in the structure and the identity of the Party.[4] It became their redemption, and they found it increasingly intolerable for ostensible fellow radicals to remain aloof from its structure. This sense of growing isolation and political impotence must figure into the account of the intellectuals' striking accentuation of party discipline in the later Twenties. Indeed, to a remarkable degree, the intellectual Bolshevists outpaced their bureaucratic counterparts in the party in their commitment to a rigorous Communist cultural policy.[5]

The conflict within the avant-garde between party writers and independents arose not simply because of changes in the orientation of the Bolshevist wing of the avant-garde but because developments in German social and political history after November 1923 revealed a grim but characteristic fault line in the political culture of the Weimar Republic. The old blindness of German moderates to the danger on the right returned; the evanescent republican militancy provoked by the Rathenau assassination had lost its elan. The collapse of the German Democratic Party's electoral constituency from 1920 to 1924 signalled the weakening of liberal resolve in the new republic, and after 1924 there occurred an erosion of liberal integrity which eventuated in the surrender of the moderates to conservative and fascist forces on both political and cultural fronts. This internal rot of the Weimar moderates has been amply documented in Modris Eksteins' compelling history of the great liberal newspapers of Weimar.[6]

As a consequence, the avant-garde became increasingly isolated from the patronage and participation of the moderate and liberal dilettants and enthusiasts. The institutional basis of the avant-garde intellectuals suffered a continual erosion over the course of the later Twenties. Censorship increased and so did social support for it, as was demonstrated in the victory of the anti-pornography *Schund und Schmutz Gesetz* (1926-1927).[7] Political trials of artists also increased. Grosz was brought to trial again. Johannes R. Becher, a leading Communist writer, was hounded through the courts for his propagandistic novel, *Levisite*.[8] In theater, Erwin Piscator was dismissed from the *Volksbühne* in the midst of a full-scale politicization crisis and even the established director Lepold Jessner came under enormous pressure as Intendant of the Berlin *Staatstheater*.

84

Within literary Berlin itself a split emerged between the "radicals" — avant-garde writers who were generally politically radical as well — and the moderate "idealist" writers who, having overcome an infatuation with Expressionism, had turned to a kind of pseudo-classical traditionalism. Foremost in this class belongs Alfred Kerr, but he was not alone. A whole group of "professorial critics" — Max Osborn, Monty Jacobs, Arthur Elösser and others — centered around the great newspaper houses Ullstein, Mosse and Sonnemann, applied their grave manner to contemporary culture and proved ponderously its failure to live up to standards.[9] In this bleak context, the leftist avant-garde of Berlin fell into internal disarray.

The dynamics of this crisis demonstrate a certain regularity. It broke out simultaneously in theater and in literature. In Piscator's political theater movement, the politicization crisis isolated "radicals" from moderates first, then culminated in a conflict among the radicals themselves. Similarly, in the *Schutzverband Deutscher Schriftsteller*, the professional association of German free-lance writers, a rift first emerged between the radicals and the moderates. When these moderates resisted efforts at politicization from the left, the radicals established an alternative organization, the *Gruppe 1925.* This group represented the most significant alliance of Bolshevists and Negativists in the Berlin avant-garde and its fate proved emblematic for the whole. In the *Gruppe 1925* the same divisiveness emerged among the radicals themselves. The Bolshevists, led by Johannes R. Becher, insisted upon *Parteilichkeit*; the Negativists, led by Alfred Döblin, insisted upon independence. The consequence was disintegration.

Erwin Piscator and Political Theater

Personally and aesthetically, Erwin Piscator identified himself very closely with the party-line and the agitational objectives of the KPD, yet it would be inadequate to contend that he merely collapsed art into politics, theater into propaganda. That contention, whether uttered in condemnation by the right or in celebration by the KPD organization, mistook Piscator's dialectical idea of the interpenetration of art and politics, theater and agitation. Piscator was a major artistic talent, and his technical innovations alone would have won him a saliency in the history of German 20th-century theater and culture, even if he had not been a politically controversial figure. But he was this as well: both artist and political agitator simultaneously. Piscator conceived of art as the highest form of political agitation in its capacity of *"enhancing every theatrical aspect into general historical significance"* and bringing the audience into full participation in the stage action.[10] Even as he strove to introduce a political significance into his artistic action, his solutions of artistic problems led to new potentials for political agitation.

Piscator considered the essential nature of his endeavor the synthesis of art and politics. The political required contemporaneity, awareness of and involvement in the large social context in which the cultural realm was embedded. A political theater required a sociological foundation. The documentary and the reportorial could raise the merely individual to a sociological plane, Piscator recognized, and the application of new technological media, especially film, could provide the resources for a documentary theater. The essence of documentary theater was to "raise the theatrical to the level of the historical."[11] That would constitute "sociological dramaturgy," a theatrical style abreast of the times.

> This period, which has deprived the individual of
> his "humanness" through its social and economic
> requirements, without replacing it with the higher
> humanity of a new society, has raised a *new hero*
> on the pedestal — *itself.* No longer is the indivi-
> dual with his private, personal fate the heroic
> factor of the new drama, but rather the
> times themselves, the fate of the masses is
> the *heroic factor in the new dramaturgy.* [12]

Political and economic forces pervaded the individual personality. "Wherever he appears, there appear with him his class and status. When he enters into conflict, whether moral, spiritual or instinctual, he enters into a conflict with society." Man could only be conceived "in terms of his relation to society." That was the lesson of documentary theater.

The decisive nature of Piscator's new "sociological dramaturgy" was *pedagogical*. Didacticism was the heart of documentary. Piscator was not interested merely in being a "mirror of the times." By transforming the specific artistic event into a collective phenomenon, documentary theater became *political* theater. For Piscator, a Marxist theater aimed "to take reality as a starting point, *to enhance the social discrepancy into an element of protest, of revolt, and of reconstruction.*"[13] Contemporary documentary theater became *Tendenz-theater*, stirring immediate political response.

Piscator's breakthrough came at the *Volksbühne*, the theater founded by the Berlin Naturalists and the Social Democrats.[14] It was, technically, the best theater in Berlin. But for Piscator there was, in addition to this artistic advantage, a political mission associated with working at the *Volksbühne*. He wished to shift the direction of that institution away from its accommodationist line back towards the radicalism of its initial impulse. The *Volksbühne* should, he believed, be a theater *of* the proletariat, i.e., in the interest of the proletariat, rather than a theater *for* the proletariat, bestowing high culture on the lowly.[15] But the dominant force in the *Volksbühne* movement had come to be cultural associations concerned to provide mass access to serious theater through special bulk admission rates. The attitude in the *Volksbühne* was, from Piscator's vantage, too "bourgeois," antipathetic to party politics and especially to the idea of proletarian class struggle. What he proposed to do was to mobilize the remnants of proletarian radicalism within the *Volksbühne* to reverse this tendency. That was a "revolutionary tactic," he realized, which would be an "education of the public even against its will."[16] If he proposed to bring politics into the artistic fare of the *Volksbühne*, Piscator also proposed to bring art into the political life and propaganda agitation of the KPD. He first integrated film into a theatrical production not in any aesthetic context, but in his 1925 program for the KPD party congress, *Trotz Alledem*, a documentary drama about the German Revolution of 1918-1919. The success of that production confirmed Piscator in his belief "that the strongest political-propaganda influence lay along the line of the strongest artistic construction."[17]

In subsequent productions at the *Volksbühne* and elsewhere, Piscator sought to follow out this program. In linking his staging innovations to his political orientations, Piscator as a director asserted his primacy over the dramatist.[18] He justified this practice with the explanation that there were no adequate revolutionary dramas available; without them, he believed he had a right to transform dramatic material not only for political effect but as his artistic prerogative.[19] At first most observers welcomed his "experiments" and remained open-minded regarding their possibilities. His production of *Stormtide* in 1926 won praise for the most part, and what criticism surfaced aimed more at the dramatist than the director.[20] But in later productions, a growing restiveness emerged in the theatrical and critical community, the fear that Piscator's staging completely swallowed drama, or more concretely that his technological innovations threatened the traditional integrity of theater.[21] Thus resistance to Piscator took two forms: against his political orientations and against his artistic practice.

Piscator precipitated a politicization crisis in theater with his guest engagement at Leopold Jessner's *Staatstheater* in September 1926, by a radical reinterpretation of Schiller's classic *The Robbers*. Piscator believed Schiller's dramas in their context had been radically revolutionary, indeed, too revolutionary for the bourgeoisie not only of the late 18th century but in 1926. Yet at the same time, for the proletariat Schiller was a century and a half out of date. Piscator decided to transform Schiller's drama to accord with contemporary proletarian radicalism. In Piscator's own words, "the bourgeois public is so divided, contradictory and decomposed in itself that one cannot take its intellectual requirements as a standard."[22] Only the proletariat offered this standard. Piscator cared neither about the public at the *Staatstheater* nor about Schiller's 18th-century artistic intentions. He wished only to reproduce the revolutionary impact of Schiller in the contemporary context. As Ihering observed, getting to the heart of the matter: "What one has here is fundamentally not the staging of a classic but the presentation of a new revolutionary play based on *The Robbers* because there are no modern revolutionary plays."[23]

An uproar greeted the production.[24] Even before the opening night the right-wing press had begun to howl that the *Staatstheater* was being turned over to *Kulturbolschewismus* and that a classic of German Idealism would be travestied in Piscator's hands. They felt fully justified in that view after the production, and their spokesman, Paul Fechter, called for an official inquiry into the circumstances surrounding a state theater commissioning the "bolshevization" of Schiller.[25] In addition he demanded the non-renewal of Jessner's contract as Intendant of the *Staatstheater.*[26] While the public applauded on the night of the performance, they also accepted the judgment of their "conservative-democratic and liberal-reactionary press" the next morning that Piscator was guilty of "besmirching the cultural treasury of the nation."[27] The concurrence of the "liberal-reactionary" bourgeois press with the radical right betokened the isolation into which Piscator's politicization of theater was hastening the avant-garde.

The climax of the crisis came at the *Volksbühne* in 1927, when Piscator took Ehm Welk's drama, *Thunder over Gottland*, which depicted a German uprising of 1400, and transformed it into a paean to world revolution, a celebration of "Bolshevism" and Lenin. The right-wing press went berserk over this "rape" of the text, this extreme *Kulturbolschewismus.*[28] In this they were seconded with no less vigor by the moderate-liberal press. Both groups demanded that the *Volksbühne* fire Piscator. The executive committee felt equally outraged and censured its director. It declared that Piscator had arbitrarily plundered Ehm Welk's work "for the sake of one-sided political propaganda," a "misuse of artistic freedom... in contradiction to the fundamental political neutrality of the *Volksbühne.*"[29]

This declaration created a full-fledged crisis. The right-wing press celebrated it as a manifestation of "Germanic Idealism." On the left, in *Die Weltbühne*, Arthur Holitscher published a call for the *Volksbuhne* to return to its original proletarian commitment.[30] In this he spoke for the radical youth organization of the *Volksbühne*, which declared itself prepared to secede in protest over the censure of Piscator. Georg Springer, a member of the *Volksbühne* executive committee, responded: "The *Volksbühne* has neither the tradition nor the intention nor the possibility of equating the term '*Volk*' in its title simply with the 'radical socialist working class.'"[31] The executive committee, indeed, took further measures against the politicization of theater by Piscator. It baned the films Piscator used in *Thunder over Gottland.* Piscator resigned in protest. The avant-garde staged a variety of sympathy manifestations for Piscator and the tumult filled the cultural press of the capital. The theater had become thoroughly politicized. After *Thunder over Gottland*, Berlin theater split into two hostile camps.

What is significant about these camps is how symmetrically they reflected the structure of cultural conceptions behind the politicization crisis. Among the critics of Piscator there were those of the extreme right and those of the liberal center. Their objections to Piscator shared little more that the empty world "idealism." For the radical right Piscator's *politicization* of theater was not offensive; only his political *convictions.* For the extreme right, in other words, art was political as a matter of course. The right attacked Piscator's Bolshevism but found cogent, indeed respected and feared, his strategy of political agitation. It put political pressure on public institutions in which Piscator worked, like the *Volksbühne* and the *Staatstheater*, to restrict left-wing activities, while it set about simultaneously creating its own political theater. In the first task, Paul Fechter led the right-wing charge, arguing on the grounds of "idealism" against the infestation of *Kulturbolschewismus* in public theater institutions. The key figure in the second right-wing endeavor was Alfred Mühr, who considered Piscator an artistic genius and the model of what the right should attempt for itself in cultural politics.

Mühr recognized Piscator as the decisive figure in German theater, the man who understood how to shake the theater public from its lethargy and charge it with the life of contemporaneity.[32] He did so via the politicization of art, Mühr noted, but it was art, too. Mere political agitation would not have had such an impact. Piscator worked with the dawning cultural energies of the proletariat, which had come to recognize its own autonomy and demanded a culture of its own. It had the will to form. By contrast the "bourgeoisie" was culturally bankrupt. It could only fall back upon a sterile traditionalism. Piscator's theater with its synthesis of theater and film, of technology and *Sachlichkeit*, was completely contemporary: not just politically but stylistically. Piscator recognized, as did his followers, the importance of expressing in art the ideals and aspirations of the times and of the class to which he belonged. This lesson had to be learned and followed to its logical conclusion precisely by those in the German *völkisch* tradition who stood in such profound opposition to Piscator's political views.

The other tack against Piscator repudiated his politicization of the "neutral" or even "sacred" domain of art and culture. This traditionalist idealism characterized not only the executive committee of the *Volksbühne* but a number of old-liberal critics — Monty Jacobs, Julius Bab, and Max Osborn among them — and even those of the "idealistic" Expressionist tradition, whose sense of avant-gardism had shrivelled into an affirmation of "artistic freedom."

These critics took up Ehm Welk as a cause against Piscator. Welk had rebelled against Piscator's staging, seeking at the last to withdraw the play from production, and walking out of the premier in great consternation. While Welk refused to associate himself with what he saw as a political persecution of Piscator, he felt entitled to protest as an artist whose intentions had been violated. He conceded Piscator had produced a fine piece of art, perhaps better that the drama as he had written it, yet he insisted that the critic Kurt Pinthus had been correct in terming it "a colossal staging *against* a play." Welk complained to the executive committee of the *Volksbühne* "against the way in which the staging turned into a political and artistic end in itself...independent of the play, indeed, introducing influences which annihilated the play."[33] Hence, critiques of Piscator's *Tendenz* and of the *Primat des Regisseurs* were linked together in a defense of the "rights of the dramatist against the director," of "idealism" and of artistic freedom from propaganda.

On the side of those who defended Piscator a similar split became apparent. The radical left defended Piscator precisely for his political convictions, insisting that art was unquestionably political and that its function had to be to evoke social revolution. But by the same token there were those in the artistic avant-garde and in the liberal press who defended Piscator on the basis of "artistic freedom."

Bernhard Diebold's "Das Piscator Drama," in many ways constituted the most serious effort of "idealist" bourgeois culture — the established culture of metropolitan liberalism — to understand and to foster what Piscator attempted, on the grounds of artistic development.[34] Diebold argued Piscator stood out both for his aesthetic radicalism and for his political radicalism. He had two distinct publics: the proletarians and the establishment. Diebold expressed no reservations about the exclusion of Piscator from the *Staatstheater* and the *Volksbühne*: Communist manifestations, he wrote, belonged in party meeting halls. Piscator's establishment audience celebrated his *artistic* experiments. Yet there was more at stake than the latest fashion or the most sensational experiment, Diebold continued. There was a "fatal seriousness" behind Piscator's theater: it had an internal force and dynamism of which the established audience was not aware. Diebold insisted that this audience take the political message seriously, recognize how directly it threatened the bourgeois position.

Having said this, however, Diebold himself plunged into an analysis of the aesthetic implications of the Piscator Theater. The most essential point to grasp, in his view, was "that Piscator turned bad drama into good plays!" Given the "impotence" of contemporary dramaturgy, Diebold continued, this was a great achievement. Piscator ended the "anarchy in drama" of which Diebold had been complaining for almost a decade, for he had simply "knocked drama dead and got rid of it."

Diebold's essay operated on the basis of an idealist notion of artistic freedom. Yet the whole point of the politicization of art was to cast the idea of "artistic freedom" irretrievably into limbo. The issue was no longer one of artistic freedom of expression but one of political freedom of expression. The autonomy of art had long since — this was Piscator's whole point — been shown up as illusory. All theater had a political content, implicit or explicit. Whether he knew it or not, whether he wished it or not, the artist was caught up in a political atmosphere, and his work immediatly subject to political appropriation.

The leading "radical" critic, Herbert Ihering noted in this context: "in a politically excited epoch one can do nothing other than produce 'political' theater..."[35] The experience of a work of art, and especially of a drama, could not be isolated from all the other experiences of life, particularly politics. "Whoever goes to an amusement theater does it often as an explicit rejection of the times. He is political in his intention to be unpolitical..." Ihering scoffed at arguments which charged political theater with hostility toward art. What really endangered art was the mystification of it into some sacred realm. Ihering believed that the experiences of the epoch were so novel and so radical that traditional forms of art could not assimilate them. For this reason he attached great importance to the documentary theater. "The journalistic-theatrical presentation of contemporary materials is not against art; it remains honorable, it does not try to be what it is not; it does not fake; it opens the way to the times and it does not block the way to art." Thereby it performed two vital services, First, it brought theater out of its elitist obsolescence and into confrontation with the experiences of the times; in a word, it made theater "relevant." Second, by gathering and presenting these materials, it created the possibility for their eventual artistic transformation.

Ihering was not alone in defending the political and the contemporary-documentary tendencies in Weimar dramaturgy. In November 1928 *Die Szene*, a journal of Berlin theater, conducted a survey inquiring "Ought Drama have a Political Thesis?"[36] The respondents represented the leading lights in German theater – of all stripes. Fred Angermeyer, Alfred Brust, Gerhard Menzel and Emil Ludwig argued art was separate from politics. Paul Kornfeld did as well. But a number of other respondents – Walter Hasenclever, Heinrich Mann, Hans J. Rehfisch, Ernst Toller and Bertolt Brecht – all urged that the question was *mal posé*. It was not a question of ought but of is: drama *had* a political thesis, and could not extricate itself from this condition.

This was not an unproblematic conclusion, for if all literature and art proved inherently political, then its appeal for universal appreciation was fundamentally misguided. Bela Balazs attacked Herbert Ihering, on Piscator's behalf, on precisely this line.[37] Balazs charged Ihering was not prepared to go all the way, to follow out to their ultimate consequences the arguments he advanced in the essay just discussed. Ihering still thought in terms of a single theater public, an undifferentiated mass, Balazs charged, but Ihering's call for commitment on the part of the dramatists necessarily shattered this illusory unity of the public:

> Commitment, as long as it is clear and unambiguous, already means party! For "public" and "mass" as the same element which has a *single* even if unconscious will, exists so little as the idea of "nation" in this sense exists. For the public is not fragmented by theater but is fragmented by its different commitments and is about the business of fragmenting theater along those lines.[38]

The only alternative was party-theater. Defense of Piscator, defense of theatrical experimentation, on the basis of aesthetic-universal categories was delusory and reactionary. There could be no middle ground.

This extreme tension introduced between art and politics, between political sympathy and party orthodoxy, signified an excruciating choice for literary intellectuals. On the one hand, they longed to have influence, and they longed to belong to a significant social movement. On the other, they retained their ideas about the universality of values and the ubiquitous humanism of art — notions that a relentless politicization threatened to annihilate. These issues were brought even more clearly to the fore in the conflict among writers in the *Gruppe 1925*.

Becher, Döblin and the "Gruppe 1925"

By the mid Twenties, Johannes R. Becher had emerged as the foremost exponent of Communism in the arts. This role was underlined after 1926, when his propagandistic novel *Levisite* brought state charges of sedition and he was subjected to a series of legal proceedings which rallied the entire intellectual left to his defense.[39] In articles from 1924 and 1925 Becher set forth the orthodox Communist view of the intellectual and the party, especially as

94

it focused on organizational questions within the domain of intellectual life. In the first article, Becher began with a critique of the state of mass culture in the post-war years, expressing a disdain for Americanism and its manifestations.[40] The experiences of war and revolution, Becher asserted, brought the finest, most idealistic artists to the terrible realization that bourgeois culture was beyond recovery. The rise of fascism made it imperative that these intellectuals affiliate with a proletarian revolution which would restore the basis for culture. In his second article, Becher continued to emphasize the duty of the intellectuals to heighten the class consciousness of the proletariat and prepare the way for revolution.[41] He criticized "bourgeois intellectuals" like Thomas Mann, Gerhart Hauptmann, Kurt Hiller and even Ernst Toller for failing to align themselves with the proletariat. On the other hand, he castigated the *Aktion-Kreis* for anarcho-syndicalist tendencies. Art had to be directed toward the strategic line set forth by the vanguard of the proletariat, the Communist Party.

Such a position had been adopted above all by the circle at the Malik-Verlag, the so-called *"Rote Gruppe."*[42] Because George Grosz and the others in the *"Rote Gruppe"* committed themselves wholeheartedly to the subordination of art to the needs of the Communist Party, Becher praised the *"Rote Gruppe"* with real enthusiasm. It served as a beginning of the Communist organization of art and culture for proletarian revolution. Becher believed Communist organization in the arts required the repudiation of all ideologies of "eternal value" in art. His program called for the affiliation of artists in an organization in conformity with the principles of the Comintern. From such an organizational position they could then work out a rigorously Marxist view on all matters of art and culture. Becher set about trying to realize this program by organizing a Communist opposition group within the *Schutzverband Deutscher Schriftsteller* (SDS), the professional association of German free-lance writers. The focus of this initial effort to create a Communist faction, starting around 1924, was the Berlin local organization of the SDS. Becher, Berta Lask and several others, among them Wilhelm Herzog, strove to turn the SDS into a political forum.

The reaction of the executive committee of the national association proved distinctly negative, as emerged in the report in *Der Schriftsteller*, the organ of the SDS, in March 1924, that "a Communist faction within the SDS...may represent a great danger to [its] continued existence."[43] The national assembly of the SDS voted to ban all party affiliation within the organization. This decision reflected the conservative character of the SDS by 1924.[44] As early as 1921 Kurt Tucholsky had taken his leave of the association. Its executive committee had come to be dominated by such men as Monty Jacobs, Max Osborn, Theodor Heuß, Robert Breuer, Fedor von Zobeltitz, Bernard Kellermann and Jacob Schaffner. Its business director was Arthur Elösser. These were men for the most part of the generation of 1890. They wrote for established journals in the Ullstein firm or the S. Fischer Verlag. They were not reactionary, but they feared radicalism with almost the same intensity that Ebert feared revolution.

The one exception in the higher echelons of the SDS was Alfred Döblin. In the same meeting which banned political organization, he was elected chairman of the SDS. In his address, "The Creative Writer and Politics," Döblin distantiated himself from the resolution. It might be the case, he conceded, that the explicit introduction of political factions within the SDS would compromise the organization's economic interest or professional solidarity, yet it remained an inescapable fact that "the writer...is, whether he knows it or not, intensely politicized, even if not in the sense of the coincidental parties. There is no unpolitical writer."[45] Döblin made it clear that he felt this political dimension was decisive in intellectual work, in creating a perspective for judgment which in the long run would influence the course of affairs. Politics was too important, he concluded, to be left to the politicians.

This commitment to politics led Döblin to a closer association with those like Herzog, Holitscher and Becher who agitated on the left. By 1925 he had grown disgusted with the SDS as an organization and he refused reelection as Chairman. In that year he and a number of the radical writers decided to form a separate group to develop their political and artistic ideals. This *Gruppe 1925* drew together all the leading left-wing writers of Berlin, yet little is known about it. The few documents establishing its existence stem mainly from Döblin and Becher, the two leading figures of the group, and from Herman Kasack. Kasack wrote of the *Gruppe 1925* in a *Festschrift* for Döblin in 1948.[46] He listed as members besides Döblin and himself: Becher, Ernst Bloch, Ernst Blaß, Bertolt Brecht, Friedrich Burschell, Georg Kaiser, Rudolf Leonhard, Oskar Lörke, Walter Mehring, Hermann Ungar, Ernst Weiß, Alfred Wolfenstein, and the list was not complete. The function of the group, according to Kasack, was "to see to it that the writer no longer live apart from the times in a contemplative idyll or in political resignation," but rather feel himself to be the conscience and spokesman of the times. Döblin himself reminisced about the group in a letter to Johannes R. Becher in May 1951. He recalled the group having been founded by Rudolf Leonhard. "The best antifascist writers of the period" belonged. "What did we do? Debate, exchange opinions, [establish] personal contacts..."[47] Becher described it to a Soviet audience in 1927 as "an effort to activate the literary life of Berlin. In the 'group' left liberal and communist writers came together. The only theme of all the debates is always 'bourgeois and proletarian-revolutionary art.'"[48]

Even after the creation of the *Gruppe 1925*, Becher and the Communists continued their struggle to create a faction within the SDS and to use it for agitational purposes. The faction was called the *Arbeitsgemeinschaft kommunistischer Schriftsteller*, and it achieved a certain notoriety in February 1926. The Berlin local of the SDS had sponsored a conference on the subject of "The Want of the Author," a favorite theme in the organization.[49] The conference began with speeches by the leaders of the SDS — Heuß, Elösser, Kuczynski, Schaffner. Toller also spoke. Then Becher, Lask and other Communists interrupted the proceedings with a demonstration and Wilhelm Herzog submitted a resolution calling for the expropriation of royal properties without compensation. Osborn, the chairman of the Berlin local, ruled them out of order and declared the meeting closed. When the radicals proposed to continue anyway, Osborn had the lights in the hall turned off. The result was a showdown. In March 1926 the Communists put a motion before the Berlin local to recall the chairman, but the motion failed and the conservatives consolidated their control of the Berlin local. The radicals turned to the literary journals to continue their struggle. Leo Lania reported on the controversial evening in *Die literarische Welt*, pointing out with irony that the proposal of the radicals had indeed been out of place, since it was a concrete suggestion in the context of ethereal "discussions of principle."[50] The aftermath, he went on, demonstrated less the economic want of authors than their want of organization.

The *Gruppe 1925* addressed the public directly in March 1926 with a "Call for the Expropriation of the Princes," signed by many Berlin radicals.[51] A month later the *Gruppe 1925* addressed the public in the pages of the *Rote Fahne*, the KPD newspaper, in a manifesto setting forth its goals as "raising the writer out of his isolation" and "representing radical-intellectual" ideas.[52] The manifesto was signed by Becher, Döblin, Kasack, Blaß, Hasenclever, Ehrenstein and Haas.

In 1928 the issue of state censorship and in particular the case of Johannes R. Becher came to be resolved by a government amnesty under the rubric of a commitment to "artistic freedom."[53] This seemed an ambiguous victory to the avant-garde, for as Alfred Döblin argued, the basis for this assertion of "artistic freedom" was the notion that art was harmless and irrelevant in concrete political affairs, and thus showed a greater contempt than censorship itself. While it did not mollify the avant-garde, the amnesty decision did result in a significant lessening of concern on the part of the moderate "idealist" intellectuals in Berlin. They did subscribe to the doctrine of "artistic freedom," since for them *Tendenz* meant a corruption of art. A work was to be defended, in their view, only in the measure that it remained "Art." These "idealists" defended Becher's novel, Piscator's theater or Grosz's political drawings not on the basis of political freedom of opinion but as works of artistic merit. Once the state had satisfied their artistic scruples, they no longer felt the need to sympathize with the unpleasant political radicals. This isolated the avant-garde even more and provoked the party intellectuals to demand a full commitment from the unattached leftists. This irked the latter into countermeasures. By the mid Twenties there emerged among a number of avant-gardists a growing impatience with the cult of radicalism, the adoption of

Communist or Bolshevik rhetoric by writers for whom it was only another fad.

A prominent instance of this change in mood came when Willi Haas, editor of *Die literarische Welt*, disputed Kurt Tucholsky's defense of the radical Berlin avant-garde against provincial detractors from the *völkisch* right. Haas had participated in the *Gruppe 1925*, but now he charged that Berlin was full of individuals who, having made a mess of things where they came from, tried to create a new identity by moving to Berlin and subscribing to "radical" ideologies.[54] For Haas, Berlin was full of phony radicalism, a literary posture which was chic but completely lacking in character or commitment. "Bolshevism," he argued, was a fad, nothing more, in the Berlin literary set. In his reply, Tucholsky agreed there were too many opportunists and shallow enthusiasts who called themselves "radicals" in Berlin. Yet implicit in his remarks remained an insistence upon real radicalism.[55]

In 1928, Haas returned to the subject of the "radicals." In his most important editorial, "We and the Radicals," he repudiated the demands of Communist critics for an explicitly "radical" commitment by his journal.[56] Despite frequent praise for serious Marxists, Haas wrote, the journal was constantly chastised from the radical side "that we are not a 'proletarian' but (in the eyes of these gentlemen the worst pejorative:) an 'intellectual' journal." As he made clear not only in this article but in a whole series of sharply polemical pieces he wrote over the next few years, Berlin "radical" willingness to talk Bolshevism but not follow it through eventually undermined its influence.[57] For Haas, the decisive criteria were commitment and quality. He had no quarrel, he claimed, with writers like Tucholsky or Egon Erwin Kisch, whose commitment to the proletariat led them to abandon art for propaganda. But he could not tolerate mediocre writers, failures by "bourgeois" standards, who merely by converting to Communism laid claim to being major spokesmen of the times.[58] That betrayed quality, art and intellect, Haas believed. It was incongruous, he wrote, for Johannes R. Becher, whom he knew and liked, to believe his poetry, simply because it proclaimed Communism, was more important than that of Goethe. Haas dismissed as unfounded or inadequate any critical appreciation which substituted sociopolitical stances for aesthetic standards, charging Herbert Ihering specifically with this fault.[59]

Becher answered Haas's essay in the November 1928 issue of *Die literarische Welt.*[60] He disputed Haas's view that there existed an autonomous aesthetic standard. Art served only as a weapon in class conflict, and whoever was not with the proletariat was against it, he asserted. Any secular, realistic intellectual would have to become a socialist since the proletariat's struggle was for the universal liberation of mankind. Communism could not be judged according to its modernity or modishness, but only according to the truth it embodied and the results it obtained. To be sure, proletarian-revolutionary art was only in its infancy, but the alternative was to allow antiquated forms of "bourgeois culture" to dominate intellectual expression and uphold the status quo.

Radical intellectuals felt an obligation to do more than criticize; they wanted to change the world, and that meant they had to put themselves at the service of the proletariat and of its party. To do this, Becher believed, they had to undergo a thorough personal reorientation. In an article for the Communist newspaper *Rote Fahne*, Becher elaborated on this key question of "The Party and the Intellectual."[61] The essay was devoted to an examination of the relation of the intellectual to party discipline. For Becher, "the intellectual does not enter the party through any triumphal arch." Rather, his "integration into the proletariat" was desperate and prolonged, for he had to begin again, give up his cultivated "individuality," and put away from himself his entire "bourgeois" heritage. Many who tried to do this fell back to "bourgeois" ways, criticizing the party and its discipline. Such criticism of the party constituted "antibolshevik" agitation and amounted to treason. For Becher, to break with the party was to abandon all that guaranteed his humanity. It reduced him to nothingness, to disorientation and despair. Therefore the intellectual had to submit to the collective will and discipline of the party.

This disintegrating issue of the intellectual versus the party would obsess the avant-garde for the remainder of its existence. In the sharp debates about the nature and autonomy of art in the *Gruppe*

1925, Becher's opposite number was the negativist Alfred Döblin. His negativism led him to insist vis à vis the Communist Party, as he had insisted vis à vis the Futurists a decade and more earlier, that it was his first responsibility to preserve "the freedom of a creative writer."[62] When within the *Gruppe 1925*, the KPD intellectuals pressed for a full party commitment, Döblin replied vituperatively: "I am a class-conscious bourgeois, a poet of the bourgeoisie; who says I desire the victory of the working class? What entitles the proletariat to make any demands on me at all?"[63] In the last days of the avant-garde, the orthodox Communists would quote these lines in righteous indignation and Döblin would be written off as an enemy of the proletariat. In 1926 it was patently obvious to all concerned that he stood very far to the left of such "bourgeois" circles as those of Thomas Mann.

Döblin made clear his commitment to *Tendenzkunst* in the context of the censorhsip struggles of 1926-1928 in his essay "Art is not Free but Influential: Militant Art." Considering the censorship of tendentious art, Döblin objected to the argument that art should be exempt and should not be censored since it was a "free" play in the realm of the ideal. The real point behind this whole campaign against *Tendenzkunst* was to enforce the economic monopoly over culture, "the chaining of artistic producers and thus of their production to one single small social stratum, at least in Germany, the propertied and their dependents."[64] According to this elite, artists were to preoccupy themselves with the ethereal and the unreal, and leave politics and economics to the ruling class. If an artist "belonged to another social stratum and produced according to its mentality," the ruling class labelled his work *Tendenzkunst* and refused to concern itself with its fate or freedom, for it was not "pure art." Their concern for the "freedom" of the artist was in fact a measure to preempt altogether the social significance art could have. The "sanctity of art" was a dangerous misconception which implied in fact that art was impotent and trivial. Art served as an active agent in social life, Döblin believed, and deserved to be taken seriously. Art was too potent to be ignored. In that sense, the state's desire to defend itself through censorship showed a healthy respect for art.

In any event, Döblin went on, censorship was not an aesthetic matter. It was political. The only legitimate reason to oppose censor-ship, he insisted, was not artistic purity but freedom of opinion in a democratic society. Opposition to censorship guaranteed the right of opposition against the opinion of those in power, and was a matter of formal democracy, not of aesthetics. Döblin went on to argue that such freedom of democratic opinion existed nowhere, not even in ostensibly democratic societies, for the interests of ruling economic groups and classes interfered. Hence the need to struggle against censorship. On the other hand, Döblin concluded, this did not mean the total subordination of art to politics, but rather the renaissance of art as a major social force. Art could not be simply political journalism.

Late in 1926 at an evening sponsored by the *Sozialistische Monatshefte* on the topic of "Art and Community," Döblin had a sharp exchange with Adolf Behne. Paul Westheim, editor of *Das Kunstblatt*, was present for the debate. In an editorial note he charac-terized Behne's position as the "recently fashionable conception which would like to turn the artist into something like a community functionary."[65] Westheim was impressed by Döblin's dissent from such a view and invited him to publish his remarks in *Das Kunstblatt*. Döblin did so in an essay entitled "Art, Daimon and Com-munity." Döblin saw Behne's statements in a kinder light than had Westheim, as "the clear, sober and honorable address of a serious man." Behne, he noted, "favors social progress, believes in a develop-ment of the human species, takes a stand for technical progress."[66] While he was not out of sympathy with Behne's politics, he disagreed profoundly about how they related to aesthetics.

Propaganda, even "humanistic" or "socialist" propaganda, could not be the criterion for art. Even Behne recognized that the doctrine that art was purely a matter of political line led to hopeless dif-ficulties. "Everyone must fail who does not resolutely accept the communist tactic of making party works, direct political propagan-da." Behne could no more accept this than could Döblin, as had been established in an earlier controversy between Behne and John Heartfield of the *Rote Gruppe*. Behne had criticized an exhibit of *Rote Gruppe* works as mere propaganda. He insisted upon aesthetic criteria and urged that the best advocates of socialism were the best artists, not the propagandists. When Heartfield reasserted the "Bolshevik" argument that art was a weapon for awakening proletarian revolutionary consciousness,[67] Behne replied that the artistic stance of the *Rote Gruppe* was unintelligent and banal, that it misapprehended the nature of art's influence, making it trivial and opportunistic.[68] Such a view was not all that far from Döblin's. Döblin insisted that art was not a product of community primarily but of the individual artistic ego. Radicalizing this subjectivist component in aesthetic creation, he argued works of art were "gestures of a completely mysterious transcendence [*Jenseits*]," for which he suggested the term Daimon.[69] "Art works are inroads of the daimonic in a developed world," he insisted. Works of art were "not very comfortable things," for this irrational origin remained evident. Works of art, rather than constituting community, proved "dangerous, malicious, individualistic." Art, Döblin concluded, favored anarchism.

In May 1926, Döblin made just this argument in the *Gruppe 1925*. As Döblin had opposed the utter etherealism of post-war Expressionism for its abandonment of objectivity, now Döblin turned to oppose the thoroughgoing utilitarianism of the prevailing journalistic and agitational conception of artifice. His "new naturalism" was to be objective and committed, but it had to remain art.

In his defense of the integrity of art as a form, Döblin provoked the criticism of leftists, and this in turn heightened his adamance. The result was intemperate rhetoric. A reporter for the *Berlin Börsen-Courier* described Döblin's statement as "a passionate rejection of the psychological, reasoned, commentated novel in which he saw no rigorous and finished art form but rather a manifestation of the civilizational degeneration (*zivilisatorische Entartung*) of the epic."[70] With understatement, the reporter commented that this provoked a "lively exchange."

In an evaluation of Döblin's whole opus through 1927, Hans Georg Brenner made a systematic critique of Döblin from the orthodox Marxist vantage.[71] Brenner began by arguing that "originally" the novel had been the reflection of contemporary affairs. It always addressed its time immediately. But, Brenner went on, this original connection had been lost, and the novel lost its direction. It was caught up in "epigonal ideologies." The tendency toward "aesthetic-philosophical prophecy" foundered against the political realities of the day which left no room for such self-indulgence. The sense of art or the artist as "elect" or "exempt" reflected the lack of impact of that same art in the real affairs of the community. The lesson of the age was that the individual had to make way for the collective, yet among artists, the stronger the literary talent, the greater the distance between artistic fantasy and contemporary affairs.

This, Brenner asserted, was Döblin's problem. While it was his great achievement in such novels as *The Three Leaps of Wang-lun*, *Wadzek's Struggle with the Steam Turbine* and *Wallenstein* "to recognize that the individual is not the center of the world (Expressionism), but rather the masses," Döblin still betrayed too much ambivalence. "Döblin does not have the power which, derived from the times, is capable of pulling together all the isolated desires and impulses" of the day. "His artistic sense of responsibillity is superior to his responsibility to the times." This found reflection in Döblin's preference for remote and exotic settings for his novels: 18th-century China, the Thirty Years War, and most recently, mythical India.[72] Contemporary problems got lost in such "historical costuming." It was the novel's function "to serve the objectification of the present," but even in the one novel in which Döblin did ostensibly deal with contemporary problems of technology, *Mountains Oceans and Giants*, he never got beyond the elites. "The relation of those who enjoy the fruits of labor to those compelled to labor, the proletariat, this question which rules the present and will set the terms of the future, does not come up in this book... Instead of the necessary sense of responsibility there arises an anachronistic art-for-art's-sake standpoint."[73] Brenner concluded: "Döblin was the only one of the last epoch of literature to overcome self-blinding individualism — only to fall back into it now?" That was the left-radical indictment of Döblin. It provoked a violent response.

The tension between Döblin and the KPD intellectuals over artistic autonomy and form came to a head when Döblin was elected to the Prussian Academy for Literary Art in March 1928. Döblin used the occasion of his acceptance speech to reiterate his views on art in an even more aggressive and contrary form. His speech was delivered on March 15, 1928 under the title "Free-Lance Writing and Literature" (*Schriftstellerei und Dichtung*). In enunciating his aesthetic principles he noted "literature is, like art in general, an autochthonous growth, it has its own structure and the laws of its growth are its [only] laws."[74] Döblin went on to identify the decisive aspects of literature as a form of art with the sovereignty of fantasy and the sovereignty of language. These were the keys to epic form, he asserted. The word was the medium of literary art, but this made literature a more problematic form of art than painting or music because the same medium of words figured in strictly utilitarian conversation. Literature was not the same as reality or its linguistic reflection. "Literature does something to reality as it is provided by our day-to-day linguistic material; the data of reality are used to show *that* one intervenes, *where* one intervenes, and *how* one intervenes." The author "ennobled" words and materials in so far as he penetrated them with intellectual purpose. This was not a scientific procedure but an aesthetic one. Döblin insisted he was making no "art-for-art's-sake" argument. He rejected the view that art had no influence on life. Only he wished to insist that literature was not the same as journalism or exposition. "Literature does not have to borrow its purposes from party offices or from manuals of ethics."

If we can understand the thrust of Döblin's observations about literature as a defense of the autonomy of art and as part of his advocacy of epic form, it still remains that these remarks came to be formulated in a manner and in a context overladen with political resonances of a profoundly disturbing nature. This was clear in his basic distinction of literature from the clearly pejorative term *"Schrift-stellerei."* Döblin maintained "literature stands in clear contra-distinction to purposive-rational free-lance writing." His review of the contemporary forms of the novel – the *Bildungsroman*, the historical novel, the milieu study, the biography – suggested that each had a confused artistic intention. In most cases, they were written with a practical end in mind: to entertain or to instruct morally or politically, or to exercise social criticism, or to lay bare the author's soul. Such novels competed with journalism, science and history for the public's attention, but had no place competing with art. Though it was the most prevalent form of contemporary writing, Döblin insisted, the genre of the novel was "a most comical and pathetic product." He declared it "incomprehensible that one could consider the contemporary novel in the same context with literature." He concluded: "This descent into the practical, into the useful and the concrete, characterizes the civilizational degeneration of the work of art [*zivilisatorische Entartung des Kunstwerks*]."

In the context of the Prussian Academy, this line was stunning coming from Döblin. The whole distinction between "*Schriftstellerei*" and "*Dichtung*" was offensive and understandably occasioned the outrage of the left. Döblin was fully aware of the ideological signficance of these terms. A year earlier he had responded to an inquiry from Emil Factor and Herbert Ihering of the *Berliner Börsen-Courier* on the subject of "The Representative and the Active Academy." Döblin was explicitly critical of the name of the new "Section for Literary Art."

> Why did they use the term "for literary art"
> [*für Dichtkunst*] apropos the Academy or Section?
> They ought to have known that a *Dichter* is a
> comical thing; didn't they know the words
> *Schriftsteller* [author] and *Schrifttum* [writing]
> — hence, Section for Writing?[15]

This concern for the socio-cultural symbolism of the title of the Academy reflected the fundamental tension between the avant-garde and the established "mandarin" mentality as well as the traditionalist-*völkisch* viewpoint. In his remarks, Döblin set into a sustained critique of the pretentious mandarinism of the idea of the *Dichter*. A writer was one who worked with words. "The word — and hence, the author, and hence a literary academy — has two elements: an intellectual element and an artistic element." Döblin argued that by the selection of the idea of *Dichtkunst* the first element had been devalued and the second blownup all out of proportion. "It looks pretty damned like in the term Section for Literary Art there is already a commitment to one of [two] views — namely the one I oppose."

For Döblin a scant year later to use the language of the anti-modernist cultural critics seemed a clear repudiation of much of what he and those with whom he had so long stood, the avant-garde radicals of *Neue Sachlichkeit*, believed. The acceptance speech may be gauged as the expression of frustration and wounded dignity of a serious and avant-garde writer at the neglect of the public, the criticism of his peers, and the pressure of the Communist Party intellectuals. It was certainly not Döblin's finest moment. Two final provocations figured into it. His published cut off his advances because his works were so unsuccessful, and his friends of the radical avant-garde expressed open contempt for his new Hindu verse-epic, *Manas*.[76] Döblin had never taken criticism well, and his natural response was to strike back. His conduct helped shatter the crucial solidarity between critical negativists and orthodox Communists.

The Establishment of the Bund proletarisch-revolutionärer Schriftsteller

Döblin's acceptance speech in the Prussian Academy in 1928 seemed a total about-face and betayal of his radical ideals. The vehemence and impropriety of his remarks in accepting his election set Becher and the other Communist intellectuals into a posture of agitated hostility, which led to the breakup of the *Gruppe 1925*. Döblin and Becher had been the moving forces in this group and their falling out and prolonged and bitter conflict betokened the collapse of the alliance of the unattached, negativist intellectuals with their Party brethren. In October 1928, Becher, Berta Lask, Egon Erwin Kisch and numerous other Communist writers formed the *Bund proletarisch-revolutionärer Schriftsteller* (BPRS) as an organization exclusively for Communist intellectuals.[77]

The BPRS was designed to fulfill all the functions Becher had hoped for in the earlier *Rote Gruppe*.[78] The thrust of Becher's opening remarks and the program which ultimately emerged from the founding congress of the BPRS made it clear that it aimed to break altogether with "bourgeois culture" and its representatives and to devote its attention to the cultivation of a true proletarian literature among working-class writers and journalists. The BPRS organization contained real proletarians, drawn primarily from the journalists of the working-class press, but bourgeois revolutionaries, like Becher, Lasch, Renn, Kisch, Weiskopf, and Hungarian émigrés, like Biha, Kurella and Gabor, dominated the BPRS leadership. They saw its goal not only as the discovery and promotion of proletarian writers but as the development of ideological purity in the domain of literature. This required a sustained critique of bourgeois notions of art and the elaboration of a Marxist theory of literature. Above all, this entailed a repudiation of those intellectuals not willing to serve in the Party. The most bitter criticism of the BPRS was directed at intellectual "fellow travellers" who cultivated their own personal and artistic autonomy. They dabbled in proletarian affairs, all the while expressing contempt for "mere propaganda" and for the cultural level and achievements of the proletarian writers.

Initially the BPRS sought to work with existing left-radical journals but the question of ideological purity versus intellectual and artistic quality ruined its association with *Die Front* and then *Die Neue Bücherschau.* The affair at the *Neue Bücherschau* typefied the whole issue. In 1925 the editor, Gerhard Pohl, invited numerous left-radicals onto the editorial committee. Becher, Kisch and Herrmann-Neisse were among those who joined. In 1929 Herrmann-Neisse published an article in *Die Neue Bücherschau* praising Gottfried Benn as an artist who devoted himself to the purity of his craft and avoided propagandizing for party-political concerns. Becher and Kisch were incensed that Pohl should have allowed this essay to appear in the journal. In August 1929, by resigning in protest, they turned the matter into a cause célèbre.

An exchange of views between Pohl and Kisch highlighted the controversy. In his letter resigning from the editorial board, Kisch wrote:

> What angered me most was the first sentence, in
> which Herrmann-Neisse attacked the "literary pur-
> veyors of political propaganda material." Who can
> that be? Barbusse? Sinclair? Becher? Whoever

> he meant, in our view the literary purveyor of
> political propaganda material towers above all
> superior world poets, above all Benns or Stefan
> Georges.[79]

Pohl recognized the seriousness of the issues involved.[80] Before addressing them, however, he cleared up some preliminary matters in the controversy. He noted that Herrmann-Neisse's article was not typical of the journal's stance but that as a member of the editorial committee Herrmann-Neisse, like Kisch or Becher, had the right to express himself without editorial interference. He went on to express his own respect for Benn's poetic achievement and to note that Herrmann-Neisse was an intellectual of enough polemical verve that if he wished to attack Barbusse, Sinclair, or Becher, he would have done so outright. The Communist writers had blown things all out of proportion in claiming persecution in the pages of *Die Neue Bücherschau*.

All that was preliminary. The real issue at stake was the responsibility of the creative writer in the contemporary situation. Pohl argued that by virtue of the war experience a whole generation of intellectuals had taken their stand on the left and that there had long prevailed a powerful and effective solidarity between strict Communists and the unattached left intelligentsia around *Die Weltbühne* and other journals of the metropolis. Pohl insisted that there existed a definite commitment to radical change in the negativists and that their position was not so distant from the Communists that a split between them was necessary or appropiate.

> You say: a writer who perceives the situation
> must carry on the struggle where the political
> forces are stored: in the Communist party...
> We say: a writer must carry on the struggle
> where he can develop his strength: in independen-
> dence...We too recognize the necessity and impor-
> tance of a revolutionary militant party of workers
> ...But we do not know what a writer is supposed
> to do in this party.[81]

For Pohl the task of the writer was to write — to portray and to explain. The writer's whole function lay in his use of words to create form. And to develop his own achievements the writer required automony. The literary impact of Becher and Kisch themselves, he argued, was not a function of their party membership but of their literary talent, and Pohl went even further: "Your sphere of influence would be greater if you spoke as independents."

The issue was set forth clearly, and Kisch responded with a concise statement of the BPRS attitude.[82] First he asserted that Benn was not worth criticizing and that what had offended him and Becher was the stab-in-the-back by their colleagues, Herrmann-Neisse and Pohl. He denied that there was anything like a generational solidarity based on the war experience which bound Communists with unattached intellectuals. The examples which Pohl provided of such solidarity for social justice were hardly valid, for what inspired the Communists was not the idea of justice but support for a fellow-party member, he claimed. Concern for toleration and justice was a "democratic" posture, which appealed most to the reactionaries at the *Berliner Tageblatt* with their obsolete ideas of liberalism. It had nothing to do with revolutionary socialism. Finally, Kisch noted, Pohl preached independence yet there could be no autonomy of art or culture from politics. The idea of artistic autonomy allowed a Remarque to water down the passionately partisan war-writing of Barbusse and make millions, while a bourgeois audience could revel in artistic-revolutionary fads, still secure in its power. This "independence of the writer" meant in reality a valueless relativism, against which socialists took a stance for *truth*. That truth was political; it was represented by the Communist Party. It meant that literature could not be "pure art" but only "party-political propaganda."

The BPRS founded its own journal, *Die Linkskurve*, in order to advocate this pure party position. In the first issue, Kurt Kersten reviewed the *Neue Bücherschau* affair, deliberately contrasting the "arbitrary" and independent behavior of Pohl to the disciplined, collective and Communist intention of the new *Linkskurve*. "The *Linkskurve* is no coincidental product, nor is it the work of a single individual who believes in the illusion of isolation, which leads either to nihilism or to the worship of success."[83] In the same issue Kurt Kläber attacked the *Literarische Welt* for its special issue on working-class poets, because it published not revolutionary – i.e., Communist party – worker-poets but rather a variety of workers, some of whom had no ideological posture at all.[84] Andor Gabor began a sustained assault on "bourgeois" literature, focusing first on the successful popular biographer, Emil Ludwig.[85] And this first issue contained a manifesto by Becher himself, designating the journal's major task as the propagation of a pure proletarian art.[86]

In the second issue, *Die Linkskurve* printed Lenin's pre-1914 essay, "Party-Organization and Party Literature," his most adamant call for subordination of literature to party propaganda requirements.[87] That set the tone of the entire issue. In what followed, there came an unsigned critique of Piscator's theater as not Communist-revolutionary enough. A second unsigned article criticized the "bourgeois" social critic of the Rhineland, Erik Reger. In the next issue, Gabor set forth the stance of the journal in an extreme and extensive position statement:

> There is no "humanity" in general, there is only
> a concrete humanity composed of classes, and –
> as it is written – the history of humanity is
> precisely the history of class struggles. Litera-
> ture is not an inspiration by the Holy Spirit, it
> is a historical image, a class product, it belongs
> to one or another class whose ideas and feelings
> it portrays, organizes and develops further.[88]

"Proletarian-revolutionary" literature was literature for class struggle. Gabor directed a long sement of the essay to a remonstrance, clearly directed at the KPD, urging the importance of a Communist culture front in creating proletarian class consciousness and rejecting the persistent classical humanism of some Party leaders and intellectuals. Then he turned to the issue of the composers of the new, proletarian-revolutionary literature. He rejected categorically the importance or utility in this cultural endeavor of "bourgeois" intellectuals, however independent, critical of the bourgeoisie or interested in the proletariat. Proletarian culture could only be made by committed writers fully versed for the new task by experience in the working class and by study of Marx and Lenin.

111

In the same issue the campaign against Pohl and against Piscator was continued. Two issues later, Gabor attacked Barbusse for allowing Hendrik de Man and Ernst Gläser to express their reservations about Marxism-Leninism in his Paris journal, *Le Monde*.[89] Gabor advised his readers against looking into such indiscriminate, "modernist" journals. In the same issue, Otto Biha defended the campaign in the USSR against the "counterrevolutionary" Pilnyak.[90] And in this issue began what soon emerged as the central polemic against unattached intellectuals in Germany itself: the attack on Alfred Döblin.

Chapter Four

THE LEFT-RADICAL CONTROVERSY OVER ALFRED DÖBLIN'S WISSEN UND VERÄNDERN!

> Those we mean are the left-radical intellectuals who already openly reject capitalism and think nothing of the reformism of Social Democracy. But...
> They are 'in principle essentially' in agreement with a radical transformation to socialism. But...
> But actually they cannot draw the consequences of their apparent agreement because they have hundreds of reservations, concerns and hindrances.
> — B. Balazs, "The Intellectuals' Fear of Socialism" (1928)

Wissen und Verändern! — The Culminating Statement of Negativism

Alfred Döblin's discontent, expressed all-too-vehemently in his inaugural address in the Prussian Academy of Art, did not signify an abandonment of his commitments to engaged writing, to political democracy or to the democratization of culture. He remained the paradigmatic Negativist. The controversies of 1928 in fact drove him to attempt a definitive formulation of his stance, one that would demonstrate the artistic integrity and intellectual responsibility of his vision while at the same time mobilizing a progressive turn in German affairs. That this was a desperately difficult enterprise cannot have escaped him. Yet his whole intellectual identity was at stake. To confirm and defend it, Döblin embarked upon his most important literary venture, the novel *Berlin Alexanderplatz*. When this novel, too, came under attack, he found himself drawn more and more explicitly to formulate his view of the intellectual calling in the Weimar context, and this culminated in a major statement, *Wissen und Verändern!* In these two works, Döblin's struggle for an intellectual identity in which neither political nor intellectual integrity would be sacrificed emerges with utter clarity. Through them, too, emerges the general dilemma of Negativism, its fate of despair and dissolution.

The *Linkskurve* launched an attack upon Döblin's new novel shortly after it was published in December 1929 in book form. A short, pointed review by Klaus Neukranz questioned the excitement surrounding the book, blaming it on a "misleading" title. The book had nothing to do with Berlin or Alexanderplatz, the centers of Communist working-class strength, Neukranz noted. Rather: "Döblin in this book expressed in unmasked form his openly declared enmity toward the organized class struggle of the proletariat."[1] Reactionary and counterrevolutionary in its misrepresentation of the working class and its silence over the bloody encounters with the security police in and around Alexanderplatz, "the book only substantiates the case that the so-called left-bourgeois writers are a political danger for the proletariat to which we must pay the sharpest attention."

In January 1930 Becher himself took up the cudgels in his essay "One Step Farther!" Becher began by proclaiming hostility toward unattached leftists:

> We must demarcate ourselves sharply from the *sympathizers.*
> This *left literature* is quite definitely not
> for us. We must before everything demonstrate
> the corrupting workings of these *sympathizers*
> in our own ranks, in the proletariat itself...
> We can only win and hold for the long term the
> most worthwhile energies among the *sympathizers*
> by relentless and open struggle...[2]

Those who remained "independent" after all the time and experience that had passed since the war and the revolution had to be written off from the Communist side. A true proletarian literature might be crude, but its message and contribution were clear. The opposite was the case with Döblin's *Berlin Alexanderplatz*. Becher termed *Berlin Alexanderplatz* "a mad construction which was incapable of life." Döblin's "transport worker" was "an artificially processed laboratory product...speaking a stenographically reproduced Berlin dialect."[3] A true proletarian-revolutionary writer's *Berlin Alexanderplatz*, by contrast, would depict real workers, members of the organized and militant proletariat.

Döblin responded swiftly to these polemics in his essay "Catastrophe on a Leftward Bent," in spring 1930.[4] In his characteristic fashion, Döblin's riposte was vehement and *ad hominem*. First he attacked the journal as an "apparatus" which produced "mechanically standardized criticism" by "assembly line." Döblin claimed the "apparatus" came "equipped with protective devices against independent thought." He charged the editorial board of the *Linkskurve* — Becher, Gabor, Kläber, Weinert and Renn — with emptiheadedness (*Begriffslosigkeit*): "to be sure, one is nothing, but one is not bourgeois. To be sure, one cannot write, but one does not write in a bourgeois fashion." Then Döblin went on to mock the accomplishments of each of these writers. He scoffed at Becher's claim of a "mighty upswing" in proletarian literature. Above all, Döblin challenged Becher's implicit pretention to "dictatorship over literature." He argued that Becher had no idea what the proletariat was really like. Playing on the title of Grosz's famous book of drawings, Döblin called for a volume to explore "the face of the ruled class." A true Marxist literature, he insisted, would strive "to show reality as it is, to demonstrate the actual requirements of the masses and on this basis and for this purpose to develop theories." Instead, Döblin concluded, Becher offered his milksop verse and his propaganda.

Otto Biha, the main editor of *Die Linkskurve*, answered Döblin in June 1930 with an essay as pointed and bitter as Döblin's.[5] Biha repudiated Döblin's estimation of Becher. Becher was known by revolutionaries throughout the world, Biha claimed, somewhat improbably, and by millions in the German working class. He had even provoked the state censors, the most telling proof of significance, while Döblin's own Buddhist mysticism interested only a few dilettantes of the upper bourgeoisie. Ludwig Renn's "mediocre" war novel, he went on, was more widely read than Döblin's entire opus. Döblin was an open enemy of the working class, Biha concluded, quoting Döblin's remarks from the debate in the *Gruppe 1925*. His novel *Berlin Alexanderplatz* tried to portray workers as "burdened with Freudian complexes" and "Hamlet souls" — maladies only of the egotistical petit-bourgeoisie (!). The novel was "the position statement of a cultural nihilist," a "typical phenomenon of degeneration in the bourgeois novel." Because Becher pointed this out with such force and clarity, the megalomaniacal Dr. Döblin had attacked the *Linkskurve*, but this petty resentment did him no good, Biha concluded, for the emerging generation of young proletarian writers would be far more interesting than Döblin. A few issues later the *Linkskurve* celebrated an even sweeter revenge against Döblin. It engineered and then announced that Döblin's novel, about to be published in Russian translation, had been cancelled by the International Bureau for Revolutionary Literature in Moscow.[6]

The attacks on Döblin from the Communist side were not restricted to *Die Linkskurve*. In *Berlin am Morgen*, the Communist writer F.C. Weiskopf trotted forth Döblin's statement of 1926 as a preliminary to a sharp critique of *Berlin Alexanderplatz*.[7] Weiskopf called Döblin an opportunist: "Döblin is a versatile spirit, a modern spirit; a spirit open to all that is new," he mocked. Döblin's effort in *Berlin Alexanderplatz* to spring the bond of the established novel form remained merely an epigonal imitation of the true innovator, James Joyce. Joyce succeeded. Döblin did not. His failure proved nonetheless instructive, for it represented the bankruptcy of the German novel. The genre and the artist belonged to the decadent bourgeoisie.

The debate did not end with the Communist rejoinders. In response to Döblin's article in *Das Tagebuch*, a young student from Bonn, Gustav Hocke, wrote an open letter to Döblin which appeared in that same journal in July 1930.[8] Having read not only the diatribe against the *Linkskurve* but also Döblin's programmatic address to the Prussian Academy, "From the Old to the New Naturalism," Hocke saw in Döblin a prominent writer, progressive but unattached, whom he could challenge to present some coherent strategy for a contemporary intellectual. He asked Döblin to specify what the role

116

of the intellectual should be. He claimed to be caught in a labyrinth of competing ideas and values in which he could not find his way. He saw himself called upon at once to be loyal to a two-thousand-year-old tradition and to throw it over entirely, to defend the bourgeoisie, to join the proletariat and to preserve intellectual autonomy. Every year a new worldview was suggested, only to be controverted thereafter. Germans had begun to look abroad for answers — to France, to America, to Russia, but Hocke claimed he wanted to remain within the German orbit. He referred to Döblin's program of shattering the monopoly of culture and bringing culture to the masses, and queried whether opening up culture to the "Moloch masses" did not mean a decline in quality, citing the work of Becher and Piscator as examples.

This was a problematic and difficult challenge for Döblin. He did not know Hocke and he was suspicious, as he noted in his response, of "what really lies behind your questions" — i.e., the political orientation of the young man.[9] Recognizing that the student had posed a fundamental issue of the time, however, Döblin resolved to give his response. His letters to Hocke were intended as self-clarification as much as instruction. If the tone of the letters proved sharp and assertive, the charge that Döblin played "Dr. All Knowing" seems quite misplaced,[10] for the endeavor at self-conception, with its implicit concommitant of social analysis, is ineluctable for any serious man of mind. As he made clear in the preface to the book *Wissen und Verändern!* into which his series of responses to Hocke had grown by 1931, he wrote not so much for Hocke specifically as for the whole "stratum of people in Germany which does a great deal for others but thinks too little about itself and for itself," the intellectuals.[11]

The best entry into Döblin's *Wissen und Verändern!* is to recognize that it arose directly out of the debate with the *Linkskurve* and continued on a far vaster and more systematic level the arguments adumbrated there. In his book Döblin set himself two goals: to specify the situation of the intellectual in Germany in 1930 and to determine his own course of action. The historical specificity of these concerns must be emphasized for they determined the substance and the structure of Döblin's reflections. These concerns revolved around the categorical demand by the German Communist intellectuals for subordination to the Party, or as they put it, "integration into the proletariat." Following out of his controversy with the *Linkskurve*, his reflections would necessarily be sharply critical of orthodox Communism. At the outset, therefore, Döblin made it clear that he nonetheless opposed capitalism and authoritarianism and believed no intellectual of conscience could stand by the ruling minority.

In this context, Döblin rebuked Hocke's cavalier attitude toward Soviet Russia. In the student's letter there were scoffing remarks about America and the USSR; indeed, Hocke used a very Spenglerian line against Russia as "a barbarian people which will overrun the declining West."[12] For Döblin, Hocke's proposal to reject Americanism and Bolshevism in favor of the "flesh and blood" of German history misunderstood the vital energies of the epoch and vastly overestimated the integrity and promise of Germany's historical development. For all his reservations about its outcome, Döblin insisted that Bolshevism in Russia had reflected a hope for social justice and a concern for the rights of the oppressed. Bluntly Döblin informed Hocke that a true intellectual of necessity had to take his stance "at the side of the proletariat."[13]

That did not mean the intellectual had to submit himself to the so-called "proletarian party," however. Indeed, the very notion of a "proletarian party" made it necessary to rethink the idea of the proletariat itself. When Döblin asked what "proletariat" meant, he found that it was a construction, not a real social entity. In an age of enormous research and proliferation of knowledge, next to nothing was known about the masses.

> Not even the working-class theorists had time
> to consider the masses, to study and to dif-
> ferentiate; they wanted to make something out
> of them too, if for their own good. They have
> seen the masses the way they wanted to see them.
> They made out of the masses the proletariat,
> which is a construction which has formed on the
> masses like a boil.[14]

The lower classes of Germany had no organizational or ideological unity. A large part of the working-class itself had no orientation whatever. A significant part of the balance organized in Catholic and "bourgeois" unions which embodied the traditional *Untertanen Mentalität*, the attitude of subservience, instilled by German authoritarianism. "Proletariat" as an idea befitted only the organized and active remainder of the working class. But here party intervened to rob even them of solidarity. They were fragmented into factions which embraced either a narrowly economistic interest politics with no social vision whatever or an authoritarian and violent revolutionary posture which dismissed all ideals as laughable and respected only force. Just this reduction of socialism to the mere interest politics or class warfare of one segment of society against another proved to Döblin that socialism had been corrupted by *party* organization. "In Germany access to the people is blocked by the parties."[15] Economic interest groups ruled and tried to force the intellectuals into subordination to party programs. This was true even of the so-called "working-class parties." Anti-intellectualism prevailed in the working class and in its parties, Döblin observed. "They will distrust you persistently."[16] He quoted Bebel's famous warning to the German Social Democratic Party, "if a bourgeois comes to you, look him over carefully; if he is an intellectual, doubly!" For all these reasons, Döblin argued the place of the intellectual was "at the side of the proletariat," not within the ranks of its party.

Döblin entered into a vituperative and adamant critique of Marxist-Leninist theory and especially its dogma of dictatorship of the proletariat. He pointed to the situation in the Soviet Union as an example of the harm that this militant and militarist class warfare caused. "The workers' movement and class struggle can bring about the destruction of the capitalist class (but) it is entirely up in the air whether it leads to a classless society and to socialism."[17] Not socialism but collectivism, state capitalism and a relentless authoritarianism: that was what the Soviet Union had become by 1930 for Döblin. Ten years and more had passed since the Bolshevik Revolution. Stalin and the apparat had already removed the gloss from the Soviet Experiment. Döblin was informed enough to have become disabsued of any residual Bolshevik utopianism. The inter-

119

national revolutionary potential and the progressive character of Bolshevism in the era 1917-1920 had been lost forever. Russian Communism represented instead a form of centralist, industrializing authoritarianism which under the banner of collectivism tended to reduce men to the mechanical agencies of its will. In this view of Russia, Döblin demonstrated parallels with the Russian Zamyatin, though he may not have read the latter's *We*. Not only did the Soviet experience by the late Twenties seem to indicate a massive flaw in the theories and practices of the left, but the comportment of the German Communist Party and above all of its intellectual representatives convinced Döblin that these were authoritarian and bureaucratic types with less concern for humane society than for the tactics of force and the regimen of strict discipline. The organized left by 1930 began to appear all too similar to the organized right, and a humane socialism seemed to be the concern of neither. The erosion of the leftist ideal corresponded to the dissension and decline in power of the leftist political organizations in Germany, and Döblin lost all hope for a united leftist front against fascism. Again, the historical condition made negativism a position of profound pessimism.

The Marxist-Leninist doctrine proved extremely dangerous.[18] First, "dictatorship of the Proletariat" turned out to resemble "good old militaristic subjection." When one accepted the "old methods of force" one could only be sure "how they begin, but not how they stop." Second, no one knew "who should be recognized as the correct proletariat in view of the fragmentation of the working class." But the greatest danger was that the party of the proletariat "destroys private capitalism but it does not say a thing about why it destroys it and for what end it desires the association of free and equal producers." "Producers" were merely "economic magnitudes," not human beings. For Döblin economic interest and revenge against capitalist exploiters were not sufficient to legitimize proletarian hegemony. "Something cannot produce what is not already within it: out of this murderously sharpened class struggle justice may emerge, but not socialism."[19]

To the doctrine of "dictatorship of the proletariat" Döblin opposed the idea of a true socialism which he defined as "freedom, spontaneous cooperation of individuals, rejection of all force, outrage against injustice and force, humanity, tolerance, a peaceful orientation."[20] A hostile critic has observed that these have less to do with socialism that with liberalism,[21] but Döblin's whole point was that a socialism which did not include these values was a step backward from liberalism. Döblin insisted that violence and negativity were not enough, nor would economic self-interest suffice. Döblin disputed the primacy of the economic over the political in historical explanation. In terms of German history it was simply not true that the bourgeoisie ever controlled Germany or that the state subordinated itself to economic interests, Döblin argued.[22] Indeed, precisely the reverse was true. In Russia, he went on, the revolution itself demonstrated the primacy of politics and ideology over economic determinism. Russia was no advanced capitalist society ripe for inevitable proletarian revolution: quite the opposite, ideological visionaries seized a political opportunity and were only now creating an industrial Russia.

Döblin went on to attack the so-called "dialectical materialist critique of ideology," the whole notion of "base" and "superstructure," in which ideas were the mechanistically determined consequence of the social origins of intellectuals and of the conditions of production. To Döblin it seemed an utter contradiction to argue such a wooden determinism and then demand of intellectuals a "commitment" − i.e., a voluntary choice − to join the proletariat. It was in emphasizing this patent logical flaw that Döblin made his remark of 1926 in which he denied the proletariat any claims over him since he was, after all, a "bourgeois" writer.

It was the issue of critical freedom − exactly what brought the intellectual to the side of the proletariat in the first place − which was at stake: autonomy meant freedom to criticize even the proletariat and its party. This whole system of objections impelled Döblin to argue for an intellectual autonomy which would still support the proletarian struggle for human liberation.

Döblin sought to establish the intellectual tradition out of which intellectuals of the unattached left could fashion a viable identity. The place to begin was to take up the most frequent rationale of the Marxist-Leninist proponents of "commitment" − Marx's Thesis on

121

Feuerbach, "The philosophers have only *interpreted* the world in various ways; the point is, to *change* it." When Marx wrote this, Döblin noted, it was a healthy measure against a nebulous idealism.

> Today, however, the sentence has a damned
> aftertaste. It seems as though we don't need
> to understand. Thought is superfluous, one
> has only to "change"...I can imagine someone
> today, myself for example, standing up and saying:
> in the last few decades an enormous
> amount has changed about the world, almost too
> much...it wouldn't be bad for a change to think
> a little bit and take command of the change in
> terms of one's thought.[23]

Döblin insisted that his concern was to reverse Marx's formulation, to go back toward the issues Marx had prematurely foreclosed with the invention of Marxism. Marx had begun fully in the spirit of socialist humanism, but in his effort to lend an increased "realism" and "science" to the new conception of man in terms of the naturalistic program of secularization, Marx made two errors. First, he reduced the whole issue to economics, and second, he proposed a resolution which partook fully of the inhumanity of German-Prussian militarist authoritarianism, the very force against which he was rebelling. Ultimately, Marx explained the problem of human development in a secular, naturalistic order in economic terms exclusively, reducing the idea of a free mankind to the specific interest of a particular class, the proletariat. And he turned the problems of human self-realization into a Gordian knot to be cut through with the brutally swift "justice" of a proletariat as militant, ruthless and vengeful as its enemy. Yet neither error should obscure, Döblin insisted, the humanist inspiration of Marx. Döblin believed there was more to Marx's initial concern, more, too, in the set of ideas with which he worked, than emerged in finished Marxism. Döblin wanted to return to the "utopian" socialism with which Marx began, rather than the "scientific" and authoritarian Marxism with which he ended.

All too many Marxists, starting at least in some measure with Marx himself, had underemphasized the active pole of human intervention in the dialectic. The Marxist-Leninists had no use for "humanism." That was all "ideology" which had to be exposed for its "class basis," its materialist determination. Döblin's program consisted in rescuing the vital elements of humanism both from this Marxist captivity and from the degeneracy of late 19th-century German *Vulgäridealismus* for which it was an empty phrase or a beautiful myth. "Sure, 'humanism' has degenerated massively into a phrase — into 'beautiful' literature — but it lives under the disfiguring tyrannical mask of Marxism itself. Just as we reject the mere phrase and the 'beautiful' literature, so we reject this cruel masquerade."[24]

All of these critiques of Marxism-Leninism are hardly original with Döblin. That does not lessen their validity or the importance he attached to them in his dispute with a circle of thinkers whose orientation did indeed betray a good deal of the *Vulgärmarxismus* Döblin — and before him with greater originality and rigor, his teacher Karl Korsch — disputed.[25] *Wissen und Verändern!*, in consequence, may be read as a literary and impressionistic essay in the line of Karl Korsch, toward the recovery of Hegel behind Marx. This movement, which George Lichtheim has paradoxically termed "From Marx to Hegel," is at the heart of leftist efforts at intellectual identity in the 20th century. As Lichtheim puts it, "the central problem now before us is not so much to change the world (that is being done independently), but to understand it."[26] This was Döblin's view.

Döblin proposed to delimit the historical development which generated socialism in order to explain how it had gone astray. There were two strands to this account: a social-historical survey of German political development and an intellectual-historical conceptualization of European cultural change. For Döblin the turning point in German history was 1525, when Luther failed to support the effort to extend freedom from the sphere of religious conscience to the worldly domain of politics and economic life. After Luther, the parallel course of *Untertänigkeit* in political affairs and *Innerlichkeit* in cultural life destroyed the progressive character of the German bourgeoisie and corrupted the German intelligentsia. Consequently, at the next great turning point, 1848, the struggle for liberation failed and both the bourgeoisie and the intelligentsia became servants of the feudal tradition. Only in view of this utter degeneracy of the German *Bildungsbürgertum* could the emergent working class have become the total obsession of a thinker like Karl Marx. In this German world Marx inherited, the proletariat had become the only hope for liberation.

In European culture it was the unintended consequence of Luther's Reformation that there emerged a new assessment of the sacred and the profane. The ascendancy of a passion for truth, instilled by the religious problems of conscience and faith, gradually led to a relentless elimination of God and religion — of all transcendence — from European culture. This notion of Christianity setting in motion an implacable will to truth, which soon turned upon and consumed Christianity itself, clearly came to Döblin from Friedrich Nietzsche.[27] But the consequence of this process was not the nihilism to which Nietzsche's bitter anti-humanism seemed to point.

For Döblin the end of secularization was not nihilism but a thoroughgoing philosophical naturalism. This philosophical naturalism found historic expression in the 19th century pantheism of Goethe and above all in the dialectical-historicist philosophy of Hegel. These represented a transference of the idea of spirit and of human eschatology to the realm of immanence — what M.H. Abrams has analyzed for modern scholarship in terms at Carlyle's paradox "natural supernaturalism."[28] Thereby spirit became the animating principle of the natural order and man's intellectual and personal existence took on a new significance as the unfolding realization of this immanent development of nature. Döblin labeled this conception "dialectial naturism" and differentiated it emphatically from mechanistic materialism and from *Vulgäridealismus*. He traced the latter degeneracy from Goethe through Wagner to Stefan George, but his greatest strictures were directed at Nietzsche's abandonment of humanism and celebration of force, destructiveness and domination.[29] This German perversion of humanism and idealism was bankrupt. It could not be salvaged, but the cultural heritage over which the mandarin masters of this *Vulgäridealismus* presided had nevertheless to be wrested from them and given over to the true bearers of progress, the masses. Hence the democratization of culture remained at the crux of Döblin's program.

In coming to his final diagnosis of the situation and task of the German intellectual in 1930, Döblin returned to his key ideas of the masses, technology and the urban-industrial future. He sharply chided Hocke for the phrase "Moloch masses" used in the student's letter. "You know as well as I do that politically and economically the masses have not been a Moloch but only a sacrificial victim, an almost willless object."[30] Döblin described the masses as "unformed, empty, uneducated or miseducated, at the same time generally simple and certain in their fundamental instinct."[31] The educated classes, the so-called "bearers of science and industry," had proven clearly reactionary, though the science and technology they administred remained thoroughly progressive. The masses, for the most part the unconscious objects of that science and technology, were in that very measure the outgrowth of social and cultural development, the implicit bearers and defenders of humanistic values, and therefore "the most important kind of people." It was the task of the progressive intellectual to go over to the side of the masses, to help them to grasp the culture of which they were the legitimate heirs.

The intellectual's function was *educative*. In moving to the side of the working class, Döblin concluded, "you do not become a renegade from your class but rather separate yourself from a class that has itself become renegade, and return to the broad platform which your class abandoned and which was left exclusively to the struggling working class to defend."[32] Progressive intellectuals had a major project in making explicit the implicit development of history. Hitherto, amid much "sorrow and feigned joy over technology," people construed society in the advanced industrial age in terms of a collective crude as the idea of an antheap. The task of the progressive intellectual was to take part in the effort to grasp contemporary social reality and to envision the social future. The instrumental breakthroughs of science and technology cried out for an adequate social vision. "Good, clear technology" and "hard science" were "emanations of the powerful, single, intellectual process of naturalism, of secularization."[33] Technical change had "achieved a great deal but it had not yet touched human society and its formation." It was "in no one's control and following no one's command." The intellectual had to help the masses from a passive to an active relationships to technical change by supplying them with a vision of human self-realization.

The task of creating a social vision of human self-realization in a urban-technological age: this was Döblin's sense of the mission of a progressive intellectual. It also fit into his larger philosophical vision of "dialectical naturism":

> If spirit works in nature and in history and
> develops both, then human thought has a new
> role, one must say, a new dignity, and that is
> to extend just this dialectical progress, first
> through the understanding of the historical
> situation and then through a responsible inter-
> vention in that situation.[34]

These ideas of social vision and dialectical intervention were at the heart of Döblin's notion of the intellectual.

The Bolshevik Response to Wissen und Verändern!

Döblin's *Wissen und Verändern!* provoked an enormous contro-versy in the radical avant-garde. As can be surmised, the *Linkskurve* intellectuals would not abide such a statement in silence. A whole spate of responses emerged on the orthodox Left. In *Die Linkskurve* itself, Armin Kesser reviewed Döblin's new work in terms of a "crisis of the bourgeois intelligentsia."[35] This crisis seemed to create a specific type of debator, Kesser observed, and "in the literary circles of Berlin this type is called Alfred Döblin." Döblin was a "wild man" but not revolutionary. He served up to the decadent bourgeoisie an artistically spiced version of social problems, only to permit them the better to scoff at radicalism and cultivate an attitude of righteousness. Kesser charged that Döblin contradicted himself by calling upon intellectuals in one breath to stand by the side of the proletariat and in the next attacking Marxism-Leninism. Döblin's understanding of dialectical materialism was flawed as well, and he misrepresented German history and class conflict in accordance with his penchant toward a three-thousand-year-old Taoism.

F.W. Weiskopf returned to the attack in *Rote Aufbau.* [36] Restating almost word for word his earlier polemic, Weiskopf came eventually to the new work. He concentrated on the phrase "at the side of the proletariat." What did that mean? he asked, especially since it manifestly did not mean support for a working class party. Trotting out Döblin's ideas of "socialism," Weiskopf dismissed them as the "old idealistic humbug" and reiterated the KPD demand that intellectuals take their place "in the proletarian front."

In 1932, Otto Biha, editor of *Die Linkskurve*, published a "contribution to the analysis of the fascist tendency in literature" in *Internationale Literatur.* [37] Entitled "The Ideologies of The Petit Bourgeois and the Crisis," one of its major targets was Alfred Döblin's *Wissen und Verändern!* Biha felt Döblin betrayed what had seemed his gradual development toward the socialist movement by making this critique of the Soviet Union and Marxist-Leninist thought. Döblin thereby served the interests of the "social fascists" – the SPD. Döblin's ideal of socialism, severing it from class struggle, constituted a mystification of working-class ideology, a utopian and pseudo-religious deviation that had nothing to do with workers and expressed rather "the dead end of the petit bourgeois." For Biha there was little or no difference between Döblin and his other targets – the religious mystic Franz Werfel and the aesthetic nihilist Gottfried Benn. All three reflected a petit-bourgeois flight from reality and hence a fascist tendency.

A more discriminating and careful Communist critique of Döblin came in the pages of *Die Weltbühne* in 1932, in Bela Balazs' article, "The Dread of Socialism Among the Intellectuals." [38] Balazs made it clear that his concern was with the negativists, not their mandarin or "idealist" brethren.

> Those we mean are the left-radical intellectuals
> who already openly reject capitalism and think
> nothing of the reformism of Social Democracy. But...
> They are all "in principle essentially" in agree-
> ment with a radical transformation to socialism.
> But...
> But actually they cannot draw the consequences
> of their apparent agreement because they have
> hundreds of reservations, concerns and hindrances. [39]

127

Balazs was concerned to persuade these authentic negativists out of their hesitancy to join the proletariat. They had an important function and their ideological lack of clarity threatened their historical efficacy. Balazs sought to diagnose this "ideological crisis of the left-radical intellectuals." It was an ideological crisis for them, not an economic one, though they experienced an economic crisis as well. The issue was strictly ideological − ethical, in their terms. These intellectuals approved of socialism as an economic order but they could not yet accept "the proletarian ideology of class struggle and revolution."

In his article, Balazs catalogued the objections and answered each from a Communist standpoint. The first objection dealt with the ostensible obfuscation of the division of mental from physical labor. It was true that under socialism, "mental labor will enjoy no special prestige as a genre of labor." But in a socialist order, "personal and intellectual achievement" would become "much more important" in planning and leadership.[40] Nor could it be argued that intellectuals as a social group enjoyed that much prestige in bourgeois society. They were tolerated by the real elites, but never actually dominated. A second objection had to do with the concern over the "vulgarization of spirit," the need of the intellectual to preserve "aristocratic isolation." This was in fact a curse of bourgeois society, not a necessity of intellectual integrity. It was an implicit protest against the bourgeois order. In the classless society the level of the masses would rise to the level of the intellectuals and there would be no isolation. A third objection juxtaposed the "mechanization and objectification" of socialism to the soul and inwardness of intellectuality. Again, Balazs argued, it was capitalism which created the reification of life, as Marx had demonstrated. Industrialization was inevitable, but the decisive question was whether technology should rule man or man technology. The false anxiety before mechanization, the Ludditism among traditionalist intellectuals which permitted them to equate Bolshevism with Americanism and reject both, was irrational. Socialism promised an industrial order in accordance with human dignity, not a technicist determinism.

Another set of objections had to do with the divergence between bourgeois ideas of culture − *Bildung* − and the Marxist worldview.

128

Balazs asked what *Bildung* meant and argued interestingly: *"Bildung* provided specifically in each period only that knowledge which aided in the development of a world view and from which one could draw consequences for a style of life."[44] Precisely this was now impossible for the bourgeoisie: "there is no longer any bourgeois *Bildung*." It had become incapable of synthesis. The only viable worldview came in proletarian *Bildung*: Marxism. To this a number of intellectuals objected, foremost Döblin, because of its "mechanistic materialism" and "mere economism." They created a straw man of *Vulgärmarxismus*, for none of this was true of Marx himself. Marx had a dialectical vision of historical development. To be sure Marx argued about the precedence of existence over consciousness. But this was not mechanistic. Otherwise, why the enormous concern in Marxism with propaganda? Otherwise why a theory of history in which active revolution was the centerpiece? Bolshevism was not doctrinaire, Balazs insisted. Marx was a Hegelian; Lenin recommended the study of Hegel. The idea of base and superstructure was not mechanical and the concept of ideology did not lead to a crisis of relativism or a crude reductionism, he went on. On the other hand, the bourgeois idea of an unchanging human nature was extremely dangerous. Ideologies changed with economic changes — though with a lag that became the more pronounced the more ethereal the level of culture involved.

Arguments against the domination of a proletarian dictatorship reflected a misguided individualism which did not recognize that personalities would have the greatest freedom of development in the classless society of Communism. Already in Russia, Balazs saw this transpiring. The concern for intellectual autonomy was also misguided. First, censorship remained only as a consequence of an ongoing civil war and would cease with the victory of socialism. To challenge *Tendenzkunst* or proletarian culture as unripe was altogether unfair, for no one claimed they were perfect forms; they were weapons in the struggle to create a society where untrammeled masterpieces could be achieved. Finally, the objection to violence was either hypocritical or stupid, for capitalism ruled by force and violence — by starvation and economic exploitation: "we have only to choose whether force and dictatorship be used for or against the proletarian."[42] The way to make the decision was to judge the ultimate goal. The goal of proletarian dictatorship was classless society. There was no alternative to the proletarian front, no other mass base which was vailable for promoting human liberation, and consequently there was nothing more dangerous than to claim to support the proletariat and then reject the party. It was not required that intellectuals become "assimilated" into the proletariat:

> No one demands assimilation from the intellectuals.
> One demands only an insight: the insight that their
> interests as intellectual workers are the same as
> those of the proletariat and not merely in the eco-
> nomic but also in the cultural domain.[43]

What was required was "community of path and struggle," but not assimilation. "Even sympathizers are valuable to the Party," Balazs asserted. "Only one condition: that they really smpathize. That means with the Party and not just with abstract and vague goals." Balazs concluded that the intellectual could not really help the proletariat. It was the proletariat which could help the intellectual by providing him with the worldview of Marxism and the realization of the Marxist program. The intellectual had only to join in.

Despite its subtlety and persuasiveness, Balazs' critique of Döblin is weakend first by an uncritical reverence for the Soviet Union, which already by 1930 sophisticated Marxists and non-Marxists had seen slipping into a rigid, bureaucratic authoritarianism under Stalin. Second, it made no distinction between the KPD and the proletariat, though empirically the proletariat, as Döblin charged, was hopelessly divided. Communist ideological phrases like "social fascism," moreover, tended to heap all those not fully in accordance with the Party into the arch-reactionary category. This very rigidity gives the lie to Balaz's contention that there was no reductionism in the Marxist-Leninist approach. *Vulgärmarxismus* was no straw man but by far the preponderant force in orthodox Communist parties. By holding up the aspiration of a Communist order — classless society, freedom and equality, etc. — Balazs was no less "utopian" than the reluctant negativists he sought to convince. These nega-tivists might accept his contention that the proletariat was the only mass base for social progress in Germany. They would agree that this meant the intellectual had to stand by it. Only what Balazs failed to recognize was the hopeless fragmentation of the proletariat and the grim prospect that in the current German situation doctrinaire party postures did little to stem the reactionary tide.

Balazs, intimate friend of Lukacs and defender, long after the latter's defection, of the aspirations of the humane Marxism of the early Twenties, reflected in his argument and in its difficulties the plight of a fullbodied Marxism in the confines of a "Bolshevized" orthodoxy.[44] Common to his vision and that of the negativists he hoped to convert was the spark of revolutionary hope awakened in 1917. But what Balazs would not recognize was that the opportunity has been foreclosed by 1930: foreclosed by the failure of the revolution in the West, and by the perdition of the revolution in Russia. Balazs's rhetoric was a plea for a perished hope: crass "Bolshevizers" of the stripe of Biha and Weiskopf had taken administrative command of the Marxist vision in the name of Lenin but in the service of Stalin. The bitter strictures of Döblin and of his mentor Korsch could not be refuted by an idealistic affirmation.

The Kracauer-Döblin Exchange: The New Negativism

The left-wing critic to whom Döblin paid the most attention and to whom he devoted the bulk of his rejoinder was the Berlin cultural editor of the *Frankfurter Zeitung*, Siegfried Kracauer. Kracauer's initial review of *Wissen und Verändern!* appeared in that newspaper on April 17, 1931. Kracauer praised Döblin's endeavor:

> In it the issue is the *determination of the position* of the German stratum of intellectuals. Where do they belong, where are they at home and not at home? Döblin has at least fixed clearly their dubious position between the fronts.[45]

Kracauer recognized that Döblin wrote his book in conflict with orthodox Communists, commenting, "his argument touches to the quick many contemporary Marxists and hence should provide a great deal for left radicals to consider."[46] Kracauer praised Döblin's efforts to demonstrate the excesses of *Ideologiekritik* and to rescue Marx from vulgarization at the hands of his followers. Despite a number of inaccuracies in Döblin's interpretations, Kracauer seemed to approve generally of his attack on "economistic" reductionism and excessive collectivism. Yet Kracauer criticized Döblin sharply for his specification of the intellectual's position as "beside the proletariat." For Kracauer that could only mean *between* the proletariat and the bourgeoisie, "this *undialectical alongside* is by all appearances unrealizable."[47] Kracauer contended that "with the best of wills I cannot recognize how Socialism is to be helped to its feet by the measures Döblin recommends." Rather, Kracauer contended, they created a real danger: "it is to be feared that against his own intentions, by the nature of his affirmative goal definition, he offers the intelligentsia he has awakened an ideology which ennables them in the name of socialism not to bother about socialism..." Kracauer believed it possible, on the basis of "dialectical materialism," to specify more authentically the course intellectuals had to pursue for the realization of socialism. Kracauer spelled this out in a second article, "Minimal Demands Upon the Intellectuals," *Die Neue Rundschau* (July 1931).

Kracauer set forth a quite specific conception of intellect in his remarks. The intellect was "nothing other than the instrument for the destruction of all mythical remains around and within us."[48] Intellectuals had to "subject to radical doubt the entirety of established positions," to confront "inherited conceptions, and especially those which seem incontrovertible, with the results of revolutionary theory and then make an accounting of what reality remains in these conceptions." For Kracauer intellect was, hence, a destructive faculty. "It must constantly debunk ideologies and thereby put all adopted intentions to the test." This meant, ultimately:

> The task of the intellectual is not simply
> to hold up the ideal — even the socialist ideal —
> but rather to bracket it, to set it into dialectical
> relation to the immediate possibilities of its realiza-

tion. The ideal only develops energy in this way,
and it is only fruitful in so far as it can be realized.[49]

Kracauer argued that socialism was the end product of a "chain of
historical situations for which a theoretically appropriate evaluation
called forth a correct practice." Intellectuals had as their domain
not so much action as thought: "a historically conditioned thought,"
however, not a pure utopianism.

In a subsequent issue of *Die neue Rundschau*, Döblin responded
in his usual abrasive manner.[50] He clearly differentiated Kracauer
from orthodox Communist critics, but he felt Kracauer made the
same false critique of his ideas. Döblin scrutinized Kracauer's alternative formulation, praising Kracauer rather patronizingly as a
"prudent and meticulous man," who nevertheless indulged in an
"uncharacteristic naivety" in defining the task of the intellectual.
Döblin argued "the intellect is more that a mere instrument of
destruction; it is above all and in the first place an instrument for
the realization of a will." Kracauer's definition of the intellectual
function pretended that this was a pure matter of truth and not of
value: "Why this game?" Döblin demanded. "In between there
pop up such turns of phrase, after all, as 'revolutionary theory,'
'historical materialism'..."[51] Döblin insisted that intellect was at the
service of will, and that will could be oriented to a host of goals
and values. Therefore a minimum demand upon intellectuals had
to specify the will and the goal. Kracauer wanted to bring the socialist ideal into dialectical relation to present possibilities for its realization. Döblin agreed that "the ideal takes power only in this way,"
but went on immediately to quarrel with Kracauer's assertion that
the ideal was "only fruitful in so far as it can be realized." Döblin
vehemently rejected this notion, arguing "Commitment works in
the long term, it works into reality [though] often it must wait a
long time to bear fruit."[52]

Döblin went on to dismiss as willful misunderstanding the
depiction of his call to stand "beside" the proletariat as a directive
to stand "between the fronts." He had expressed a clear commitment. "It must be immediately clear as a matter of principle that
[the intellectual] thereby takes a stand in real and practical terms

against that part of the population in Germany which calls itself
the bourgeoisie and that he places himself at the side of the workers."[53] The workers represented the social force which worked
on behalf of the goal values of human liberation and solidarity,
and the intellectual had to take his stand with them. Yet he should
not subordinate himself to the workers' parties so long as they
failed to demonstrate a clear commitment to these goal values.
Döblin again specified the points that remained problematic about
their posture: "The points are: the harsh centralism, the scientism,
the militarism which this doctrine encourages and out of which
its authoritarian spirit is growing, the economistic narrowing of
thought which occasionally comes very close to the borders of a
crass metaphysical materialism."[54] The economic struggle, however
important, was only partial and should not be allowed to obscure
the goal values of a naturalistic socialism toward which the total
struggle for human liberation had to tend. The challenge was to
create a more authentic ideal of human realization, a more total
ideal of solidarity, Döblin argued.

Ostensibly Kracauer criticized Döblin from a more orthodox
Marxist posture. As Döblin noted, such phrases as "dialectical
materialism" and "revolutionary theory" dotted Kracauer's com-
ments. Yet what really separated Kracauer and Döblin? Both insisted
upon at least a functional differentiation of the intellectual from
the proletariat. Both saw the intellectual defined by his thought,
not his social origins. Both presupposed and preserved the idea of
critical freedom as indispensable in the intellectual function and
both accepted the implication that the impact of the intellectual
was mediated. The difference remained that for Kracauer intellect
had a purely critical function. It served to challenge and debunk
traditional — "mythical" — values and to expose ideologies as forms
of legitimation for social injustice. Intellect should be fully absorbed
in this destructive enterprise, Kracauer believed. It did not have need
to spin out utopias; its ideal was realized fully in the concrete historical integration of theory and practice.

Döblin emphasized far more a didactic function. For Döblin,
the intellectual was the bearer and disseminator of a tradition of
secular humanist values about which he felt far less skeptical than

Kracauer. His attitude toward tradition, while hardly uncritical, made provision for a positive heritage of humane values in tradition, and hence he rejected the exclusively critical orientation of Kracauer. Even more importantly, he insisted that intellectuals were called to formulate utopias, to envision alternative futures and to provide social orientations upon which human action might be based.

The distinction between the posture of Kracauer's "immediate unity of theory and practice" and this orientation to social vision was the willingness to posit "affirmative goal definitions." For Kracauer this was impractical, undialectical and "utopian" in the pejorative Marxist sense. But did he himself really spell out the concrete tactical connection between intellectuals and proletarian organization and mobilization? What did "immediate unity of theory and practice" actually signify? What was Kracauer's attitude regarding the dominion of party directives and the doctrinaire quality of KPD thought? Knowing Kracauer's attitude toward the U.S.S.R. might have made his position more definable, but he characteristically shirked stating his own position not only vis à vis the U.S.S.R. but toward the KPD and the German proletariat in its various concrete organizational manifestations. In Kracauer we get a foretaste of that "Marxism without the proletariat" which would become the stock in trade of Frankfurt School Post-Marxism. Kracauer's stance in 1930 amounted to an unwillingness to make explicit criticism of the left. That may be the distinguishing feature of his relation to the proletariat. Whether this posture is more "dialectical" than Döblin's it certainly seems less candid.

Where did Kracauer stand? Are we dealing here with an orthodox Marxist or with another species of negativist? To answer this we must explore Kracauer's intellectual perspective in the light of other writings. His work set out from the crisis of historicism and relativism as it was expressed in the sociological writings of Simmel, Weber, Scheler and Mannheim.[55] He knew Bloch and reviewed works by Lukacs. His perspective, then, was anchored in the most sophisticated social theory of the Twenties. How he interpreted these matters himself comes clear in an early essay, "Those who Wait," from 1922.[56]

There he wrote of the crisis of consciousness of the intellectuals before instrumental rationality. Free from every commitment of faith, they spent their days for the most part "in the loneliness of great cities." In the bustle of affairs they would forget "their own inward existence." But then a "burden" at the "center of their beings," a "deep sorrow which grows out of the knowledge of their captivity in a specific intellectual situation," would reawaken in them their "metaphysical suffering for want of a higher meaning in the world." Kracauer described the syndrome through which these intellectuals passed as *Entleerung*, emptying: a liberation from attachment to God, to religion, to tradition. They evinced a lost capacity for faith and a lost sense of community. In place of the communal, they substituted the autonomous individual. In place of the eternal they substituted the historical. But this historicization did not resolve the metaphysical crisis. The result was relativism.

There were three ways to deal with this intense crisis, this "horror vacui" experienced by the intellectual, in Kracauer's view. First, there was skepticism as a principle. This position — one thinks of Max Weber — accepted the complete impossibility of an absolute and accepted the disenchantment of the world as inevitable. It recognized the agony of the dilemma yet reacted with passionate hatred against anyone who tried to retrieve or revive the absolute. The second path was taken by the "short-cut men": those who took anything to believe in and threw themselves utterly into it with a forced faith, a too-rapid surrender of doubt amounting to self-deception. Such men were "intellectual desperados." The last way was simply to wait. Those who wait — this was Kracauer's title for the essay — were neither convinced skeptics nor desperate believers, but agnostics awaiting resolution. They dwelled, Kracauer wrote, in a "lingering openness." This posture was one which could not even accept the condition of emptiness itself as a basis for self-conception.

Kracauer recognized the decisive measure in which the intellectual was caught up in a crisis of relativism and he proposed a twofold strategy: on the one hand, a relentless critique of all established ideas and ideologies on the basis of the *Ideologiekritik* derived from Marx, and on the other hand, a "lingering openness" toward the possible return of some absolute truth or meaning after all the illusions had been purged away. Kracauer wished above all to avoid the short-circuit of the "intellectual desperado" who grasped at a new dogma to restore lost faith.

In "The Mass Ornament," (1925) Kracauer developed the idea of history as a "battle between weak and distant reason and the forces of nature" as these manifested themselves in mythological constructions. "In serving the breakthrough of truth, the historical process becomes a *process of demythologizing* and effects a radical dismantling of those positions continually occupied anew by the natural process."[57] Here Kracauer articulated the idea of critical intellect which featured in his exchange with Döblin. In this process of "disenchantment of the world," capitalism played a major role. It introduced a form of rationality which, in combination with "bourgeois revolutions," broke the domination of nature and myth in many spheres. But capitalism was "obscured" reason: "Capitalism does not rationalize too much but *too little.*" It was too abstract to "encompass human beings." Capitalism's "abstract and general determinations of meaning" were not "capable of grasping the actual substance of life."[58] The flaws of instrumental rationality were patent, but a return to organicism was the path of a "short-cut man."

> Such an objection is too hasty when it is raised
> in favor of that false mythological concreteness
> which sees as its goal organism and form. By re-
> turning to this type of concreteness the ability
> once acquired to think abstractly would indeed
> be abandoned; however, the abstractness would
> not be overcome...[59]

The problem for the intellectual was how to bring about a full realization of reason. The rational disenchantment of the world was not complete. But the persistence of "obscured reason" in capitalism could only be transcended if "its base — the economic system — undergoes an essential change." The solution of the intellectual dilemma was a social transformation, Kracauer concluded.

Because Döblin seemed willing to indulge in "affirmative goal definition," Kracauer feared he would contribute to this coopting of the intelligentsia and this distraction of the masses. There could only be one antidote: a rigorous concentration on *Ideologiekritik.* Kracauer insisted upon anchoring the intellectual's action in the present and in the critical function, for this alone would preempt the "short-cut man." He proposed to debunk all ideologies for the sake of an ultimate liberation and an ultimate culture whose positive attributes he did not even believe it possible to conceive. This fore-closure of the past and of tradition and refusal to embrace a new faith prematurely made Kracauer a far more thoroughgoing negativist than even Döblin.

In opting for critique combined with a "lingering openness," Kracauer moved toward the bleak post-humanist posture of the "critical Marxists" of the era of fascism, a new generation of culture. The leading spirit of that new generation would be Theodor Adorno, whom Kracauer tutored in philosophy, and who was one of his closest intellectual associates. Kracauer was instrumental in bringing Adorno together with another close friend, the critic Walter Benjamin, whose esoteric allegorical style of criticism was to be the single most important influence in Adorno's elaboration of "negative dialectics." Indeed, the whole argument which Kracauer brought to bear against Döblin was drawn from the collective vantage of this nascent "Frankfurt School," the dominant left-independent intellectual posture of the generation of the Thirties and thereafter in German culture.[60]

Chapter Five

A NEW "BOLSHEVISM"? –
BRECHT'S IDIOSYNCRATIC COMMUNISM

> What baseness would you not endure, so that
> Baseness may be eliminated?
> If you could finally change the world, what
> Would you be too fine to do?
> Who are you?
> Sink into filth
> Embrace the butcher, but
> Change the world: it needs it!
>   – B. Brecht, *The Measures Taken* (1930)

Bertolt Brecht presents a most difficult case with regard to the problem of art and politics. The problem is to discern the evolution of his views on Marxism and the Communist Party in Germany and Russia as they bore on his political stance and on his artistic theory and practice. During the mid-Twenties, Brecht, despite avowed Marxism, remained significantly detached from *Parteilichkeit*, indeed sceptical altogether of the "Bolshevik" line on cultural politics. Brecht had expressed distaste for Bolshevik egalitarianism as early as 1921 after a lecture in Munich by Alfons Goldschmidt. He remained quite cool about Bolshevik ideology in the mid-Twenties. "As long as Bolshevism is a matter of views, it does not do much for me," he wrote in 1926. The ideological postures of left and right could be "completely false." One had to judge them by their practice.[1] He felt a general sympathy for leftist criticism: "the crowd on the left is good as long as it struggles." But he had serious reservations about their program. Once again, it was the idea of egalitarianism that stuck in his craw. "It just comes down to this: whether one wants to chop happiness into so many small pieces."[2] Brecht argued adamantly that this was neither advisable nor possible. Happiness "would vanish like snow if someone approached it for this end."

While 100,000 Marks was a lot of money, five batches of 20,000 Marks did not amount to much, Brecht pointed out. The real animus behind Brecht's critique was a vision of life reduced to dull uniformity.

> Should people squat between their photographs and
> their meatballs, next to fix-priced women,
> before uniform pipes in their fresh-painted
> uniform huts? That is no happiness, for it
> lacks chance and risk. Chance and risk, the
> greatest and most ethical things in existence.[3]

Brecht's complaint about the evil of great men — that there were too few of them, not a mass, not a proletariat — found its counterpart in Brecht's wish to raise the proletariat to the level of greatness and morality of the great men — of chance and risk — not reduce all men to the satisfaction of petty security.[4]

Brecht preserved his sense of greatness as an artist and refused bluntly to be subsumed as an agent of "class struggle." He drew a remarkable distinction between "revolutionary" art and art subordinated to class struggle in another note from the mid-Twenties.[5] Great artists of all times had a legitimate claim on the title "revolutionary," Brecht contended, because they were "collective" — by which he meant they expressed grand social visions. He contrasted their work with that of "lesser literati." These writers were completely caught in the ebb and flow of "momentary conditions," and were therefore subject to the constraints of the moment. Their "inward instability and outward dependency" made it easy for "terror" to direct their output. Hence they were "always partly reactionary, partly revolutionary, according to social relations." Such writers *were* subordinate to the practical considerations of the class struggle but "the practical methods of revolution" were not revolutionary, according to Brecht. They were too instrumental, too compromised by the conflict. This meant great writers had to preserve their distance from the pragmatic struggles. Great writers, Brecht wrote, "find it difficult to join in the class struggle, they handle it as already decided and they occupy themselves with those new, collectively desired relationships which are the objective of the revolution. The revolution of great writers is eternal."[6] The essence of great – i.e., "revolutionary" and "collective" – art was, Brecht argued, to "serve great interests." "Eras without great interests have no great art," he contended.

The relation of art to interest was very problematic in an epoch of transition, Brecht recognized in a second striking note. There were several quite distinct social strata with competing interests. Great art could come of a commitment to "only *one* of these strata," the one that embodied the progressive evolution of society.[7] It remained, however, that though a great writer would write for this stratum, what he wrote might not elicit the stratum's response or support.

From the outset Brecht labored under no illusions as to his reception by the proletariat. He felt the efforts of writers to satisfy the views of the proletariat were "unspeakably comic."[8] Yet he was concerned to create great art and in his epoch this seemed to compel him to work in the interest of the proletariat. He turned to Marxism for its sociology and its conception of the historicity of art forms, and to the proletariat because it was the only great cause out of which he could create great art. He had no intention of becoming a mere propagandist. In a draft for the important Prologue to *Mann ist Mann*, Brecht set forth the implications of the artist choosing to create art in the interest of the proletariat. "The proletariat takes the alarming standpoint that art is harmful, since it draws the masses away from struggle."[9] This view struck Brecht as "alarming" on two counts. First, it did not accord with the historical role of art in the rise of the bourgeoisie. "Art sent the bourgeoisie on its way to the struggle." Yet, secondly, even this realization could lead to the wrong conclusions. "It is comprehensible but not pleasant that the proletariat now wishes to command art to send the masses to their own struggle." That was to misunderstand the nature of art, Brecht insisted, for it was not simply an ideological marching order. "A proletarian art is just as much art as any other: more artistic than proletarian." This mean that art would definitely be "unusable" in "times of conflict." But that was beside the point. Art was not simply agitation. It was not even "a matter of views."

> Art is — regarding both its emergence and
> its influence — something collective...I maintain
> therefore, that a view about art current in our
> left-wing circles is false. I take this opportunity
> to note that there are an enormous number of false
> views on the left, only not quite so many as on the
> right.[10]

Brecht insisted that he expected revolutionary socialism to transform the country in his lifetime, but he argued that as far as art was concerned, his advice to artists would remain "that it would be best if they went about doing what they enjoyed without further ado: otherwise they would not do good work."

Taking Brecht's ideas about art and politics around 1926 and contrasting them to Grosz's *Die Kunst ist in Gefahr*, it would appear that Brecht disagreed totally with the views of the "Bolsheviks." In 1924-1925 Brecht drafted a "conversation with George Grosz" in which he pointedly challenged the posture of Grosz and the Malik-circle regarding art and politics.

> You and I, George Grosz, are against injustice
> (like everybody else). But we would be less against
> it if it could be committed by the proletariat.
> I mean to say: it can't be injustice that 'forced
> you to take up your brushes'...I don't believe,
> Grosz, that overwhelming compassion for the
> exploited or anger against the exploiter one day
> filled you with an irresistible desire to get
> something about this down on paper. I think
> drawing is something you enjoyed, and people's
> physiognomies were so many pretexts for it.[11]

Brecht went on to analyze Grosz's *The Face of the Ruling Class* in terms of a paradox: Grosz prefered as the subject-matter of his art a type for which politically he felt nothing but loathing, and this suggested a decisive reversal of the causal flow of Grosz's art and politics. "Politically you regard the bourgeoisie as your enemy not because you are a proletarian but because you are an artist. Your political position (which unlike you I treat as secondary, you see) is a position in relation to your subject-matter." Significantly, Brecht's insight into Grosz's artistic sensibility proved more apt than the latter's own manifestos.[12] But the main point is Brecht was quite prepared to consign *bourgeois* art to the dustbin of history, but not art itself. He was first and foremost an artist.

Brecht's major dramatic idea of these years was the cycle *Entry of Humanity into the Big Cities.* The key drama in this cycle was to be a play entitled *Joe Fleischhacker.* The initial idea for *Joe Fleisch-hacker* came around 1924, close to the time Brecht resettled in Berlin. He wanted to juxtapose two plots: on the one level, he wanted to depict the manipulations of wheat speculators and their impact on food prices and the economic cycle; on the other, he wished to depict the urbanization of families out of the countryside and their fate under capitalism. Joe Fleischhacker was to be a Chicago wheat tycoon whose rise and fall wreaked havoc upon the immigrants. Not only Upton Sinclair's *The Jungle* but also the writings of Frank Norris, especially *The Pit*, can be discerned in this design. Norris's wheat-trilogy served as a major literary influence on the work.[13] Brecht became fascinated with the commodities market and began collecting news articles on wheat speculation starting in March 1925, stimulated by drastic fluctuations in world grain prices in the mid-Twenties and their impact on the German agricultural sector and German food prices.[14] It was a fateful preoccupation which would lead him to Marx.

Brecht discovered, as he pursued his research into the wheat exchange, that "these events were not explicable, that is, accessible to reason, and that means simply irrational." Even an interview with a lifelong broker on the Chicago exchange could not resolve the contradictions of capitalist speculation. "The planned drama was never written; instead I began to read Marx."[15] While this celebrated autobiographical account suffers from Brecht's penchant for fictive enhancement, this direct relation of his interest in Marxism with problems of his theatrical practice must be underscored. Certainly Brecht plunged into Marxism with a vengeance in the summer of 1926. Elisabeth Hauptmann noted in her diary on October 26, 1926: "Brecht obtains works on socialism and Marxism and asks for lists of the basic works he should study first. In a letter a little later in the holiday he writes: 'I am now eight feet deep in *Das Kapital.* Now

I want to know all the details..."[16] Brecht's fascination with Marx led him to proclaim Marx "the only audience for my plays," and to claim that only after reading *Das Kapital* did he understand his own plays.[17]

It remains that the Marxist sociologist Fritz Sternberg was correct in maintaining to Brecht: "It was not through Marx that you came to recognize the decline of the drama. It was not through Marx that you came to speak of the epic theater. For, let us put it quite gently, Epic theater, that is you, dear Mr. Brecht."[18] Brecht met the sociologist through the painter Rudolf Schlichter in the winter of 1926-1927. In their initial conversation, Brecht said he had written a play, *Drums in the Night,* on the theme of a sexual-romantic relationship but that since then the erotic and individual had proven inadequate as a basis for his dramaturgy. Sternberg immediately explained that individualistic drama was obsolete and that a modern author had to operate in the sociological dimension. His ideas fit precisely the tendency which Brecht's own thought had pursued over the year 1926, and the two men entered into spirited weekly discussions revolving around Sternberg's thesis that a modern writer could not work up a comprehension of reality from intuition or personal experience, but only through "ratio," i.e., study in a formal manner.

The turn to the sociological entailed great risk for a creative writer, Sternberg cautioned Brecht, for it could block his purely personal writing style. "In fact in the first few years we knew each other, he did write only very little," Sternberg noted.[19] Nevertheless, Brecht insisted upon making the intellectual switch. He not only met with Sternberg but attended the MASCH (Marxistische Arbeiter Schule) in Neukölln, directed by Hermann Duncker, and took private lessons in Marxism from the maverick philosopher Karl Korsch. Out of all this he evolved his idea of "sociological dramaturgy." Elisabeth Hauptmann noted in 1926 that Brecht "recognized that the current dramatic forms were not suited to reflecting such modern processess as the world distribution of wheat or the life-story of the times — in a word, all human actions of consequence."[20] In developing his conception of "sociological dramaturgy" Brecht derived from Marxism above all the ideas of the social determination of behavior and the historicity of cultural forms. As Marx had argued that Greek forms of art could no longer be creative in a world of automatic machinery and the stockmarket, Brecht felt that certain literary forms were obsolete. Just as there were no absolutes or perennials in human nature for Marxism, there were no such perennial themes or artistic styles. Despite the avowedly Marxist inspiration for this stance, it must be remarked that such a stance is just as characteristic of modernism as it is of Marxism.

From the exchange of views between Brecht and Sternberg in the *Berliner Börsen-Courier* in late spring 1927 we may come to a more concrete appreciation of Brecht's concept of "sociological dramaturgy." Sternberg began the exchange in an open letter to Brecht entitled "The Downfall of the Drama."[21] In it he proclaimed that the collapse of contemporary drama was a historical necessity which followed from the intellectual decline of the age itself. He tied the collapse to an epochal transformation, the end of the age of individualism. The dilemma of the creative intellectual of the 20th century, in his view, revolved around the question of what remained to be done since "the collective has once again become determining, since machines are in control and history is determined only by the millions."[22] The mechanization of the individual created a situation in which collectives − classes − formed the only reality. In this context, the *Dichter* lost his orientation and dwindled into a mere *Literat*, i.e., subordinate to the organizational imperatives of the institutions which employed him, rather than an independent creator. The only possibility for a new dramatic art was to turn to the new "collective agents of history" as new *dramatis personae* for a new theater.

Brecht's response to Sternberg was published in June 1927. Entitled "Shouldn't We Abolish Aesthetics?" it is a decisive theoretical statement of Brecht's new theatrical stance. Addressing himself to Sternberg, Brecht wrote: "When I invited you to look at the drama from a sociological point of view, I did so because I was hoping that sociology would be the death of existing drama."[23] For Brecht sociology was the only science appropriate to the new epoch. It alone knew how to explode the mystique of the "eternal" appeal of drama. The only appeal that was eternal, Brecht commented, was to see dramas; everything else − content, form, staging, etc. − changed with the times. Only the sociologist knew how to evaluate the decline of the capitalist age. Only via sociology could art come to an assessment of its own morass. A sociologist based his judgment on the "vital interests" of society, not on aesthetic values. He judged in terms of true or false, not good or bad. There was no point in trying to improve aesthetically what was sociologically false. The sociologist alone, Brecht concluded,

> knows what is false; he is no relativist, he
> goes by interest of a vital sort; he takes no
> pleasure in being able to prove everything but
> only wishes to establish what is worth proving;
> he in no way accepts responsibility for every-
> ting, but only for one thing. The sociologist
> is our man.[24]

It is in this context that one may understand Brecht's contention that Karl Marx was the only true audience for his dramas.

Brecht declared his loyalties to Marxism in the summer of 1926 largely because of the intellectual insight it allowed him, not on the basis of any attachment to the Communist Party. In these years Brecht studiously avoided party affiliation, studying his Marxism with such non-party theoreticians as Fritz Sternberg and Karl Korsch. When he joined the *Gruppe 1925* in the wake of his "conversion experience" of the summer of 1926, he gravitated naturally to the position of Alfred Döblin. In the context of that organization, Brecht was like Döblin, a left-radical but still "bourgeois" writer who did not subordinate his artistic autonomy to propagandistic concerns and who did not belong to the KPD. In these years a particularly close bond emerged between Brecht and Döblin. To-gether they listened to the lectures of Korsch, whose Marxism took a decidedly anti-Comintern, anti-Soviet tone. Together they visited the Luxemburgist sociologist Fritz Sternberg to discuss the problem of art and politics. Writing to Döblin from Augsburg in 1928, Brecht reflected on those discussions:

> It would be wonderful if we could have those
> weekly discussions again this winter. I de-

rived a great deal from them. I always knew
that your kind of literature could give expression to the new world order, but now it also
becomes clear to me that it fills just that
niche that is being formed by the current
Marxist interpretation of art.[25]

That interpretation cannot have been the line advocated by the
BPRS. Brecht's Marxism was anchored in the now heretical "Praxis"
tradition of his mentor Korsch, and in the disputes in the *Gruppe
1925* Brecht felt greater sympathy for Döblin's positions than for
those of Becher.

At the same time, Brecht became attracted to the theatrical
radicalism of Erwin Piscator, and their relationship serves further
to clarify Brecht's complex position. In many senses a parallel
tension emerged between the two theatrical giants as had led to the
rupture between Döblin and Becher.

The two men came into personal contact in the context of
Piscator's production of *The Robbers*. Brecht had a longstanding
interest in the problem of restaging classic dramas, having himself
adapted Marlowe's *Edward II*. He despised the piety of traditionalist staging, which tended to wrap the classics in plaster and make
them useless. He wanted the public to be "able to extract the material value from these finished works," i.e., elements of plot, language,
or characterization, which could be salvaged almost like scrap parts.[26]
Piscator's *Robbers*-production avoided that plaster-coated reverence
for the classics, and Brecht approved. He was particularly taken
with Piscator's explanation that his intention had been to show the
public "that 150 years is no small thing."[27] Brecht took this to mean
Piscator intended to sabotage, to make unenjoyable, all non-contem-
porary drama, a project he applauded heartily.

In the fall of 1927, as a result of these impressions, Brecht and
his circle formally joined Piscator's theatrical collective. Piscator
appreciated his new ally and promised to stage Brecht's drama,
Joe Fleischhacker, under the title *Die Weizen*, as part of the new
season of his theater. But the relationship became strained over the
course of 1928. The primacy of the director offended Brecht, who
believed the real impulse for theatrical transformation had to come

from a new drama, his new drama. He disparaged in Piscator "a certain tendency...to misuse technology for a certain cheap symbolism."[28] But Brecht went beyond this to dispute the political merits of Piscator's theater. He wrote: "the requisitioning of the theater for the purposes of class struggle offers a danger to the real revolutionizing of the theater."[29] Proponents of class conflict "usurped artistic means" by employing new forms like jazz and film to revolutionize staging. "Revolutionary spirit via stage effects could not revolutionize theater," Brecht insisted. In another comment, he elaborated: "Nowadays one is inclined to consider the Piscator experiments at the renovation of theater as revolutionary. But it is this neither in relation to production [i.e., dramaturgy] nor in relation to politics but only in relation to theater [i.e., staging]."[30] Brecht went so far as to charge that Piscator's theater was "not the effort of politics to take control of the theater but of theater to take control of politics." The differences with regard to theatrical practice reflected a divergent view of the mediation between art and politics.

In 1928, Brecht engaged in a radio conversation with Fritz Sternberg and Piscator concerning his first play, *Drums in the Night*, which had turned out to be his most frequently produced play of the Twenties.[31] This dialogue spelled out the differences between Brecht and Piscator on the relation between *Tendenz* and *Parteilichkeit*. Earlier in the Twenties, in his "Conversation with George Grosz," Brecht noted that after the play had been performed in some fifty theaters, with the wrong sort of people liking it, the drama began to trouble him.[32] Those most offended by the drama, he noted, were the radical Marxist revolutionaries, who felt its cynicism directed against them. With his newfound Marxist loyalties, Brecht felt it necessary to clarify the play's meaning in context. In his "Conversation with Grosz" he noted: "My interest in the revolution, whose job it was to serve as background, was about as great as the interest felt in Vesuvius by a man who wants to boil a kettle on it. Moreover, my kettle seemed to me a very large affair compared with the volcano in question."[33] This was severe self-criticism, yet Brecht felt justified in believing that in the character Kragler ha had unwittlingly captured the essence of the November Revolution, the "catastrophic revolutionary who sabotaged the revolution." The Kraglers were considered revolutionaries, but in fact "they made the revolution because their own country, which some of them hadn't seen for four years, had changed." As Brecht put it most succinctly: "The problem for the Kraglers was how to become bourgeois."

When he came to discuss the play with Sternberg and Piscator it was with the intention of discerning how to stage it ten years later so that it served the didactic function of stimulating true revolutionary consciousness. It quickly emerged, however, that Brecht and Piscator had substantially different views of how the play could serve this function. Piscator initially insisted that Brecht's play did not depict the situation of 1918 as it really was. Brecht's Kragler seemed to have no idea of the importance of the revolution.

> But you had Liebknecht, Luxemburg...
> Everybody knew the proletarian slogans.
> Only a half-wit could avoid them. Can
> Kragler remain so ignorant and apart?
> Then he's an individual case, not a typical
> worker.[34]

Piscator demanded changes in the play. Kragler had to become a true proletarian hero, or he had to be shown as an enemy of the revolution. Otherwise the "tragedy" of the German Revolution would be obscured. Brecht loathed the word "tragic" and objected that his play had nothing to do with tragedy. Sternberg intervened to make an essential point. The play certainly required more background on the 1918 Revolution; it was essential to move from the individual to the collective, the sociological dimension, he noted, supporting Piscator. But, he went on, it was wrong to project KPD militancy back onto 1918. Of eight million returning veterans only two percent turned Spartacist, he pointed out. Piscator avoided the issue by arguing that to project backward was the essence of *Zeittheater*, "raising things in a present-day light." For Piscator, a play like *Drums in the Night* had to evoke the militant immediacy of 1928 Communism if it were to have a didactic-political function. But Brecht felt this would falsify the 1918 play. When Piscator

149

insisted that Brecht's own perspective had shifted from a poetic to a "scientific" understanding of the revolution, Brecht countered that Kragler nevertheless represented the reality of 1918 far more realistically than the exceptional revolutionaries of Liebknecht's stripe. Piscator demanded to know why such a play should even be produced if this were so, and Brecht replied: as a historical lesson to explain why 1918 was a failure.[35]

It was enough to make the play *historical*, to use distance, the shifted viewpoint from 1918 to 1928, as the didactic force of the presentation. Just because Kragler behaved in a fashion so alien to a true revolutionary considering him from a 1928 vantage, the play could be instructive. Not the tragedy of Kragler, but the objectivity of his behavior as historically conditioned — *that* was the key.

In this discussion the different temperaments and the different perspectives of the two artists come clearly to the fore..

Piscator launched his productions frontally at an immediate problem of society, marshalling all his technical devices to assault the audience and stir them to protest and revolt. Piscator's political theater was unabashedly propagandistic. Brecht, who felt his theater was equally revolutionary, had a far more subtle approach. He set out from the premise that classical drama was in fact an alien world and he sought to make it significant by virtue of its distance. Precisely this distance insured the grandeur of the work while stimulating change in the contemporary sensibility by alerting it to an alternative pattern of human action. By presenting characters, as in *Mann ist Mann*, so that their natures changed as their circumstances did, Brecht felt he introduced a social-critical potential into theater, that he challenged his audience to a critical appreciation not only of the play but of their condition. Brecht aimed, that is to say, far more at the intellect than at the will. He wished to appeal to the capacity of judgment in the audience while Piscator wished to stir their commitment to action. And this pronounced difference may be read back directly to their relation to Marxism and to politics. Piscator entered left-radical politics out of the fire of his own war and revolutionary experience. Brecht turned to Marxism to resolve an intellectual problem.

150

The main focus of Brecht's concern at the close of the Republic was the question of the role of the intellectual in relation to the institutions of culture on the one hand and to the proletariat on the other. The centerpiece of these considerations remained his conviction of the total obsolescence of individualism and idealism, and their attendant German mystiques of *Persönlichkeit, Innerlichkeit* and *Bildung.* In the last aspect he was not far from Döblin, but what made all the difference was their attitudes toward collectivism. As Döblin moved away from collectivism at the close of the Republic, Brecht became more emphatically collectivist. This emerged most clearly in his fragmentary essay on the idea of the masses.[36] Mass society, Brecht argued, could no longer be perceived exlusively from the vantage of the individual. To reach a unified totality, a unity, one could not try to divide the mass, but only to organize and unify it. Only the mass could be an authentic unity. Rather than the divisibility of the mass, it was the divisibility of the individual which had to be emphasized. Nor did the individual ever confront the mass as a totality. He dealt with and through groups within the mass. These groups mediated between him and the totality of mass society. Within the mass there were multiple collectivities: mankind was "an apparatus which is only partially organized." As these collectivies consolidated, the individual personality was shattered. He retained his "uniqueness" only in his divisibility, his membership in several collectivities.

The heart of Brecht's "sociological dramturgy" had been to replace the individual perspective with a collective one, to assay behavior not from within the individual — i.e., in terms of motives and personal psychology — but rather from without, in terms of the institutions and historical conditions in which that behavior was enmeshed. In Marxist terms Brecht reoriented his entire thought to the principle that "social existence determines consciousness." If there is about Brecht a measure of "crude thinking," it resides precisely in his willingness to follow this idea regorously to its ultimate conclusions. This "behavioristic" Marxism was offensively reductionist to the more humanistic Marxists, to say nothing of traditional humanists, yet it remained quite different from orthodox Dialectical Materialism in tone, for Brecht's emphasis on institutional structures of culture aimed all the more emphatically at their openness to human transformation. Hence by referring intellectual and cultural affairs constantly to practice, to the institutions of intellectual life and their accommodation and subordination to industrial capitalist principles, Brecht's thrust was consistently toward change.

As he developed this orientation to the institutional transformation of culture and more collectivist-activist Communism, Brecht moved away from his old political-intellectual associates, Döblin and Sternberg, and even from his more rigorous mentor, Karl Korsch.

In "Of My Teacher," Brecht made a pointed critique of the cultivation of autonomy on the part of Korsch. "It would appear that he has made himself free from all kinds of unpleasant tasks. Oftentimes it seems to me that he would be able to do more for the cause of freedom if he were not so insistent upon his own freedom."[37] With those lines Brecht raised the issue of the intellectual's obligation to the proletariat. His attitude remained independent, but he began to assert the necessity for a full commitment. What this meant to him emerges from a series of political fragments from around 1929. In one such fragment Brecht wrote "a review of the motives which might turn a young intellectual into a revolutionary is an activity which produces extreme pessimism." It was not enough to feel moral outrage, Brecht insisted. "A generally held disapproval of a few human qualities does not produce a revolutionary." That had been the problem with Expressionist utopianism. "The sight of thirty-year-olds today, who ten years ago inspired such hopes, is truly depressing...what began as an emotion ended as a hangover."[38] Brecht felt nothing but contempt for this "idealistic-pathetic" sympathy for the proletariat. It had proven useless in 1918-1919 and it would be of no use for the Marxist revolution. Neither the ideological purism of his teacher Korsch nor the sentimental sympathy of an Ernst Toller seemed practical avenues for Brecht. The struggles against a capitalism brutal enough to use crass violence and subtle enough to work within the collective structures of automated production could only be violent conflict which would offend the gentle sensibilities of "idealists." Intellectuals had to commit themselves to the proletariat and to revolution.

Brecht saw two difficulties to be overcome in this commitment. The first was accommodating the party bureaucrats. "The current leadership of the party is hard for the intellectual to comprehend, for it is an intellectually inferior but powerful and cunning little bureaucracy, which has no grand vision but which keeps the masses together effectively."[39] Since the bureaucracy performed this task so well Brecht dismissed cavils over its intellectual mediocrity. He conceded that the bureaucracy might not be able to lead a revolution. Indeed, he went further and argued that in a revolution its interests would no longer be the same as those of the proletariat. In this lay the key opportunity for the intellectuals: to attack the bureaucracy only at those points where its interests did not correspond with the needs of the proletariat. Hostile intellectuals tended to do just the opposite, however, embarrassing themselves with elitism and compromising the proletarian cause.

There was a second aspect of tension between "humanist" intellectuals and the party: their failure to realize that the conservatives were right to consider socialism a continuation and even intensification of tendencies in capitalism. The American industrialists built capitalist enterprises whose technical structures and collective organization belonged to the coming world of socialism. A revolutionary had to accept industrial society; he could not be hostile to mechanization and the material world. Otherwise he was envisioning a reactionary "pensioner's utopia." With these remarks Brecht reasserted the cardinal thesis of Döblin's "Spirit of the Naturalistic Epoch," the juxtaposition of capitalism and socialism as urban-industrial orders over against a traditionalist, "idealist" humanism. Brecht embraced the scientific-technical epoch without reservation. The evil of capitalism would be set right, but the antiquarian aspirations of the intellectuals would never be realized.

Out of his considerations of this problem, Brecht developed a capsule sociology of the intellectuals. His major contention was that the intellectuals were a separate social group and that "the frequent claim that it is necessary to immerse oneself in the proletariat is counterrevolutionary."[40] Intellectuals always sought to assimilate into the ruling class, Brecht observed, and with the rise of working-class socialism, "they frequently attempt to merge with the proletariat." Brecht felt that proved "there are not different kinds of intellectuals, two types as it were, proletarian ones and others who are bourgeois, but that there is only one type." In this stance Brecht differed both from orthodox Communists and from the position of Döblin.

The intellectual was a separate species from the proletariat, and hence it was quite appropriate for the proletariat to distrust him. Two issues remained: what were the uses of the intellectual for the proletariat and how could the intellectual be mobilized for the revolutionary cause? In "What does the Proletariat Need Intellectuals For?" Brecht described three functions: first, to "drive holes through bourgeois ideology;" second, to "study the forces which 'move the world;'" and third, to "develop pure theory further."[41] In general, Brecht noted in "The Difficult Situation of German Intellectuals," the main function which the proletariat delegated to the intellectuals was leadership. In all of these contexts, the intellectual served the proletariat *by being an intellectual*, i.e., by virtue of "a dynamic, politically speaking a liquidating intellect."[42]

To make use of the intellectuals, the proletariat had to appeal not to their sympathies but to their interests. Brecht believed intellectuals would serve the revolutionary cause because "only through the revolution can intellectuals hope to bring to fruition their intellectual activity." The basis for solidarity was the idea of *freedom*. In "On Freedom" Brecht elaborated:

> The majority of mental workers (intellectuals)
> who are for the revolution expect from it pri-
> marily *freedom*. They feel oppressed by the lack
> of freedom which is the impact of the capitalist
> system. They can be won over most swiftly if one
> demostrates to them that the ruling political con-
> ditions mean frightful restraints on the develop-
> ment of science, of all human investigation and
> useful practice.[43]

154

Of course, this demand for intellectual freedom, for personal freedom, was naive. This was proven, Brecht held, by the German Revolution of 1918. It had set up a whole range of such freedoms but without changing the political and economic structure. Thus the freedoms were exceedingly ephemeral. To secure freedom there had to be concrete liberation, he argued. The basic oppression was economic. Liberation had to come at the level of economy, "because political and all other freedom depends on economy." Hence intellectual freedom could only come with general liberation, with social revolution, and this meant the revolution took precedence over individual freedom, over intellectual scruple, over all the residuals of "humanism."

Brecht demostrated what this meant in a new and extremely controversial *Lehrstück, The Measures Taken*, written in the spring of 1930 with the Communist composer Hanns Eisler. It was Brecht's most unconpromising statement of his Communist convictions and it left many on the left — indeed, even some in the KPD — aghast. The story of *The Measures Taken* is simple.[44] Communist agents are sent out from Moscow to propagate the revolution in China. At the border they are joined by a young comrade who pledges to help with the mission. But he gets carried away again and again by his feelings of pity, moral outrage, and rebellion, and ends up endangering the mission so seriously that his colleagues are forced to kill him. The drama is presented as the report of the four returning agents to the control committee in Moscow and their justification of the action.

The construction of the play is spare to the point of severity. A chorus and four actors form the entire cast. The chorus remains almost constantly in character as the control committee in Moscow, but the four agents portray the events they report, becoming first one character then another in the course of the performance, while always remaining in the original persona. This layering of roles creates a critical distance in the portrayal — a decisive element in Brecht's idea of epic theater. At the same time it renders the four original figures anonymous as individuals and heightens their collective and functional roles. In addition to this structural severity and the use of the chorus as a vehicle for segmenting and discussing the action, there is a parallel severity in the language. The simplicity and the directness of this linguistic tone accentuates the didactic thrust of the work, but also lends it a stark grandeur, which comes to the fore especially in the choral songs.

The first chorus was entitled "Praise of the USSR."[45] It was Brecht's most emphatic statement of affirmation of the Soviet Union as the hope of oppressed mankind. The entire play concentrated upon the militancy of Communism, and upon the importance of creating revolutionary consciousness, with the Bolshevik Revolution the manifest model. Interestingly, at the outset of the play the young comrade welcomes the four agents to the border district in the expectation that they will have brought all kinds of material or organizational support for the realization of socialism in the border area. Instead, they inform him that their mission is to spread across the border the "doctrines of the classics and of the propagandists: the ABCs of Communism; to bring to the ignorant instruction regarding their condition, to the oppressed, class consciousness, and to the class-conscious the experience of the revolution."[46]

This stress on propagating the "ABCs of Communism" and on fomenting revolution in China is utterly out of harmony with the doctrine of "building socialism in one country" to which the Soviet Union under Stalin was dedicated.[47] It is unlikely in the extreme that this was unknown to Brecht. He had constant conversations with Karl Korsch on the subject of the Soviet Union, and Korsch's caustic criticisms of the Bolshevik regime and of Stalinism were well known to him.[48] Yet Brecht insisted upon giving the Soviet Union a more sympathetic interpretation than Korsch, and *The Measures Taken* can be construed as an attempt to rescue what was important about the Russian socialist enterprise both from the negative criticism of Korsch and the negative practice of Stalin. For Brecht, the essence of Communist practice was ideological instruction. Propagating the truths of Marxism was the paramount consideration, and it was for the sake of this propagation, not as a measure to consolidate party control, that the young volunteer's life was taken. A reading which sees the play as a prior justification of Stalin's purge trials simplifies and thereby distorts the real intellectual and ethical problems of the play.[49]

156

Brecht's drama explored the agonizing issue of means and ends, the same dilemma of intellectual purism and political engagement which had wracked the German avant-garde in the revolutionary moment of 1918-1919. Like Herzog then, Brecht came to the hard judgment that scruples must be put at risk, innocence lost, if, in the context of a reality shot through with violence and betrayal, a humane order was to be won. Brecht charged that many of those who stressed intellectual purity were in fact evading responsibility. This was the thrust of his criticism of Korsch. But Brecht was willing to press the argument that the end might justify the means to a point where it taxed all the tactical resiliency of a committed intellectual, and seemed to offer a ruthlessness indistinguishable from tyranny or terrorism:

> Whoever struggles for Communism must be able to
> struggle and not struggle, to tell the truth and
> not tell the truth, to provide service and not
> provide service, to keep promises and not keep
> promises, to put oneself in danger and avoid danger,
> to be recognizable or not recognizable. Whoever
> struggles for Communism has only one virtue of all
> virtues: that he struggles for Communism. [50]

Putting on this "disfiguring tyrannical mask of Marxism" (Döblin's phrase) Brecht was testing the limits of his own sensibility as much as those of his contemporaries. Hence the brutal challenge which was the heart of the drama:

> What baseness would you not endure, so that
> Baseness may be eliminated?
> If you could finally change the world, what
> Would you be too fine to do?
> Who are you?
> Sink into filth
> Embrace the butcher, but
> Change the world: it needs it! [51]

This was the terrible lesson Brecht offered the intellectuals: that dark times leave them no option but to act, casting all scruple aside. "Only

157

with force is this murderous/ World to be changed, as/ Every living person knows./ It has not yet been granted us,/ We said to ourselves, to avoid killing..."[52]

There can be no palliation of this argument. It stands in gory clarity as an ultimate challenge. It asks for a total submission to the requirements of political efficacy. Hence, Brecht was perfectly consistent to include a chorus in praise of the party: "The individual can be annihilated/ But the party cannot be annihilated/ For it is the vanguard of the masses..."[53] But just by this radical formulation, Brecht's work signified the inconsistency of his stance with its rhetoric, for Brecht never subordinated himself completely to the party. And this provides us with the perspective to grasp the complex relation between work and author. Brecht was probing his mind and conscience for the limits to which he might have to push his personal sensibility if he put on the armor and the shield of Marxism. The play was a thought-experiment, chilling in its lucidity, but consistent with the harsh either/or mentality, the penchant to push things to the extreme, which Brecht adopted at the close of the Republic to ward off the debilitating melancholia into which so many of his former allies were sinking. Within the armor of this purposive ruthlessness, Brecht could act and create while others were reduced to hopeless paralysis. In steeling himself against all pity and emotion, Brecht armed himself for the brutality which swept up Germany and the world in the era of Hitler and Stalin.

The Measures Taken can be read as an almost point by point rejection of Döblin's *Wissen und Verändern!*, though it was composed before Döblin's letters to Hocke appeared. In the young comrade Brecht located all the idealistic and humanitarian sentiments of "socialism" as Döblin defined it, and systematically demonstrated their lack of efficacy in the tactical struggle for human liberation. Döblin could not possibly have accepted such a view. With *The Measures Taken*, in fact, Brecht clearly parted company with the left-radical humanists and Negativists. *Die Weltbühne* attacked his postures as brutal and dangerous.[54]

But Brecht was not accepted into the ranks of the orthodox either. *The Measures Taken* proved acutely embarassing to the Communists. Kurella attacked Brecht for failing to understand true

158

Communism.[55] He contended that the young comrade was the true Communist and the four agent false. Brecht was only a philosophical, not a materialistic Marxist; his perspective was so formal that it distorted rather than represented. Kurella termed Brecht a petit-bourgeois revolutionary. He felt he had mastered Communist doctrine, but his theme — the primacy of reason over feeling — remained purely intellectual, and he had no concrete sense for the circumstances and practices of class conflict which were of the essence in true Communism. Even later Communist critics have found it more comfortable to side with Kurella than admit Brecht's orthodoxy.[56]

To be sure, Kurella and Biha tempered their criticism of *The Measures Taken* by greeting Brecht's willingness to become a Communist.[57] But at the height of this controversy there appeared in Berlin a Communist intellectual who would see to it that for the next decade and more Brecht would not be comfortable among the orthodox: Georg Lukacs. Helga Gallas has demonstrated that with Lukacs's appearance in the editorial circles of *Die Linkskurve*, Brecht's experimental modernism "for the sake of socialism" became the main target of the journal and above all of Lukacs's own essays.[58] That conflict would persist for years and split the intellectual world of Communism profoundly regarding modernism in art.

Brecht did not let up in his campaign of scandalous behavior after *The Measures Taken*. His next exploit involved his most popular dramatic work, *The Three Penny Opera*. Brecht contracted in the fall of 1930 to produce a *Three Penny Film*. In accordance with his new militancy he resolved to accentuate the didactic and tone down the "culinary" of the original. Brecht portrayed Macheath in the film version as rising to the position of a respectable banker, thus making the parodistic implication of the original drama into a flat demonstration of the continuity of crime and capitalism in the film.[59] Naturally enough, the film company was not happy with this transformation, and it decided to have Leo Lania compose a film-script based on the theater version without the collaboration of Brecht. Brecht filed suit against the film company for a million marks on the grounds of breach of contract, claiming that he had the right to review and change the final version of the film. That final version — script by Lania, directed by G.B. Pabst — was entirely unacceptable, he contended. The resulting trial attracted a great deal of press coverage. It was seen as a conflict between artistic freedom and the capitalist film industry. Brecht lost the first trial. Instead of appealing, he settled with the film company for the substantial sum it was willing to pay to avoid the appeal and the unfavorable publicity. After all this transpired, Brecht presented an account of the whole episode in an essay in his *Versuche*, 1931, entitled *The Three Penny Trial*. It became the culminating statement by Brecht on the issues of the Twenties.

The purpose of his suit, Brecht claimed in the essay, was to "experiment" with the bourgeois notion of justice.[60] He had never had the expectation of winning; he only wanted to test some hypotheses in a "sociological experiment." Those hypotheses centered on the idea that there was an unresolved contradiction between the ideology and the practice of bourgeois institutions. Hence Brecht proposed to compare the ideology of justice and "autonomy of art" to the practice. In his view the only real measure of culture was the manner in which its institutions actually functioned. Hence he would take the bourgeois ideology at its word and demand justice, demand the protection of his artistic autonomy and his individual rights over against the interests of a major capitalist concern. And for this reason he set his damage claim so high — to see how much monetary value was attached to these ideals.

Brecht revelled in the contradictions and absurdities this "experiment" unleashed. He found himself praised in liberal-humanist newspapers for his moral idealism in pressing his suit on behalf of artistic freedom and the sanctity of the artistic personality. He laughed all the harder when these same newspapers became outraged over his acceptance of a settlement after the first trial, when they were prepared to finance his appeal themselves. Principle and morality were not the issue for Brecht, nor was he squeamish about making money. He wanted to see the gears of capitalist culture grind. He quoted the various "issues" which the press and the court drew from his case. Many newspapers proclaimed with high pathos "the primacy of literature... must be preserved without compromise." The issue was formulated in terms of a debasement of art into a mere money-making commodity through film. Another set of issues arose

160

– namely those regarding the film as an art form. Some contended that film necessarily reduced artistic-intellectual quality because of the audience to which it was addressed. A number of newspaper commentators went so far as to suggest that a true artist have no dealings whatever with the corrupting realm of film.

On the other side, the defenders of the film company argued that Brecht sold the film rights and that the monetary compensation represented full quittance, so that he had no further say regarding the artistic quality of the resulting film. That argument was inappropriate since the film company had given him such rights in the contract itself. But the court essentially upheld a variant of this thesis, accepting the most important argument made by the film company: that it had invested 800,000 Marks in the film and could not simply throw that money away because Brecht did not like the finished product. The issue was simply a matter of economic rationality, the argument provided, for a film production by virtue of its enormous technical and capital investment was a different sort of enterprise from theater or publishing and could not be governed by the same laws of copyright and intellectual property. Above all, given the requirements for a mass distribution to cover the costs of investment, the particular political or ideological views of the author could not be respected in the way they could be in theater or publishing. In any event, this argument ran, the whole idea of artistic personality was megalomaniacal and obsolete. Cynically, it was added that after all Brecht had never shown himself particularly committed to intellectual property rights, since the *Three Penny Opera* itself was full of plagiarisms, and Brecht had openly declared intellectual property an antiquated matter he no longer took seriously.

As for Brecht, his view of the matter was simple. Obviously in a capitalist society the practical interest of production and the protection of an 800,000 Mark investment would outweigh the claims to abstract justice and to artistic freedom or integrity. And if they did not, this "would only have proven that our laws are completely obsolete."[61] Brecht wished to demonstrate exactly this – that capitalism had gone so far in the domain of culture that to judge it by ideal values was to fly in the face of reality. Hence he set about systematically refuting all the idealistic balderdash raised in support of his claim or in support of his artistic freedom. With that it emerged that justice was not the issue which most concerned Brecht. He wanted to establish what in reality constituted the culture of an advanced capitalist society like Weimar Germany.

Capitalism was consistent in its practice, because it had to be. But as a result it was forced into inconsistency in ideology.[62] The instrumental rationality of capitalism was progressive exactly in its destruction of bourgeois ideology. This dissension between ideology and practice was the essential point of Brecht's entire "sociological experiment." He affirmed the instrumental rationality of capitalism in the court's verdict, protecting the production and investment of the film company over against antiquated ideas.

> The transformation of intellectual
> values into commodities (works of
> art, contracts, trials are commodities) is
> a progressive process and one can only agree
> with it — provided, of course, that this
> progress is conceived as continuing progress
> and not progress completed, that therefore
> the phase of the commodity too is considered
> as something to be transcended by further
> progress.[63]

But that was not to affirm capitalism itself. "Reality will come to a point at which the only hindrance for the progress of capitalism is capitalism itself," he concluded.[64]

The argument Brecht advanced here had appeared earlier in his writings. Capitalism meant progress on the line toward socialism precisely in the technical transformation and the collectivization of human life, precisely in the debunking of traditional culture. The power of the technological mystique, he noted, disturbed intellectuals. They were filled with a "mixture of contempt and awe" by its mighty intervention in the spiritual realm, yet they were powerless to resist it. Brecht himself affirmed without hesitation this demystification of the world of art:

> We witness the irresistible and hence the accep-
> table decay of the individualistic work of art.

162

It can no longer reach the market place as a unity;
the condition of tension of its contradictory
unity must be destroyed. Art is a form of human
commerce and is therefore dependent on the factors
which in general determine human commerce.[65]

This meant that the "work of art" of the old ideal was transformed into a commodity along the lines of general capitalist organization, and the intellectuals had to come to terms with the consequences: "If the concept 'work of art' is no longer tenable for that which emerges when a work of art is transformed into a commodity, then we must surrender this concept cautiously and carefully but without dread..."[66] For there was no evading the process, and it was essential to salvage the progressive aspect of this transformation.

If the new media decisively transformed the situation of culture, it became a matter of great importance to know how the artistic producers stood in relation to the media. "The socialization of these means of production is a life and death issue for art," Brecht wrote.[67] The artists had to have access to the new media if they were to perform their creative function. Those who argued that art had no need of film did not comprehend this crucial fact. "To tell the intellectual worker he is free to renounce the new media of production is to suggest to him a freedom outside the process of production."

The emergence of film had changed the whole structure of intellectual-artistic productions. Capitalism worked in a "revolutionary manner" in film: "It annihilates vast stretches of ideology in its concentration on 'external' behavior, in dissolving everything into processes, in surrendering the hero as the medium, or man as the measure of all things, in destroying the introspective psychology of the bourgeois novel."[68] Not just film-makers but novelists had to face the challenge. "The transformation by the times leaves nothing untouched, but always grasps the totality."[69] It was simply not the case that some forms of art remained as before while others underwent the technical transformation. "The old forms of mediation are not left unchanged by the newly emergent forms and do not remain on an equal footing with them. The person who sees the film reads a story differently."[70] Moreover the author himself was transformed by viewing a film. "One cannot reverse the technical transformation of literary production," Brecht insisted, and this meant that the literary author had to grasp and integrate the technical and what the technical made accessible, and above all the manner of technical transformation itself, in his literary creation.

> Film provides (or could provide) applicable infor-
> mation regarding human behavior in detail. Its
> magnificent inductive method — [the method] which
> it at the very least makes possible — can be of
> incalculable importance for the novel, in so far
> as the novel itself can still mean anything.[71]

The author of a technical age had to handle things as though "with instruments," i.e., from outside. This meant that the old bourgeois ideals of "Art," of the novel as "inwardness," were obsolete. Instead of personal constructions, worldviews drawn from the interior, the art of a technical epoch had to learn from the detail of reality. One could not simply come to new media with a ready-made notion of "Art" which the media had to embody. Those who tried to make conventional "Art" with the new medium of film ended up simply making "fodder." As against this, the new media offered the prospect for a new comprehension of reality not only in their content but in their instrumental operation itself. "These apparatuses can serve like nothing else in overcoming the old untechnical, anti-technical, religiously rooted, 'auratic' idea of 'art'."

The triumph of instrumental rationality — its decisive, irreversible erosion of the residual of transcendent values like "Art," "justice," "individuality," etc. — created a crisis for the intellectual both in relation to the instruments of production and in relation to his audience. It became manifestly absurd to complain on aesthetic grounds regarding political freedom of expression. This was a clear reversal of causal flow, for politics, not aesthetics, assumed primacy. Intellectuals, Brecht concluded, *"must demand political art not for artistic but for political reasons"* (italics in original).[72] Brecht insisted upon "the transformation of art into a pedagogical discipline," and the employment of all available media to this end. For him, art meant comprehension of reality: "in order to grasp reality with the new apparatus, one has to be an artist, or at the very least someone who enjoys reality, but absolutely not an aesthetic dilettant..."[73] But this constructive art had nothing to do with the old, sacrosanct ideal of "Art." The effect of the new technical world was to debunk the old pieties of humanist culture.

So-called "progressive" intellectuals cherished "the conviction that the masses do not know their own interests as well as the intellectuals know them." They were obsessed with using art to "improve public taste." Brecht made the outrageously provocative suggestion that "the tastelessness of the masses is more deeply rooted in reality than the taste of the intellectuals." He asserted "the masses have less aesthetic and more political interests and at no time has Schiller's suggestion to make political education a matter of aesthetics been so manifestly pointless as today." Artists had to recognize that the repudiation of their "progressive" offerings had less to do with bad taste than with political realities. "We approach the epoch of mass politics," Brecht wrote, yet the intellectuals persisted in viewing it from the perspective of the individual. They could do no more than project their own individual psychology onto the masses, and that was manifestly fallacious.

> The masses of our epoch, directed by common
> interests, constantly transforming themselves
> according to these but always functioning as
> a unity, follow quite definite laws of thought
> which are not generalizations of individual
> thought. These laws have only been inadequately
> researched.[74]

It was a primary task of intellectuals, therefore, to comprehend the laws of mass behavior.

That in turn led to a recognition of the reactionary significance of the old ideals of humanism, taste and art in buttressing the class consciousness above all of the petit bourgeois. Artists had to break free from these notions to develop an effective posture of political didacticism aimed at organizing and mobilizing the masses. The purpose of art was not to distract the masses but to activate them, and this meant that a mechanistic interpretation of class struggle had to be replaced by an activistic approach. Brecht pointed to three

165

strategies aimed to achieve this: first, the economic organization of the Soviet Union, where, as he saw it, "work really determines morality;" second, the great American comedies, presumably of Chaplin; and finally, behaviorism. "Behaviorism is a psychology which follows out the requirements of commodity production, seeking to master methods of influencing consumers: hence an active psychology, progressive and revolutionary par excellence."[75]

Brecht remained the sanguine, hard-headed intellectual he had been when he set out from his metaphorical Black Forest to his new home in the asphalt city a decade before. Confronted with technocracy, concretely in the cooptation of Weimar theater and generally in the capitalist stage of rationalization, Brecht retained his affirmative attitude towards technological progress and the age of science and technology. Brecht was a freelance writer by choice, an artist whose entire intellectual experience and career opportunity were grounded in the modern development of capitalist and technical institutions of intellectual life. Howevermuch he was critical and even subversive of these institutions, he had no doubt that they were both more up-to-date and more in accordance with any ultimate socialist order than the anti-technological and traditionalist mandarinism which hankered after a "pensioners' utopia." Hardened by his experience in the market, Brecht exuded self-confidence and enjoyed the paradoxical success of his nonconformity. Not for him any mandarin lament, left or right in ideological inspiration, which equated the scientific-technological epoch definitively with reification. The distinction between technology and technocracy remained central to his thought and to his practice. Capitalism was only a stage in the development of the scientific and technological epoch, and some day that epoch would find capitalism itself the obstacle to its full realization. That day would mark the socialist revolution's dawn, and Brecht had no doubt it would be a violent revolution, an active struggle, not an internal collapse.

In the interval, Brecht resolved, with typically brash and straightforward self-confidence, to turn the tables on technocracy, to steal back the media in a reverse cooptation, an *Umfunktionierung* which would make the media useless for the manipulative intentions of the technocrats and more serviceable for a future socialist order.[76] It

166

was his serene conviction that his epic theater would serve this function of "constructive sabotage" even as the kind of thinking it would provoke in its audiences would illuminate the potential for human change and therewith the prospect for social imrpovement.

Just as Brecht refused to abandon his conviction of technological rationality, he refused to abandon his commitment to the democratization of culture. To be sure, he found it necessary to abandon his youthful and exuberant confidence in the "sporting public," yet the premise of his entire literary practice was that there was a "special character of relaxed interest in the audience," a cultural responsiveness which tallied with a potential for political rationality.[77] This faith in the progressive potential of the modern masses was part of Brecht's insistently populist-democratic notion of Marxism. Brecht could be assimilated neither to the Leninist view of a docile mass in need of domination by a vanguard party nor to the Frankfurt School view of the masses as so infused with "authoritarian" dependency structures that they were worthless for the purposes of human liberation.

Brecht, by 1930, had mellowed into a rationalist, a progressive scion of the Enlightenment. He believed in social progress: i.e., in its probability, not its necessity. He believed, with due skepticism, in real intellectual influence, confident that *"eingreifendes Denken"* was both possible and mandatory for a progressive intellectual. As for the grand scruples of the philosophical and humanist tradition, Brecht maintained far more effectively than Döblin that posture of modernist, casual indifference represented in "The Spirit of the Naturalist Epoch," that touchstone of Berlin Negativism. Brecht was an intellectual at home in his time. He showed no signs in 1930 of any metaphysical pathos. He was perfectly comfortable with a secular, hedonistic materialism, confident that, after all, the important things were not all that esoteric and a little straightforward thought — *"plumpes Denken"* — would get to the heart of things.

This is not to suggest that Brecht was insensitive to the dilemmas of the age which ground up such intimates as Alfred Döblin. However, like the agents in his harrowing drama, *The Measures Taken*, he proposed to face reality unflinchingly and do what was necessary to change the world. Howevermuch he might regret the moral costs,

167

they were not to sway him from his relentless execution. Only to posterity, to a time spared such savage choices, did he feel compelled to reveal how much the poise of the Thirties cost his own sensibility:

Remember
When you speak of our failings
The dark time too
Which you have escaped.
For we went, changing countries oftener
than our shoes,
Through the wars of the classes, despairing
When there was injustice only, and no rebellion.

And yet we know:
Hatred, even of meanness
Contorts the features.
Anger, even against injustice
Makes the voice hoarse. Oh, we
Who wanted to prepare the ground for
friendliness
Could not ourselves be friendly. [78]

Epilogue

THE NEW NEGATIVISTS AND BRECHT:
THE CASE OF BENJAMIN

> Pessimism all along the line. That's
> right, entirely. Mistrust of the
> efficacy of literature, mistrust of
> the efficacy of freedom, mistrust
> of the efficacy of European mankind,
> above all mistrust, mistrust, mistrust
> of all reconciliation — between classes,
> between peoples, between individuals.
> — W. Benjamin, "Surrealism: The
> Last Snapshot of the European
> Intelligentsia," (1929)

While Bertolt Brecht was clearly associated with the generation around Alfred Döblin, he evaded that generation's utter desolation at the collapse of the Republic. His very survival strategy made him unacceptable not only to them, but to the two emergent schools of leftist intellectualism of the Thirties and beyond. He was disparaged by the orthodox Communists under the leadership of Lukacs and he was disdained by the heterodox Frankfurt School "Marxists" led by Adorno. His position was, in short, anomalous.

At best one can identify Brecht with a new mutation of "Bolshevism," that is, a willfully metaphorical identification with, rather than a literal allegiance to Marxism-Leninism. Just as German "Bolshevism" had from the outset of the Weimar period been an image cultivated with benign indifference to the Russian realities, so too Brecht's "Communism" of 1930 was unique for its intellectual and artistic independence even while it professed to be strenuously orthodox. Brecht acted as though he were in line with the Communist Party, yet he never entered it or accepted its organizational directives. He expressed his identification with the proletarian cause, yet he labored under no illusions about his status as a "writer of the grand bourgeoisie" (*großbürgerlicher Schriftsteller*).[1] He was willing to extend to Soviet Marxism and even the Stalinist establishment a more generous recognition than they warranted or were willing to reciprocate, yet he was quite aware of this, and he scrupulously avoided putting himself at their mercy.

If Brecht's posture was anomalous, it remains by that very fact illuminating for the orthodoxies it flaunted. Brecht was a thorn in the side of party-line Communists, as the long and bitter conflict with Georg Lukacs attested. That conflict has been amply documented.[2] Of greater relevance to the current study is Brecht's conflict with the new negativists, for it suggests the transitions which negativism underwent in departing the specific circumstances of the Berlin Twenties to become a structuring perspective of general 20th-century culture. In this context, the key to the issues between Brecht and the circle around Adorno is the mercurial critic Walter Benjamin, who became Brecht's most important intellectual ally of the years 1929-1934.[3]

As has been noted, Walter Benjamin was a major intellectual source and even in some measure cultural idol of the new negativists, especially Theodor Adorno.[4] When Benjamin became associated with Brecht in 1929, consequently, it provoked great consternation in these circles. Many of Benjamin's intimate friends of the period before 1929, figures as different in orientation as Gershom Sholem and Adorno, felt Benjamin was deflected from his true course by the association with Brecht.[5] If, indeed, Benjamin changed course more than Brecht during the period of their association, it would be wise to consider whether that turn might have had other reasons than the supposed influence of Brecht. To put this another way: did Benjamin's theoretical and critical work bring him to his new turn? To grasp this, one must have a sense for what Benjamin pursued prior to his association with Brecht and how he changed thereafter.

It is neither possible nor appropriate to attempt a full rendering of Walter Benjamin's thought in his study. All that can and will be attempted is a sketch of certain key notions. For this sketch, the interpretations of Jürgen Habermas and Bernd Witte have been especially important.[6] In the briefest compass, Walter Benjamin was a Jewish mystic for whom the possibility of orthodox religiosity had dried up, and an esoteric scholar for whom the possibility of an academic appointment had similarly dried up. As a result, he felt himself outcast, a free-lance journalist in an urban-industrial exile. Professionally, Benjamin was never as adjusted to the free-lance context as Brecht. But the contrast went much deeper. Benjamin's sensibility was thoroughly incongruous with that of Brecht. Far from the hedonistic, matter-of-fact and even crude secularism of Brecht, Benjamin was full of metaphysical pathos. His sensibility was far closer to that of another haunted Jew, Franz Kafka, whose work he once described as "an ellipse with two foci that are far apart and are determined, on the one hand, by mystical experience (in particular, the experience of tradition) and, on the other, by the experience of the modern big-city dweller."[7] As Martin Jay has observed, that description could be applied to Benjamin himself without amendment.[8]

Benjamin's mystical experience of tradition constitutes the point of departure for understanding his esotericist complexity. For Benjamin, history was always at risk of perishing into nothingness, of becoming mute fate, bleak fixity, inert myth.[9] When Kracauer argued against Döblin that intellectual criticism should rescue reason from the ossifying embrace of myth and nature, he drew upon Benjamin's sense of history. Benjamin saw culture as the effort to preserve the past through reappropriation of those few moments when experience was liberated from the fixity of fate and endowed with a meaning. These rare epiphanies, preserved in the amber of works of art, constituted what Benjamin meant by tradition. Shielded within the symbolic autonomy of the work of art, the meaning and presence of the original epiphany could be preserved and eventually retrieved by posterity. But art works could only yield up their meaning if their "aura", the aesthetic distance in which they were encased, were penetrated and their burden of experience reappropriated.

This was the function of criticism. Benjamin advocated a style of "allegorical" criticism which anticipated in many ways the "strong misreading" or deconstructive criticism of the latest generation of literary negativists.[10] His allegorical and metaphorical method of criticism — so esoteric, mystical and mysterious that it was repudiated by the German university mandarins as incomprehensible — sought

171

to use the work of art as a means of springing truth free not only from its artifice but from the constricting world of the given phenomena.[11] In his own words, Benjamin asserted "criticism is the mortification of the works."[12] Jürgen Habermas adds a very important gloss to this powerful phrase. "Critique of art...aims, it is true, at the 'mortification of the works,' but critique commits such destruction only in order to transpose what is worth knowing from the medium of the beautiful into that of the truth — and thereby to *rescue* and *redeem* it."[13] For the modern critic, the assumption is that art is not itself adequate communication. Ever since Hegel, art has been considered inherently obscure and mythical and therefore in need of discursive redemption. As a consequence, the critic has tended to become more important than the artist, and this was certainly a tendency in Benjamin's own self-conception as a critic.[14]

Benjamin recognized that this conception of criticism shattering the "aura" of a work of art, violating its symbolic autonomy to liberate its crystallized meaning, was part of a larger cultural development which Max Weber termed the "disenchantment of the world." This *Entzauberung* on the part of critics, Benjamin believed, could be redemptive as well as destructive, for if it shattered the intricate aesthetic seals which shielded the preserved meanings, it also retrieved them and restored them to a live context for the few who had the intellectual wherewithal to contemplate the work of art.

This esotericist and contemplative pursuit was at the heart of the European avant-garde experience, Benjamin believed. In particular, it was the acute self-sonsciousness and artistic mission of symbolist art in France. The great Symbolists struggled on behalf of a highly esoteric transcendence against the pervasive disenchantment of the world in industrial urban society.[15] The project of distilling and then preserving what Mallarmé called *l'azur* was passed on from Baudelaire, Rimbaud and Mallarmé through Apollinaire to the Surrealists.[16] In his dedication to an indecipherable transcendence, Benjamin felt a deep and abiding affinity for this French avant-garde, and he saw the crisis of this avant-garde sensibility as a reflection of his own. In his key essay of 1929, "Surrealism: The last Snapshot of the European Intelligentsia," Benjamin found the terms in which to couch his own dilemma.[17] Modern technical-industrial society was intervening both institutionally and technically to disrupt the redemptive dialectic of art and criticism. At the level of institutions, the obduracy of the bourgeoisie had finally shaken the avant-garde from "an extremely contemplative attitude into revolutionary opposition."[18] Yet Benjamin was quite conscious that this opposition was grounded not in a sense of duty to revolution but rather a sense of duty toward traditional culture. At the level of institutional organization, the literary intellectual was confronted with the challenge to reconcile his individualist, contemplative and idealist dialogue with tradition with the mounting pressures of politics. The avant-garde, Benjamin recognized, faced a crisis in the "humanistic notion of freedom." Instead of the traditional and, in his view, "ossified" idea of freedom, Benjamin determined that the avant-garde would have to turn to politics.

The force behind this new conviction resided in the second dimension of the disruption modern technological civilization introduced into the intellectual's relation with tradition. What traumatized Benjamin and drew him from his redemptive critical role to a sense of immediate activism was his realization that the intellectual penetration of aura via criticism had been eclipsed by a new and far vaster force for the "destruction of aura," namely technology itself. In his most famous and problematic essay, *The Work of Art in an Age of Mechanical Reproduction*, Benjamin argued that mechanical reproduction, substituting "a plurality of copies for a unique existence," brought about a "tremendous shattering of tradition."[19] Historical uniqueness, persistence through time and the fate undergone through that persistence, helped constitute that hermetic and potent aura of works of art. But with mechanical reproduction that quality of an original was being made obsolete. "We are in the midst of a vast process in which literary forms are being melted down, a process in which many of the contrasts in terms of which we have been accustomed to think may lose their relevance."[20] In contrast to redemptive criticism, mechanical reproduction threatened to destroy not only the mythic container but also the authentic experience encoded within, leaving the world utterly bereft of meaning.

The disenchantment of the world, the triumph of instrumental rationality through technology, was what brought Benjamin to a

173

reconsideration of his intellectual mission by the close of the Twenties. On the one hand, technology's destruction of aura endangered meaning and threatened mankind with nihilism of value and aridity in art. On the other hand, that same disenchantment opened art to mass access and promoted the democratization of culture. Benjamin's desperate endeavor at the close of the Twenties was to accentuate the liberating aspect of the rise of mechanical reproduction in art, to see it primarily as the elimination of the "cult value" of the work of art. Thereby it would cease to be an object of individual contemplation and enjoyment and become an opportunity for mass art, for collective reception.

Benjamin obviously knew of Kracauer's conception of "distraction" as the inevitably manipulative character of the new mass media.[21] He was aware, too, of the gathering belief in the inherently degenerate quality of "mass culture" generally.[22] Yet he chose to put a positive face on what was occurring. He held out the prospect that the turn from art as a cult object to art as a collective document could have progressive possibilities. In place of the old "ritual value" of auratic art, based upon the intimacies and authenticities of the artist, the new art would be based on a new "exhibition value" in which mass meanings would be primary.[23] This, in turn, would have deeper implications. "The instant the criterion of authenticity ceases to be applicable to artistic production, the total function of art is reversed. Instead of being based on ritual it begins to be based on another practice — politics."[24]

The concepts of the democratization of culture and the politicization of art to which Benjamin turned in his recognition of the intellectual crisis of *Entzauberung* led him to Marxism. He found the "dialectical" and "materialist" philosophy of Georg Lukacs's *History and Class Consciousness* somehow reconcilable with his own allegorical criticism.[25] But was is really? Benjamin needed to reconstitute his sense of intellectual mission and cultural prospect around the idea of the politicization of art. Marxism seemed to offer an approach to this issue by juxtaposing artistic and intellectual forms with the placement of their intellectual creators in the economic structure of production.[26] But could such a point of view be derived from Benjamin's own earlier theorizing? Jürgen Habermas argues forcefully that Benjamin's advocacy of the politicization of art was not a consequence of his previous thinking. "He may have had good reasons for seizing upon this concept — it did not, however, have a systematic connection to his own theory of art and history."[27] Habermas suggests that what led Benjamin to align himself with the new Marxist standpoint and hence with Brecht was not the logic of his theory but the historical context of his life and the emergency of his need to find "an immanent relation to political praxis."

Habermas is certainly correct to argue that there was nothing inherently Marxist about Benjamin's theory of history and criticism. Benjamin's move from esotericism to Marxism was a real turn in his intellectual life, grounded in the social-historical crisis of the moment more than in any logical tendency of his thought. Yet it will not do to deny any connection between the earlier theory and the new turn, for the crisis of meaning to which the disenchantment of the world was carrying tradition, art and the intellectual forced Benjamin to a reconsideration of the possibilities of the new technological age and to a new consideration of the masses and of political activism. If he superimposed a second body of theory upon the first, the existential mediation between the two bodies of theory derived from the bleak situation which the first theory implied and the second promised to avert. In short, Benjamin turned to the theory of the politicization of art and the equation of technical progress with revolutionary praxis to avert the dead end into which he saw culture moving on the line of the disenchantment of the world. It was a leap of faith, personal and paradoxical, which endeavored to rescue the sacred values of tradition by reconceiving and hence reconstituting them as the political values of a socialist society.

When he cast about for some figure to justify this aspiration, some artist whose practice seemed to exemplify this operation, he fastened upon Bertolt Brecht. What drew Benjamin to Brecht was his emphatic insistence upon intellectual commitment to the socialist cause, a commitment which went beyond abstract sympathy and expressed itself in concrete practice. In that program of *eingreifendes Denken* and *Umfunktionierung*, Brecht offered the intellectual in the age of technocracy the prospect for both artistic and political

175

integrity. Brecht represented literary engagement without sacrifice of quality, the reconciliation of the politicization of art with avant-garde modernism. Benjamin became associated with Brecht in 1929 in order to pursue this Marxist program for the arts.

A new, more concrete and pragmatic, even programmatic, note emerged in Benjamin's critical practice. Instead of the esotericist impetus to project his messianic aspirations into the most profane forms, Benjamin began to advocate an engaged and a didactic form of art. If one considers his reviews of 1929, in particular those of Walter Mehring's cabaret lyrics and of Döblin's *Berlin Alexanderplatz*, it is apparent that Benjamin had become concerned with the pedagogical or mobilizational potential of literature. Benjamin argued Mehring's lyrics did not deserve the title *Gebrauchslyrik* for, in explicit contrast to Brecht's, his was not a poetry intended for practical use.[28] It was the poetry of a secure, upper-class dilettant. Similarly, Benjamin demonstrated how much Döblin's epic retained of the specifically bourgeois form of the novel, despite Döblin's explicit effort to introduce epic form.[29] Döblin remained too caught up in the heritage of Flaubert, too much a part of bourgeois individualism to exert the didactic, mobilizing function which Benjamin now sought in literature. As he put it most explicitly at the conclusion of his review of Mehring: "These things have no power to transform; they will not entail any regroupings [in society]. For they are not inspired by the baseness of the bourgeois public, but by its masochism."[30] Only Brecht seemed to Benjamin to have a real sense for the issue of debunking a degenerate bourgeoisie and eliciting a mass response, a social regrouping. A friend and collaborator of Willi Haas, he shared the latter's irritation with the "radicals" and also the latter's penchant for lumping together the ardent Bolshevists around Becher with the critical negativists around Döblin and Ihering.[31] In one of his most famous essays, "Left-Wing Melancholy" (1930), Benjamin launched a full-scale polemic against the Negativists in the context of a review of Erich Kästner's poetry. Benjamin asserted that the Berlin "radicals" reflected "bourgeois decadence" and "had nothing to do with the working-class movement."

Benjamin concluded his argument with the contention that "left-radical journalists of Kästner's, of Tucholsky's or Mehring's type are a mimicry of the proletarian for decadent strata of the bourgeoisie."

While this left-radical intelligentsia had been responsible for all the intellectual currents of the past fifteen years, from Activism through Expressionism to *Neue Sachlichkeit*, its bankruptcy was finally revealed in this last phenomenon, for its "left-radicalism" was "left of all possibilities." It in fact betokened abandonment of political action, a concern "to enjoy oneself in negativistic peace."[32]

Benjamin tried to explain this fallacy in terms of developments in Germany in which "under the pressure of economic circumstances, many of her productive minds underwent a revolutionary development in terms of their *mentality* — without at the same time being able to think through in a really revolutionary way the question of their own work, its relationship to the means of production and its technique."[33]

Without this concrete awareness of how ideas were anchored in the socio-economic infrastructure, they allowed themselves to think abstract sympathy for progressive causes sufficed. More, they thought themselves freed from the domination of the instruments of production, a "free-floating" stratum involved in liberated "intellectual labor." This was the self-deception of the German avant-garde from Heinrich Mann to Alfred Döblin. Their sense of literary engagement never went beyond the literary, he charged. It was simply a matter of opinions. That was what Benjamin drew from Döblin's *Wissen und Verändern!* Its contradictions demonstrated

> where the concept of the "man of mind" as a
> type defined according to his opinions, in-
> tentions or predispositions, but not accor-
> ding to his position within the production
> process, must lead. This man, says Döblin,
> should find his place *at the side* of the pro-
> letariat. But what sort of a place is that?
> The place of a well-wisher, an ideological
> patron. An impossible place.[34]

Sympathy was not enough. It was insufficient to be for the proletariat, for socialism. "The best 'tendency' is wrong if it does not prescribe the attitude with which it ought to be pursued."

even if one could grant Benjamin a general sense of his contention, one which would read technical and formal for didactic, it remains that this does not at all signify an insight into the contextual and specifically economic-structural dimension of production. The gap between the two can only be ignored by begging the question, and this is what occurs in the third and crucial domain of ambiguity in Benjamin's argument. Generalizing his formula and applying it to artists who have substantially enriched the technical arsenal of their media, it is obvious that Benjamin's equation of technical progress with political progress is specious. As his friend Willi Haas noted in his debate with the "radicals," progressives have by no means held a monopoly on the formal-technical development of artistic media.[40] Benjamin did not resolve the conflict of quality versus commitment; he tried to make an anomaly, Brecht's epic theater, into a rule.

Even there one encounters difficulties. One must query Brecht's confidence in his epic theater. There is ample evidence that the impact of his most powerful dramas simply outpaces and in some measure undercuts the structures of dramaturgical theory and didactic ideology which Brecht attached to them.[41] Even his celebrated *"Verfremdungs-Effekt"* must be regarded with a measure of skepticism. Even if one were to grant that epic theater elicited a more thoughtful response in its audience, that is still insufficient grounds for the belief that what the audience thinks upon leaving the theater coincides with Brecht's didactic intentions. On a more general level, two further points should be made. First, epic theater has proven no more immune to cooptation than any other artistic form. Brecht has become a "classic" and is wrapped in that very "plaster" he so loathed. And this betrays the second point, Brecht's conception of *Umfunktionierung* and the attendant hope of intellectual autonomy and impact, of "constructive sabotage" of technocracy, has succeeded no better than any other avant-garde oppositional posture. At best it has given the intellectual a more acute consciousness of his captivity; it has not shown a path out of the "iron cage."

There is a final, somber point about the commitment Brecht and Benjamin advocated. They salvaged their identities from the manifest disintegration of the traditional literary-artistic self-conception by an ardent "Communism" for which the disenchantment of the world could be construed as a movement towards a collectivist socialism. The translation of art and inspiration into collectivism and intellectual service to the cause of socialism entailed a profession of loyalty to Communism not without grave difficulties. The orthodox party had no room for their subtleties and deviations. If Brecht and Benjamin chastised Döblin for his suggestion that intellectuals stand "at the side of the proletariat" because this was an "impossible place," their own effort to stand at the side of the party was no less impossible. The virtually ritual affirmation of the "revolutionary proletariat," the Communist Party and the Soviet Union by Brecht and Benjamin in the early Thirties seemed to verge on that "short-cut" leap Kracauer condemned. To affirm these positions all the while resisting the authority of these entities and preserving artistic and intellectual autonomy seemed to make these postures self-deceptive or naive and to invite the charge of dilettantish "radicalism" as Willi Haas diagnosed it at the close of the Twenties. It is quite clear that this was Haas's view of Brecht, for instance; and it would also appear that Döblin came to this view as his relation with Brecht soured.[42]

It was also this penchant for simplistic affirmation which Adorno repudiated in his friend's new turn of thought and blamed upon the baleful influence of Brecht's "crude thinking." Adorno's new negativism made a clean break with hope.[43] He perceived technology as inherently disposed to technocratic domination; its intervention via the new media created an "entertainment industry" in which mass culture irresistibly desolated high culture much as bad currency drove out the good. At the same time, from his vantage, the social institutions which professed a liberating mission were themselves instruments of domination and the strata upon whom the hopes of human liberation had been projected had shown themselves utterly incapable of heroic action. For the intellectuals in the face of these realities to "engage," to offer themselves for service in any institution or movement, was to betray their mission as intellectuals. There could be no participation without contamination. All that remained was philosophy, the old project which survived by virtue of society's

Press, 1965). For a survey of German reaction, see W. Laqueur, *Russia and Germany* (London: Weidenfeld & Nicolson, 1965).

3 Comment in C. Bertrand, ed., *Revolutionary Situations in Europe. 1917-1922: Germany, Italy, Austria-Hungary* (Montreal: Interuniversity Center for European Studies, 1977), p. 59. See also his essay, "The Communist Movement in the German Revolution, 1918-1919: A Problem of Historical Typology?" *Central European History* 6:3 (Sept. 1973).

4 On SPD reaction to Bolshevism, see above all P. Lösche, *Der Bolschewismus im Urteil der deutschen Sozialdemokratie* (Berlin: Colloquium, 1967). For other perspectives see A. Lindemann, *The 'Red Years': European Socialism versus Bolshevism, 1919-1921* (Berkeley & L.A.: U. of California Press, 1974); R. Wheeler, *USPD und Internationale* (Frankfurt/Berlin: Ullstein, 1975); and two older essays: W. Tormin, "Die deutsche Parteien und die Bolschewiki im Weltkrieg," in H. Neubauer, ed., *Deutschland und die Russische Revolution* (Stuttgart: Kohlhammer, 1968); and W. Mähl, "The Anti-Russian Tide in German Socialism, 1918-1920," *American Slavic and East European Review* 18:2 (April 1959).

5 P. von Örtzen, *Betriebsräte in der Novemberrevolution* (Düsseldorf: Droste, 1963), p. 76-77.

6 Quoted in D.K. Buse, "Ebert and the German Crisis, 1917-1920," *Central European History* 5:3 (Sept. 1972), p. 245n. On Ebert and the revolution, see the sharply critical R. Hunt, "Friedrich Ebert and the German Revolution of 1918," in L. Krieger & F. Stern, eds., *The Responsibility of Power* (Garden City: Doubleday, 1967).

7 U. Kluge, *Soldatenräte und Revolution* (Göttingen: Vandenhoeck und Ruprecht, 1975).

8 G. Feldman, "German Business Between War and Revolution: The Origins of the Stinnes-Legien Agreements," in G.A. Ritter, ed., *Entstehung und Wandel der modernen Gesellschaft* (Berlin: De Gruyter, 1970).

9 G. Feldman, *Iron and Steel in the German Inflation* (Princeton: Prince-U. Press, 1977).

10 E. Prager, *Geschichte der USPD* (Berlin: Freiheit, 1922). D. Morgan, *The Socialist Left and the German Revolution* (Ithaca: Cornell U. Press, 1975). R. Wheeler, *op. cit.*; H. Krause, *USPD: Zur Geschichte der Unabhängigen Sozialdemokratischen Partei Deutschlands* (Frankfurt/Cologne: Europäische Verlagsanstalt, 1975).

11 The best account of the SAG is Morgan, *op. cit.*, but see also J. Mischark, *The Road to Revolution: German Marxism and World War One* (Detroit: Moira, 1967) for a narrative of the internal conflicts of the split in April 1917. On the Spartacists the literature is flawed with strong bias pro and con and the best introduction is the documentation of the Spartacists themselves — the *Spartakusbriefe* (Berlin: KPD, 1920) and H. Weber, ed., *Der Gründungsparteitag der KPD. Protokoll und Materialien* (Frankfurt: Europäische Verlagsanstalt, 1969). The best, if obviously partisan, source

on the *Revolutionäre Obleute* is Richard Müller's two volume memoir: *Vom Kaiserreich zur Novemberrevolution* (Berlin: Malik, 1922) and *Der Bürgerkrieg in Deutschland* (Berlin: Phoebus, 1925).

12 F. Bey-Heard, *Hauptstadt und Staatsumwälzung: Berlin 1919* (Stuttgart: Kohlhammer, 1969), pp. 73ff; K.H. Luther, "Die nachrevolutionären Machtkämpfe in Berlin, Nov. 1918 bis März 1918," *Jahrbuch für die Geschichte Mittel- und Ost-Deutschlands*, vol. 8 (1959), p. 187ff; U. Kluge, *op. cit.*, p. 86ff; F. Opel, *Der deutschen Metallarbeiter-Verband während des ersten Weltkrieges und der Revolution* (Hannover & Frankfurt: Norddeutsche Verlagsanstalt O. Gödel, 1957) p. 80ff; D. Morgan, *op. cit.*, p. 121ff.

13 D. Morgan, *op. cit.*, p. 133.

14 Däumig and Müller churned out a mass of material regarding the theory of councils in *Der Arbeiterrat*, their journal of 1919-1920, and in independent pamphlets. Däumig's speech to the first Councils Congress is printed in the protocols of the Congress proceedings. His criticism of that Congress was published in *Der erste Akt der deutschen Revolution!* reprinted, with his speech to the USPD party congress in March 1920, in *Die Parteien und das Rätesystem* (Charlottenburg: Deutsche Verlagsanstalt für Politik und Geschichte, 1919). His speech to the Second Councils Congress was issued as a pamphlet, *Der Aufbau Deutschlands und das Rätesystem* in April 1919. Müller published his speech to the Second Councils Congress at the same time: *Was die Arbeiterräte wollen und sollen.* Later he published "Das Rätesystem in Deutschland," in I. Jezower, ed., *Die Befreiung der Menschheit* (Berlin: Deutsches Verlagshaus, 1921).

15 It is fruitful to consider the pamphlets and position statements on the council movement these groups generated in the hectic days of November-Dezember 1918. See, for example, *Die Parteien und das Rätesystem, op. cit.*; D. Schneider & R. Kuda, eds., *Arbeiterräte in der Novemberrevolution. Ideen, Wirkungen, Dokumente* (Frankfurt: Suhrkamp, 1969). For a full examination of the varying stances on the council idea, see H. Dähn, *Rätedemokratische Modelle. Studien zur Rätediskussion in Deutschland 1918-1919* (Meisenheim a. Glan: Hain, 1975).

16 See the stenographic proceedings of the First Council Congress for the utterly unsuccessful effort to seat Luxemburg and Liebknecht: *Allgemeiner Kongreß der Arbeiter und Soldatenräte Deutschlands vom 16. bis 21. Dezember 1918 im Abgeordnetenhause zu Berlin.* (Berlin, 1919).

17 R. Löwenthal, "The Bolshevization of the Spartacist League," in D. Footman, ed., *International Communism* (London: Chatto & Windus, 1960).

18 H. Bock, *Syndikalismus und Linkskommunismus von 1918-1923* (Meisenheim a. Glan: Haim, 1969). G.P. Bassler documents this as follows: "Among the many testimonies, the recently published memoirs of Karl Retzlaw, *Spartakus* (Frankfurt, 1971), p. 49, are most revealing. Until many years after he had become a socialist and communist, he had not read one line

185

44 *Ibid.*, p. 32.

45 *Ibid.*, p. 44.

46 Lewis, *op. cit.*, pp. 22-23.

47 W. Herzfelde, "The Curious Merchant from Holland," *Harpers Magazine* 187 (November 1941). This was reprinted in his autobiography, "Immergrün," included in *Unterwegs: Blätter aus fünfzig Jahre* (Berlin: Aufbau, 1961), Herzfelde's selected works. In addition, Herzfelde wrote of Grosz in connection with the Malik-Verlag and the journal *Neue Jugend.* See his introduction to the reprint of *Neue Jugend*, "Aus der Jugendzeit des Malik-Verlags" (Zurich: Limmat, 1967); his essay, "How a Publishing House was Born," in Raabe, ed., *The Era of Expressionism*, and especially W. Herzfelde, ed., *Der Malik-Verlag 1916-1947.* (Ausstellung, Dez. 1966-Jan. 1967, Deutsche Akademie der Künste zu Berlin (DDR)). Finally, Herzfelde has written about his brother Helmut (John Heartfield) and his relation to Grosz in *John Heartfield: Leben und Werk* (Dresden: Vlg. der Kunst, 1976); in "Mein Bruder John Heartfield," in R. Hülsenbeck, ed., *Dada – eine literarische Dokumentation* (Hamburg: Rowohlt, 1964); and in "John Heartfield und George Grosz; zum 75. Geburtstag meines Bruders," *Weltbühne* (June 15, 1966).

48 J.R. Becher, "An Friede," *Neue Jugend* I:7 (June 1916), p. 123. The new journal was presented as a continuation of the previous journal in order to deceive the censors, hence the first issue of the new journal appeared as Vol. I, Nr. 7, and started with p. 123.

49 "Nachwort," *Neue Jugend* I:7 (June 1916), p. 146.

50 B.I. Lewis, *op. cit.*, pp. 51-52.

51 *Neue Jugend*, May 23, 1917, p. 3.

52 Grosz, "Kannst du radfahren?" in *Neue Jugend*, June 1917.

53 H. Kessler, *Diaries of a Cosmopolitan* (London: Weidenfeld & Nicolson, 1971), p. 60.

54 *Ibid.*, p. 66.

55 *Ibid.*, p. 62.

56 *Ibid.*, p. 64.

57 E. Piscator, *Schriften* (Berlin: Henschel, 1968), Vol. II, p. 281.

58 On Piscator see: Piscator, *Das politische Theater* (Berlin: Henschel, 1968); M. Ley-Piscator, *The Piscator Experiment: The Political Theater* (New York: J. Heinemann, 1967); and C. Innes, *Erwin Piscator's Political Theater* (Cambridge U. Press, 1972).

59 Piscator, *Das politische Theater*, p. 11.

60 Piscator, "Oh, Betreßt von Blutkokarden," *Die Aktion* 9:51/52 (1919).

61 Piscator, *Das politische Theater*, p. 21.

62 W. Herzfelde, "Aus der Jugendzeit des Malik-Verlags," p. 14.

63 Kessler, *op. cit.*, p. 62.

64 W. Mehring, *Berlin Dada* (Zurich: Die Arche, 1954), pp. 67ff.

65 *Ibid.*, pp. 64-66.

66 Kessler, *op. cit.*, p. 81.

67 Piscator, *Das Politische Theater* (Berlin: Henschel, 1968), p. 22.

68 *Ibid.*, p. 25.
69 Mehring, *op. cit.*, p. 65. Kessler, *op. cit.*, p. 86.
70 Kessler, *op. cit.*, p. 88.
71 *Ibid.*, p. 90.
72 *Ibid.*, p. 91.
73 *Ibid.*
74 Richter, *op. cit.*, p. 113.
75 Kessler, *op. cit.*, p. 94.
76 *Ibid.*, p. 54 ff, Richter, *op. cit.*, p. 123 ff.
77 Hecht, *Letters from Bohemia*, (Garden City: Doubleday, 1964), pp. 142-144.
78 W. Mehring, *Berlin Dada*, pp. 40-42.
79 K. Riha, *Moritat, Song, Bänkelsang*, p. 69, makes this stylistic observation, arguing that this was an innovation in this genre of poetry.
80 W. Mehring, *Das politische Cabaret* (Dresden: Kammer, 1920), p. 10.
81 *Ibid.*, p. 9.
82 "Mit Samthandschuhen," *Das politische Cabaret*, pp. 12-13.
83 *Ibid.*, p. 14.
84 "Berlin – dein Tänzer ist der Tod!" in *Das politische Cabaret*, p. 21.
85 Lewis, *George Grosz: Art and Politics in the Weimar Republic*, pp. 77-78.
86 Notice in *Der Gegner* 2:4, p. 119.
87 Grosz, *Das Gesicht der herrschenden Klasse* (Berlin: Malik, 1921).
88 The trial raised a storm of protest on the left, with articles in the *Welt-bühne, Tagebuch and Aktion*, but Grosz and Heartfield were convicted and fined.
89 R. Boyer, "Profiles: Artist" (1. "Demons in the Suburbs," November 27, 1943; 2. "The Saddest Man in All the World," December 4, 1943; 3. "The Yankee from Berlin," December 11, 1943) *New Yorker Magazine*.
90 Quoted in catalogue *George Grosz: Leben und Werk*, p. 54.
91 See above all, Schickele, "Die Politik der Geistigen," *März* (1913) Vol. I., pp. 405-407; 440-441; Vol. II., pp. 30-31. On p. 440, Schickele explicitly associates the new orientation of the German literary intellectuals with the Dreyfusards. Schickele was born in 1883 in Alsace. With Otto Flake and Ernst Stadler he founded several Alsatian literary journals of a Neo Romantic character at the turn of the century. In 1904 he became editor of *Das neue Magazin* in Berlin. Thereafter he spent several years as a reporter in Paris. In these years he became a close friend of H. Mann. In 1910, Schickele contributed to the inauguration of Expressionist poetry with the volume *Weiß und Rot*. In 1914 he became editor of *Die Weißen Blätter*. See F. Bentmann, ed., *René Schickele: Leben und Werk in Dokumenten* (Nürnberg: Carl, 1974); and Schickele's *Werke in drei Bänden* (Cologne/Berlin: Kiepenheuer & Witsch, 1959) Vol. 3 for his essays, diaries and letters; there is also a bibliography of secondary literature on Schickele in this volume.
92 R. Schickele, "Revolution, Bolschewismus und Ideal," *Die Weißen Blätter* 5:6 (December 1918), p. 125.

1919," in E. Kolb, ed., *Vom Kaiserreich zur Weimarer Republik*.

3 *Die gesetzliche Verankerung der Arbeiterräte. Das Protokoll von Weimar* (Berlin: SPD, 1919).

4 J. Erger, *Der Kapp-Lüttwitz Putsch* (Düsseldorf: Droste, 1967).

5 F.L. Carsten, *The Reichswehr and Politics, 1918-1933* (London: Oxford, 1966).

6 A. Milatz, *Wähler und Wahlen in der Weimarer Republik* (Bonn: Bundeszentrale für politische Bildung, 1965).

7 Kessler, *Diaries of a Cosmopolitan*, pp. 95-110.

8 The most penetrating assessment of this shift is R. Wheeler, " 'Ex oriente Lux?' The Soviet Example and the German Revolution, 1917-1923," in C. Bertrand, ed., *Revolutionary Situations*.

9 On these interpreters of early Soviet affairs see W. Engelberg, "Die Sowjetunion im Spiegel literarischer Berichte und Reportage in der Zeit der Weimarer Republik," in *Literatur der Arbeiterklasse* (Berlin/Weimar: Aufbau, 1971).

10 Jung wrote about Bolshevik culture as early as November 1919 in *Die Aktion*, then later for *Der Gegner* and *Proletarier*. In 1924 two books by Jung on Bolshevism were published: *Das geistige Rußland von heute* (Berlin: Ullstein, 1924), and *Der neue Mensch im neuen Rusland* (Vienna: Verlag für Literatur und Politik, 1924).

11 See *Der Malik-Verlag, 1916-1947* (Exhibition Catalogue, Deutsche Akademie der Künste zu Berlin (DDR), December 1966 – January 1967), ed., W. Herzfelde. For a historical survey of this output, see H. Denkler, "Auf dem Wege zur proletarisch-revolutionären Literatur und zur Neuen Sachlichkeit: Zur frühen Publikationen des Malik-Verlags" in W. Rothe, ed., *Die deutsche Literatur in der Weimarer Republik* (Stuttgart: Reclam, 1974).

12 *Der Gegner* 1:8/9 (Dec. 1919). The prior line of *Der Gegner* was left-radical, but not quite "Bolshevik." See the lead editorials of Karl Otten, one of the coeditors: "Sozialismus aus Angst vor dem Kommunismus," *Der Gegner* 1:5 (July 1919) and "Die Ratlosigkeit der geistig Hochmütigen," *Der Gegner* 1:6 (August/September 1919).

13 S. Großmann, "Hat Berlin eine Zukunft?" in L. Brieger & H. Steiner, eds., *Zirkus Berlin: Bilder Berliner Lebens* (Berlin: Almanach, 1919).

14 T. Wehrlin, "Blick nach Osten," *Das Tagebuch* 1:6 (1920).

15 Paquet's series is in *Das Tagebuch* 1:7 and following issues; Ross's articles begin simultaneously.

16 S. Großmann, "Der Typus Radek," *Das Tagebuch* 1:9 (1920).

17 Goldschmidt's reports begin in *Das Tagebuch* 1:33; and Russell's in *Das Tagebuch* 1:38.

18 W. Herzog, "Wahrheit über Sowjetrußland!" *Das Forum* (March, 1920).

19 D. Angress, "Lunacharski und Deutschland 1917-1924," in G. Rosenfeld, ed., *Deutschland-Sowjetunion. Aus fünf Jahrzehnten kulturellen Zusammen-*

arbeit (Berlin: Humboldt U. Press, 1966), p. 319. Also see S. Fitzpatrick, *The Commissariat of Enlightenment: Soviet Organization of Education and the Arts Under Lunacharsky, October 1917-1921* (Cambridge: Cambridge University Press, 1970).

20 A. Bogdanov, "Über proletarische Dichtung," *Die Aktion* 11:21/22 (1921).

21 A. Lunacharsky, "Proletarische Kultur," in L. Rubiner, ed., *Die Gemeinschaft* (Potsdam: Kiepenheuer, 1919), p. 265.

22 W. Herzfelde, "Gesellschaft, Künstler und Kommunismus," reprinted in W. Fähnders & M. Rector, eds., *Literatur im Klassenkampf: Zur proleta-risch-revolutionären Literatur-Theorie 1919-1923* (Frankfurt: S. Fischer, 1971), p. 134-135.

23 On Münzenberg and the IAH see his own *Solidarität: Zehn Jahre Internationale Arbeiterhilfe 1921-1931* and H. Gruber, "Willi Münzenberg's German Communist Propaganda Empire 1921-1923," *Journal of Modern History* 38:3 (September 1966).

24 The idea of the "Rote Gruppe" originated in opposition to the "Novembergruppe" association of artists in 1918. See the "Open Letter to the November Group" in *Der Gegner* 2:8/9 (1920). The actual "Rote Gruppe" coalesced somewhat later, issuing a manifesto in the *Rote Fahne* #57 (1924) which was reprinted in D. Schmidt, ed., *Manifeste, Manifeste* (Dresden: Verlag der Kunst, 1965), pp. 318 ff.

25 Grosz, "Statt einer Biographie," *Der Gegner* II:2/3, p. 68.

26 Grosz, "Zu meinen neuen Bildern," *Das Kunstblatt* V:1 (January 1921), p. 11.

27 E. Piscator, "Über Grundlagen und Aufgaben des proletarischen Theaters," *Der Gegner* 2 (1920/21), reprinted in Fähnders and Rector, eds., *Literatur im Klassenkampf*, p. 194 ff.

28 F.W. Seiwert, "Das Loch in Rubens Schinken," *Die Aktion* 10 (1920) quoted in *ibid.*, p. 224.

29 F.W. Seiwert, "Aufbau der proletarischen Kultur," *Die Aktion* 10:51/52 (1920).

30 O. Steinicke, "Das Proletariat und die bürgerlichen Intellektuellen," *Prolet* 1:1 (1919).

31 H. Lindemann, "Proletariat und Intellektuelle," *Prolet* 1:2 (1919).

32 E. Mühsam, "Die Intellektuellen," *Die Aktion* 11:3/4 (1921).

33 K. Offenburg, "Intellektuelle und Proletariat," *Die Aktion* 11:27/28 (1921).

34 F. Pfemfert, editorial note commenting on F. Seiwert, "Die Funktion der Intellektuellen in der Gesellschaft und ihre Aufgabe in der proletarischen Revolution," *Die Aktion* 13:25/26 (1923).

35 G. Lukacs, *History and Class Consciousness* (Cambridge: MIT Press, 1971); K. Korsch, *Marxism and Philosophy* (London: NLB, 1970); on the rise of this movement see: P. Breines, "Praxis and Its Theorists: The Impact of Lukacs and Korsch in the 1920s," *Telos* No. 11 (Spring 1972); R. Jacoby, "Towards a Critique of Automatic Marxism: The Politics of Philosophy from Lukacs to the Frankfurt School," *Telos* No. 10 (Winter 1971).

36 On Lenin's ideas regarding Marxist theory and praxis, see M. Liebman, *Leninism under Lenin* (London: Cape, 1975); for a sympathetic philosophical construction of Lenin's late thought see P. Piccone, "Towards an Understanding of Lenin's Philosophy," *Radical America* 4:6 (Sept./ Oct., 1970); also: R. Jacoby, "Lenin and Luxemburg: Negation in Theory and Praxis," *ibid.* For less sympathetic consideration, see I. Fetscher, "From the Philosophy of the Proletariat to Proletarian *Weltanschauung*," in his *Marx and Marxism* (New York: Herder & Herder, 1971) and the vehemently anti-Leninist work of Pannekoek, *Lenin as Philosopher* (London: Merlin, 1975).

37 F. Wolf, "Kunst ist Waffe," reprinted in *Zur Tradition der sozialistischen Literatur in Deutschland* (2nd. ed.; Berlin/Weimar: Aufbau, 1967), pp. 34-55.

38 Grosz & Herzfelde, *Die Kunst ist in Gefahr*, reprinted in D. Schmidt, ed., *op. cit.*

39 *Ibid.*, p. 342.

40 *Ibid.*, p. 344.

41 *Ibid.*, p. 346.

42 *Ibid.*, p. 347.

43 *Ibid.*, p. 351.

44 *Ibid.*, p. 358.

45 This "negativism" in Grosz resulted from the cooling of the utopian potential of Bolshevik Russia. See: Grosz, *Ein kleines Ja und ein großes Nein*, Chapter 11: *Rußlandreise 1922*. Grosz turned away from direct, party-line agitation. His visit to the USSR in 1922 had left him cynical about Lenin and about Tatlin, the two idols of his earlier infatuation. Moreover, Grosz was never one to fit quite comfortably into the structures set by party functionaries.

46 S. Fitzpatrick, *The Commissariat of Enlightenment*, Chapters 5/6.

47 Quoted in H. Marshall, *Mayakovsky*, (New York: Hill & Wang, 1965), p. 32. On Lenin and art see: Polonsky, "Lenin's Views on Art and Literature," in M. Eastman, *Artist in Uniform*; H. Marshall, "Introduction" to *Mayakovsky*, pp. 29-33; P. Reddaway, "Literature, the Arts and the Personality of Lenin," in Shapiro & Reddaway, eds., *Lenin, The Man, the Theorist, The Leader* (New York: Präger, 1967); L. Fischer, *The Life of Lenin* (New York: Harper & Row, 1964), pp. 488-496.

48 A. Kaun, *Soviet Poets and Poetry*, (Berkeley & L.A.: University of California Press, 1943), p. 111.

49 See R. Löwenthal, "The Bolshevization of the Spartacist League," in D. Footman, ed., *International Communism* (Carbondale: Southern Illinois U. Press, 1960); and H.M. Bock, *Syndikalismus und Linkskommunismus von 1918-1923* (Meisenheim am Glan: Hain, 1969).

50 L. Peter, *op. cit.*, pp. 136 ff; and on Jung, the literature cited above.

51 On the Comintern intervention in Central European Marxism, see the

194

documents in J. Degras, ed., *The Communist International 1919-1943* (New York: Oxford U. Press, 1956) and H. Gruber, ed., *International Communism in the Era of Lenin: A Documentary History* (Ithaca: Cornell U. Press, 1967) and *Soviet Russia Masters the Comintern: International Communism in the Era of Stalin's Ascendancy* (Garden City: Anchor, 1974).

52 The best account is W. Angress, *Stillborn Revolution: The Communist Bid for Power in Germany 1921-1923* (Princeton: Princeton U. Press, 1963). See also R. Löwenthal, *loc. cit.*; H. Weber, *Die Wandlung des deutschen Kommunismus: Die Stalinisierung der KPD in der Weimarer Republik* (Frankfurt: Europäische Verlagsanstalt, 1969), Vol. I., pp. 35-43; and O.K. Flechtheim, *Die KPD in der Weimarer Republik* (Frankfurt: Europäische Verlagsanstalt, 1963).

53 See S. Bahne, "Zwischen 'Luxemburgismus' und 'Stalinismus': Die 'ultra-linke' Opposition in der KPD," *Vierteljahreshefte für Zeitgeschichte* 9:4 (Oct. 1961); H. Weber *op. cit.*, Vol. I., pp. 53-185.

54 See W.-D. Rasch, "Bertolt Brechts marxistischer Lehrer," in Rasch, *Zur deutschen Literatur seit der Jahrhundertwende* (Stuttgart: Metzler, 1967); K.-D. Müller, "Brechts *Me-Ti* und die Auseinandersetzung mit dem Lehrer Karl Korsch," *Brecht Jahrbuch 1977* (Frankfurt: Suhrkamp, 1977). Korsch, *Revolutionary Theory*, ed. D. Kellner (Austin: U. of Texas Press, 1977), esp. Kellner's introduction.

55 S. Bahne, *loc. cit.*, pp. 362 ff; H. Weber, *op. cit.*, Vol. I., pp. 54-98.

56 H. Weber, *op. cit.*, Vol. I., p. 72.

57 *Ibid.*, pp. 81-85.

58 *Ibid.*, pp. 149-155.

59 *Ibid.*, p. 97.

60 K. Korsch, "The Present State of the Problem of Marxism and Philosophy," (1930), reprinted in *Marxism and Philosophy*, p. 101.

Chapter Three

1 On the RAPP see E. Brown, *The Proletarian Episode in Russian Literature 1928-1932* (New York: Columbia, 1953); R. Maguire, *Red Virgin Soil* (Princeton: Princeton U. Press, 1968); and G. Struve, *Soviet Russian Literature* (Norman: U. of Oklahoma Press, 1957).

2 J.R. Becher, "Über die proletarisch-revolutionäre Literatur in Deutschland," in *Zur Tradition der sozialistischen Literatur in Deutschland* (Berlin/Weimar: Aufbau, 1967; second edition) (henceforth, *Zur Tradition*), p. 32.

3 H. Gallas, *Marxistische Literaturtheorie* (Neuwied/Berlin: Luchterhand, 1971).

4 *Aktionen, Bekenntnisse, Perspektiven* (Berlin/Weimar: Aufbau, 1966); see also *Zur Tradition*. For a critique see J. Rühle, *Literature and Revolution*

(New York: Praeger, 1969).

5 Gallas, *op. cit.*, p. 25-30.

6 M. Eksteins, *The Limits of Reason* (London: Oxford U. Press, 1975).

7 The conflict over the law filled the journal *Der Schriftsteller* especially in late 1926 and caused a shake-up in the SDS leadership. Theodor Heuß, a longtime leader of the organization, supported the law and was forced to resign his office in the SDS as a result. The law won easy public acceptance despite the writers' protests, demonstrating to weakness of the forces for freedom of expression.

8 See *Aktionen, Bekenntnisse, Perspektiven* for detailed documentation of this case: Part One of the volume is dedicated to *"Der Hochverratsprozeß gegen Johannes R. Becher."*

9 The pejorative "professorial" comes from the leading progressive critic of the Weimar years, Herbert Ihering. He first used it in *Die vereinsamte Theaterkritik*, a pamphlet from 1928, reprinted now in Ihering, *Der Kampf ums Theater und andere Streitschriften 1918 bis 1933* (Berlin: Henschel, 1974). Ihering "discovered" Brecht and consistently fostered his career in Weimar theater, along with Erwin Piscator and other key figures of the literary left. See his memoirs, *Begegnungen mit Zeit und Menschen* (Berlin: Aufbau, 1962), for more on his criticism of the establishment critics and support for the literary left in Weimar.

10 E. Piscator, "Rechenschaft (II)," in Piscator, *Aufsätze, Reden, Gespräche: Schriften, Bd. 2* (Berlin: Henschel, 1968) (henceforth, *Schriften II*), p. 58.

11 Piscator, *Das politische Theater*, p. 133.

12 *Ibid.*, p. 131.

13 *Ibid.*, p. 132.

14 On the *Volksbühne* see H. Braulich, *Die Volksbühne. Theater und Politik in der deutschen Volksbühnenbewegung* (Berlin: Henschel, 1976); F. Knellessen, *Agitation auf der Bühne. Das politische Theater der Weimarer Republik* (Emsdetten: Lachte, 1970); and Piscator himself in *Das politische Theater.*

15 Piscator, *Das politische Theater*, p. 48-52.

16 *Ibid.*, p. 51.

17 *Ibid.*, p. 70.

18 Piscator, "Paquets 'Sturmflut' in der Berliner Volksbühne," *Schriften II*, p. 17.

19 Piscator, *Das politische Theater*, pp. 128-129.

20 See the reviews in G. Rühle, ed., *Theater für die Republik* (Frankfurt: S. Fischer, 1967), p. 690-695; Knellessen, *op. cit.*, p. 83-89.

21 This controversy is reflected in the following articles: G. Stark, "Piscators Regieabsichten in der Sturmflut-Inszenierung," *Die Szene* 16:5 (1926); and R. Weinmann, "Die schöpferische Tätigkeit des Regisseurs und seine Freiheit gegenüber dem Autor," *Das blaue Heft* 8:12 (1926). C. Innes, *The Political Theater of Erwin Piscator* devotes the bulk of his study to these issues.

196

22 Piscator, *Das politische Theater*, p. 88.

23 H. Ihering, "Piscators 'Räuber'-Inszenierung," in Ihering, *Von Reinhardt bis Brecht* (Berlin: Aufbau, 1959), Vol. II., p. 223.

24 See the reviews in G. Rühle, ed., *op. cit.*, p. 721-727, and the assessment of Knellessen, *op. cit.*, p. 103-104.

25 Fechter, Review in Rühle, ed., *op. cit.*, p. 725-727.

26 On the controversy surrounding Jessner, see especially F. Ziege *et. al.*, *Leopold Jessner und das Zeit-Theater* (Berlin: Eigenbrödler Vlg, 1928); and the spirited defense of Jessner in *Das Tagebuch* by Ihering, Vol. 7, No. 50 (1926); Vol. 8, No. 1 (1927); and Vol. 8, No. 8 (1927); and by the editor Stefan Großmann, Vol. 9, No. 3 (1928); and Vol. 10, No. 15 (1929).

27 Piscator, *Das politische Theater*, p. 87-88; H. Ihering, *Der Volksbühnenverrat* (1928), reprinted in *Der Kampf ums Theater*, p. 246ff; S. Großmann, "Volksbühnen-Verrat," *Das Tagebuch* 9:21 (1928).

28 Piscator, *op. cit.*, p. 95ff; Braulich, *op. cit.*, pp. 122-123.

29 Documents reproduced in Piscator, *Das politische Theater*, p. 102; see the pamphlet by Ihering and Großmann's commentary cited in note 27, and also Braulich, *op. cit.*, p. 123-142; Knellessen, *op. cit.*, p. 109-113.

30 A. Holitscher, "Zur Krise der Volksbühne," reprinted in Piscator, *Das politische Theater*, p. 98-99.

31 G. Springer, "Zur Krise der Volksbühne," reprinted in *ibid.*, p. 99.

32 A. Mühr, *Kulturbankrott des Bürgertums* (Dresden/Berlin: Sibyllen, 1928).

33 E. Welk, "An den Vorstand des Verbandes deutscher Volksbühnen Vereine e.V." reprinted in *Das politische Theater*, p. 106.

34 B. Diebold, "Das Piscator-Drama," *Die Szene* 18:2 (February 1928) p. 33ff.

35 H. Ihering, "Etappendramaturgie," *Der Kampf ums Theater*, p. 232.

36 "Soll das Drama eine Tendenz haben?" *Die Szene* 18:11 (November 1928).

37 B. Balazs, in *Berliner Börsen-Courier*, February 1927, reprinted in Piscator, *Das politische Theater*, pp. 92-94.

38 *Ibid.*, p. 93.

39 See note 8 above.

40 Becher, "Deutsche Intellektuelle, Ein Aufruf," in F. Albrecht, *Deutsche Schriftsteller in der Entscheidung* (Berlin/Weimar: Aufbau, 1975), p. 581 ff.

41 J.R. Becher, "Bürgerlicher Sumpf/Revolutionärer Kampf," (1925) reprinted in Albrecht, *op. cit.*

42 See the founding manifesto of the *Rote Gruppe* in D. Schmidt, ed., *Manifeste, Manifeste* (Dresden: Verlag d. Kunst, 1965), pp. 318-319; and "Offener Brief an Die Novembergruppe," *Der Gegner* 2:8/9 (1920/1921), p. 297ff.

43 Annual Report, February 1924, in *Der Schriftsteller* 11:2 (March 1924), p. 8.

44 Such an interpretation is based on an examination of the journal *Der Schriftsteller* for the entire period of the organization, especially the reports of the Annual Meetings.

45 Döblin, "Schriftsteller und Politik," *Der Schriftsteller* 11:3 (May 1924), p. 13.
46 H. Kasack, "Begegnungen mit Alfred Döblin," *in Alfred Döblin zum 70. Geburtstag* (Wiesbaden: Limes, 1948), p. 19.
47 Döblin, *Briefe* (Olten & Freiburg: Walter, 1970), p. 421.
48 Becher, "Über die proletarisch-revolutionäre Literatur in Deutschland," in *Zur Tradition*, p. 32.
49 "Ortsgruppe Berlin," *Der Schriftsteller* 12:1 (February 1926), pp. 8-9; and "Ortsgruppe Berlin," *Der Schriftsteller* 12:2 (March 1926) p. 18.
50 L. Lania, "Die Not der Schriftsteller," *Die literarische Welt* 2:9 (1926).
51 The Manifesto is reprinted in Schmidt, ed., *op. cit.*, p. 367.
52 H. Gallas, *Marxistische Literaturtheorie* (Neuwied/Berlin: Luchterhand, 1974), Chapter I.
53 See *Aktionen, Bekenntnisse, Perspektiven*, p. 120ff., and L. Kreutzer, *Alfred Döblin: Sein Werk bis 1933* (Stuttgart: Kohlhammer, 1970), p. 138ff.
54 W. Haas, "Berlin," *Die literarische Welt* (1927) No. 17. One of his targets, probably, was Bertolt Brecht. See Haas, *Bert Brecht* (New York: Ungar, 1970).
55 K. Tucholsky, letter in "Zur Psychologie des Marxismus und der 'radikalen' Literaten. Zwei Briefe an den Herausgeber," *Die Literarische Welt* (1927) No. 19.
56 W. Haas, "Wir und die Radikalen" *Die literarische Welt* (1928) No. 43.
57 Other essays of importance by Haas in *Die literarische Welt* are: "Die Theaterkritik von heute," (1929) No. 22; "Egon Erwin Kisch und die 'neue Sachlichkeit'," (1930) No. 1; "Restauration?" (1930) No. 43; "Schmock hie und drüben," (1931) No. 1. See Haas's memoirs, *Die literarische Welt* (Munich: List, 1960).
58 Haas, "Wir und die Radikalen," *loc. cit.*
59 Haas, "Die Theaterkritik von heute," *loc. cit.*
60 J.R. Becher, "Antwort eines 'Radikalen'," reprinted in *Zur Tradition der sozialistischen Literatur in Deutschland* (2nd ed., Berlin/Weimar: Aufbau, 1967) (Henceforth, *Zur Tradition*), p. 123ff.
61 J.R. Becher, "Partei und Intellektuellen," *Rote Fahne* (November 25, 1928), reprinted in *Zur Tradition*, p. 127ff.
62 "Die Freiheit eines Dichtermenschen," *Die Neue Rundschau* (June 1918), reprinted in *Aufsätze zur Literatur* (Olten & Freiburg: Walter, 1963), p. 23ff.
63 A. Döblin, in *Welt am Abend*, March 16, 1926; cited in several diatribes against Döblin by Communists in 1930-1931. See, e.g. O. Biha, "Herr Döblin verunglückt in einer 'Linkskurve'," *Die Linkskurve* 2:6 (June 1930).
64 A. Döblin, "Kunst ist nicht frei, sondern wirksam: ars militans," *Aufsätze zur Literatur*, p. 99.
65 P. Westheim, editorial note to "Kunst, Dämon und Gesellschaft," *Das*

Kunstblatt 10:3 (1926), p. 184.

66 A. Döblin, "Kunst, Dämon und Gesellschaft," in *Aufsätze zur Literatur*, p. 84.

67 J. Heartfield, "Grün oder – Rot?" *Die Weltbühne* 22:11 (1926).

68 A. Behne, "An den Verein Kommunistischer Künstler," *Die Weltbühne* 22:12 (1926).

69 A. Döblin, "Kunst, Dämon und Gesellschaft," *loc. cit.*

70 Quoted in L. Huguet, *Bibliographie Alfred Döblin* (Berlin: Aufbau, 1972), p. 137.

71 H.G. Brenner, "Alfred Döblins Werk und die Zeit," *Die neue Bücherschau* Jg. 7. F.S. Schrift 1, p. 20ff.

72 Döblin was acutely sensitive to this criticism; he had made it of himself in 1922: "psychologically I am for myself a leave-well-enough-alone and I can approach myself only through the distance of epic narration. Hence via China or the Holy Roman Empire," in "Autobiographische Skizze," *Das literarische Echo* (April 1, 1922), reprinted in W. Muschg, ed., *Die Zeitlupe: Kleine Prosa von Alfred Döblin* (Olten & Freiburg: Walter, 1962), p. 57. But he grew tired of having it thrown at him. In 1924 he wrote, "Critics had charged me with never being able to work without an enormous historical apparatus. They questioned my imagination, in other words; that made me angry." – "Bemerkungen zu 'Berge Meere und Giganten,'" *Aufsätze zur Literatur*, p. 348.

73 Brenner, *loc. cit.*

74 A. Döblin, "Schriftstellerei und Dichtung," reprinted in *Aufsätze zur Literatur*, p. 94.

75 A. Döblin, "Die repräsentative und die aktive Akademie," in A. Döblin, *Die Vertreibung der Gespenster. Autobiographische Schriften. Betrachtungen zur Zeit. Aufsätze zur Kunst und Literatur*, ed. M. Beyer (Berlin: Rütten & Löning, 1968), p. 384-386.

76 See Brecht's remarks in *Gesammelte Werke* (Frankfurt: Suhrkamp, 1967) (henceforth *GW*), Vol. 18, p. 63. See also the observations of L. Frank in the survey, "Reportage und Dichtung," *Die Literarische Welt* 2:26 (1926); and the critical review by K. Herrmann in *Die neue Bücherschau* Jg. 5, Folge 5, H. 6, p. 258-259.

77 On the BPRS see H. Gallas, *Marxistische Literaturtheorie* (Neuwied/Berlin: Luchterhand, 1974); Fähnders & Rector, *Linksradikalismus and Literatur*; and E. Simons, "Der Bund proletarisch-revolutionärer Schriftsteller Deutschlands und sein Verhältnis zur Kommunistischen Partei Deutschlands," in *Literatur der Arbeiterklasse* (Berlin: Aufbau, 1971).

78 J.R. Becher, "Bürgerlicher Sumpf/Revolutionärer Kampf," in F. Albrecht, *Deutsche Schriftsteller in der Entscheidung*, p. 581 ff. and "Unsere Front," *Die Linkskurve* 1:1 (August 1929).

79 Letter to *Die Neue Bücherschau*, reprinted by G. Pohl, *Die neue Bücherschau* 7:9 (September 1919), p. 463.

80 Pohl, "Über die Rolle des Schriftstellers in dieser Zeit," *Die neue Bücherschau* 7:9 (September 1929).

81 *Ibid.*, pp. 465-466.

82 E.E. Kisch, "Über die Rolle des Schriftstellers in dieser Zeit," reprinted in *Zur Tradition*, p. 141ff.

83 K. Kersten, "Der Jahrtausendputsch der Literatur-Nihilisten," *Die Linkskurve* 1:1 (August 1929), p. 22.

84 K. Klaber, "An die Leser der 'Literarischen Welt'," *ibid.*, p. 24ff.

85 A. Gabor, "Emil Ludwig: Juli 1914," *ibid.*, p. 33ff.

86 J.R. Becher, "Unsere Front," *ibid.*, p. 1ff.

87 This was not Lenin's position on art and culture after 1917. See Ch. 2 note 47.

88 A. Gabor, "Über proletarisch-revolutionäre Literatur," *Die Linkskurve* 1:3 (October 1929), p. 3ff.

89 A. Gabor, "Die bunte Welt des Genossen Barbusse," *Die Linkskurve* 1:5 (December 1929), p. 5ff.

90 O. Biha, "Der Fall Pilnyak und die Folgen," *ibid.*, p. 13.

Chapter Four

1 K. Neukranz, "Berlin Alexanderplatz," *Die Linkskurve* 1:5 (December 1929), pp. 30-31.

2 J.R. Becher, "Einen Schritt weiter," *Die Linkskurve* 2:1 (January 1930), pp. 2-3.

3 *Ibid.*, p. 4.

4 A. Döblin, "Katastrophe in einer Linkskurve," *Das Tagebuch* 11:19 (May 1930) reprinted in *Schriften zur Politik und Gesellschaft*, p. 247.

5 O. Biha, "Herr Döblin verunglückt in einer 'Linkskurve'," *Die Linkskurve* 2:6 (June 1930), p. 21.

6 *Die Linkskurve* 2:10 (October 1930), p. 36.

7 F.C. Weiskopf, "Die Pleite des großen deutschen Romans. Döblin, der deutsche normaleinheits-Joyce," in *Materialien zu Alfred Döblin 'Berlin Alexanderplatz'* (Frankfurt: Suhrkamp, 1975), p. 100ff.

8 G. Hocke, letter to Döblin, *Das Tagebuch* 11:27 (July 1930), reprinted in Döblin, *Der deutsche Maskenball von Linke Poot/Wissen und Verändern!* (Olten & Freiburg i.B.: Walter, 1972), p. 129ff.

9 A. Döblin, reply to Hocke, *Das Tagebuch* 11:27 (July 1930), reprinted in *ibid.*, p. 132.

10 This is the title of a harshly critical review by Emanuel Ben Gurion in *Neue Revue* 2:3/4 (1931/1932).

11 A. Döblin, Reply to Hocke, *loc. cit.*, p. 128.

12 Hocke, letter, *loc. cit.*, p. 130.

13 Döblin, *Wissen und Verändern!*, *op. cit.*, p. 135.

14 *Ibid.*, p. 249.

200

15 *Ibid.*, p. 144.
16 *Ibid.*, p. 143.
17 *Ibid.*, p. 140.
18 *Ibid.*, p. 206.
19 *Ibid.*, p. 140.
20 *Ibid.*, p. 141.
21 L. Kreutzer, *Alfred Döblin: Sein Werk bis 1933* (Stuttgart: Kohlhammer, 1970), p. 141ff.
22 Döblin, *op. cit.*, p. 221 ff.
23 *Ibid.*, p. 221.
24 *Ibid.*, p. 248.
25 Döblin studied with Korsch along with Brecht. See L. Kreutzer, *op. cit.*, p. 143 ff.
26 G. Lichtheim, *From Marx to Hegel* (New York: Herder & Herder, 1971), p. viii.
27 Nietzsche developed this perspective in several works, esp. the fragments on "European Nihilism" gathered in *The Will to Power* (New York: Vintage, 1967), pp. 7 ff. and *On the Genealogy of Morals* in *Basic Writings of Nietzsche* (New York: Modern Library, 1966), pp. 439 ff.
28 M.H. Abram, *Natural Supernaturalism* (New York: Norton, 1971).
29 A. Döblin, *op. cit.*, p. 182.
30 *Ibid.*, p. 248-249.
31 *Ibid.*, p. 249.
32 *Ibid.*, p. 172.
33 *Ibid.*, p. 187.
34 *Ibid.*, p. 203.
35 A. Kesser, "Das Labyrinth des Dr. Döblin," *Die Linkskurve*, 3:9 (September 1931), pp. 28-30.
36 F.C. Weiskopf, "Gute Ratschläge für Herrn Hocke — oder Alfred Döblins Rettung der deutschen Intellektuellen," reprinted in *Zur Tradition*, p. 337 ff.
37 O. Biha, "Die Ideologie des Kleinbürgertums und die Krise," *Internationale Literatur* 2 (1932), p. 208.
38 B. Balazs, "Die Furcht der Intellektuellen vor dem Sozialismus," *Die Weltbühne* (1928) in four parts.
39 *Ibid.*, p. 93.
40 *Ibid.*, p. 94.
41 *Ibid.*, p. 132.
42 *Ibid.*, p. 167.
43 *Ibid.*, p. 208.
44 L. Congdon, "The Making of a Hungarian Revolutionary: The Unpublished Diary of Bela Balazs," *J. of Contemporary History* 8:3 (1973), pp. 57-74.
45 S. Kracauer, Review, reprinted in I. Schuster & I. Bode, eds., *Alfred Döblin im Spiegel der zeitgenössischen Kritik* (Berlin/Munich: Francke, 1973) p. 284.

46 *Ibid.*
47 *Ibid.*, p. 282.
48 S. Kracauer, "Minimalforderungen an die Intellektuellen" *Die Neue Rund-schau* (July 1931), p. 73.
49 *Ibid.*, p. 74.
50 A. Döblin, "Nochmals Wissen und Verändern!" *Die Neue Rundschau* (August 1931).
51 *Ibid.*, p. 186.
52 *Ibid.*, p. 198.
53 *Ibid.*, p. 187.
54 *Ibid.*, p. 194.
55 On Kracauer, see the brief review of his career in Witte, "Introduction to S. Kracauer, 'The Mass Ornament'," *New German Critique* 5 (Spring 1975).
56 S. Kracauer, "Die Wartenden," in *Das Ornament der Masse. Essays* (Frankfurt/M: Suhrkamp, 1963), p. 106.
57 S. Kracauer, "The Mass Onrament," *New German Critique* 5 (1975), p. 71.
58 *Ibid.*, p. 74.
59 *Ibid.*, p. 72.
60 See T. Adorno, *Negative Dialectics* (New York: Seabury, 1979); on Adorno and his intellectual origins, see: S. Buck-Morss, *The Origin of Negative Dialectics* (New York: Free Press, 1977); G. Rose, *The Melancholy Science: An Introduction to the Thought of Theodor W. Adorno* (London: Macmillan, 1978); M. Jay, *The Dialectical Imagination* (Boston: Little-Brown, 1973).

Chapter Five

1 Brecht, "Die Ansichten trügen," GW 20:16.
2 Brecht, "Über den Sozialismus," GW 20:16-17.
3 *Ibid.*
4 Brecht, "(Alles Unglück der Welt)," GW 20:16; and see his poem "Von den großen Männern," GW 8:146.
5 Brecht, "Terror gegen Literatur," GW 18:16.
6 *Ibid.*
7 Brecht, "Über die Eignung zum Zuschauer," GW 15:92.
8 Brecht, "Aus Über Kunst und Sozialismus," GW 15:66.
9 *Ibid.*, p. 65.
10 *Ibid.*, p. 66.
11 Brecht, "Conversation with George Grosz," in *Collected Plays*, (New York: Vintage, 1971) Vol. I., p. 373 ff.
12 Evidence of Grosz's political attitudes by 1927 or 1928 can be found in a story Hans Richter told of a dinner party with Grosz. A man who had just returned all aglow with news from the Soviet Union thought he would have

a willing audience in Grosz. As the man went on, Grosz sank into a black rage, then suddenly slammed his fist into the man's astonished face. H. Richter, *Dada: Art and Anti-Art*, p. 135.

13 Seliger, *Das Amerikabild Bertolt Brechts* (Bonn: Bouvier, 1974), p. 109 ff.

14 On the economic situation see I. Svennilson, *Growth and Stagnation in the European Economy* (U.N. Economic Committee for Europe, 1954).

15 Brecht, "Der Lernende ist wichtiger als die Lehre," GW 20:46.

16 E. Hauptmann, "Notes on Brecht's Work," *Brecht as They Knew Him* (New York: International, 1974), p. 53.

17 Brecht, "Der einzige Zuschauer für meine Stücke," GW 15:129.

18 F. Sternberg, Open letter to Brecht, *Berliner Börsen-Courier*, June 6, 1927, reprinted in F. Sternberg, *Der Dichter und die Ratio. Erinnerungen an Bertolt Brecht* (Goettingen: Sachsen und Pohl, 1963) p. 67.

19 *Ibid.*, p. 66.

20 E. Hauptmann, *loc. cit.*, p. 52.

21 Reprinted in Sternberg, *op. cit.*, pp. 58-64.

22 *Ibid.*, p. 61.

23 Brecht, "Sollten wir nicht die Ästhetik liquidieren?" GW 15:126.

24 *Ibid.*, p. 128.

25 Brecht, "Brief an Alfred Döblin," GW 18:64-65.

26 Brecht, "Materialwert," GW 15:105ff.

27 Brecht, "Wie soll man heute Klassiker spielen?" GW 15:112.

28 Brecht, "Das neue Theater und die neue Dramatik," GW 15:138-139.

29 Brecht, "Über eine neue Dramatik," GW 15:175.

30 Brecht, "(Notiz über das) Piscatortheater," GW 15:139.

31 This conversation is published in English only, in Manheim and Willett, eds., *Collected Plays*, I., p. 379ff.

32 Brecht, "Conversation with Grosz," in *Collected Plays*, I., p. 374.

33 *Ibid.*, p. 377.

34 Conversation with Piscator and Sternberg, *loc.cit.*, p. 379.

35 *Ibid.*, p. 382.

36 Brecht, "(Notizen über Individuum und Masse)," GW 20:60ff.

37 Brecht, "Über meinen Lehrer," GW 20:65-66.

38 Brecht, "Musterung der Motive junger Intellektuellen," GW 20:47.

39 *Ibid.*, p. 49.

40 Brecht, "Schwierige Lage der Deutschen Intellektuellen," tr. as "Intellectuals and Class Struggle," in *New German Critique* 1 (Winter 1974), p. 20.

41 Brecht, "Wozu braucht das Proletariat die Intellektuellen?" GW 20:54.

42 "Intellectuals and Class Struggle," *loc. cit.*

43 Brecht, "Über Freiheit," GW 20:56.

44 Brecht, *Die Maßnahme*, GW 2:631ff.

45 *Ibid.*, pp. 635-636.

46 *Ibid.*, p. 635.

47 See E.H. Carr, *Socialism in One Country 1924-1926* (2 vols.; New York: Macmillan, 1958-60) and R. Tucker, ed., *Stalinism: Essays in Historical Interpretation* (New York: Norton, 1977).

48 On Brecht and Korsch see: W.D. Rasch, "Bertolt Brechts marxistischer Lehrer," in Rasch, *Zur deutsche Literatur seit der Jahrhundertwende* (Stuttgart: Metzler, 1967), pp. 243-273; and K.D. Müller, "Brechts *Me Ti* und die Auseinandersetzung mit dem Lehrer Karl Korsch," *Brecht Jahrbuch 1977* (Frankfurt: Suhrkamp, 1977), pp. 9-29.

49 This is Adorno's move in the key essay, "Commitment," in *Aesthetics and Politics*, ed. R. Taylor, (Mondon: NLB, 1977), p. 187.

50 Brecht, *Die Maßnahme*, GW 2:638.

51 *Ibid.*, p. 652.

52 *Ibid.*, p. 661.

53 *Ibid.*, p. 657.

54 See M. Esslin, *Brecht: The Man and His Work* (Garden City: Anchor, 1971), p. 157 ff.

55 A. Kurella, "Ein Versuch mit nicht ganz tauglichen Mitteln," reprinted in *Zur Tradition*, p. 351.

56 E. Schumacher, *Die dramatischen Versuche Bertolt Brechts*, pp. 344ff.

57 See Biha, "Die Maßnahme," *Die Linkskurve* 3:1 (1931), pp. 12-14.

58 H. Gallas, *Marxistische Literaturtheorie* (Neuwied/Berlin: Luchterhand, 1974), p. 135 ff.

59 Brecht, *Die Beule. Ein Dreigroschenfilm*, in *Brechts Dreigroschenbuch* (Frankfurt: Suhrkamp, 1973), I., p. 102.

60 Brecht, *Der Dreigroschenprozeß*, GW 18:139ff.

61 *Ibid.*, pp. 153-154.

62 *Ibid.*, p. 204.

63 *Ibid,.* p. 201-202.

64 *Ibid.*, p. 204.

65 *Ibid.*, p. 181.

66 *Ibid.*, p. 201.

67 *Ibid.*, p. 158.

68 *Ibid.*, pp. 170-171.

69 *Ibid.*, p. 159.

70 *Ibid.*, p. 156.

71 *Ibid.*, p. 157.

72 *Ibid.*, p. 178.

73 *Ibid.*, p. 161.

74 *Ibid.*, p. 179.

75 *Ibid.*, pp. 171-172.

76 On Brecht's theory of *Umfunktionierung*, see esp. H. Brüggemann, *Literarische Technik und soziale Revolution: Versuche über das Verhältnis von Kunstproduktion, Marxismus und literarischer Tradition in den theoretischen Schriften Bertolt Brechts* (Reinbek: Rowohlt, 1973), esp. pp. 139-177.

77 The description is from W. Benjamin, "What is Epic Theater?" in *Illumina-tions* (New York: Schocken, 1969), p. 148.

78 B. Brecht, "To Posterity," *Poems 1913-1956* (London: Methuen, 1976), p. 319-320.

Epilogue

1 See his conversations with Benjamin, reproduced in the latter's *Under-standing Bertolt Brecht* (London: NLB, 1973).

2 On the Brecht-Lukacs conflict, see: K. Völker, "Brecht und Lukacs: Analy-se einer Meinungsverschiedenheit," *Kursbuch* 7 (Sept. 1966); W. Mitten-zwei, "Die Brecht-Lukacs Debatte," *Sinn und Form* 19:1 (Feb. 1967); J.-F. Anders & E. Klobusicky, "Vorschlag zur Interpretation der Brecht-Lukacs-Kontroverse," *Alternative* 15:84/85 (1972); L. Baier, "Streit um den Schwarzen Kasten: Zur sogenannten Brecht-Lukacs-Debatte," *Text und Kritik. Sonderband Bertolt Brecht I.* (Munich: Boorberg, 1972); F. Vassen, "Die Expressionismus-Realismus-Debatte: Georg Lukacs und Bertolt Brecht," in Vassen, *Methoden der Literaturwissenschaft II: Marxisti-sche Literaturtheorie und Literatursoziologie* (Düsseldorf: Bertelsmann, 1972); K. Berghahn, "'Volkstümlichkeit und Realismus': Nochmals zur Brecht-Lukacs Debatte," *Basis: Jahrbuch für deutsche Gegenwartsliteratur* 4 (1973); C. Fritsch & P. Rütten, "Anmerkungen zur Brecht-Lukacs Debat-te," in *Rhetorik, Aesthetik, Ideologie: Aspekte einer kritischen Kulturwis-senschaft* (Stuttgart: Metzler, 1973); E. Lunn, "Marxism and Art in the Era of Stalin and Hitler: A Comparison of Brecht and Lukacs," *New Ger-man Critique* 3 (Fall 1974); D. Löffler, "Politische Anschauungen und ästhe-tische Theoriebildung in der Brecht-Lukacs-Kontroverse," *Bertolt Brecht Ta-gung. Acta Universitatis Wratislavensis* No. 266. *Germanica Wratislaviensia* XXII (1975).

3 On the Brecht-Benjamin connection see: B. Witte, "Krise und Kritik: Zur Zusammenarbeit Benjamins mit Brecht in den Jahren 1929 bis 1933," in Witte, et. al., *Walter Benjamin: Zeitgenosse der Moderne* (Kronberg/Ts: Scriptor, 1976), pp. 9-36; P. Mayer, "Die Wahrheit ist konkret. Notizen zu Benjamin und Brecht," *Text und Kritik. Sonderband Bertolt Brecht I.* (1972); B. Lindner, "Brecht/Benjamin/Adorno – Über Veränderungen der Kunstproduktion im wissenschaftlich-technischen Zeitalter," in *ibid.*; D. Thiele, "Brecht als Tui oder Der Autor als Produzent?" in H. Claes & W. Haug, eds., *Brechts Tui Kritik* (Karlsruhe: Argument Vlg., 1976).

4 S. Buck-Morss, *The Origin of Negative Dialectics*, passim and M. Jay, *The Dialectical Imagination*, pp. 177 ff, for Benjamin's influence on Adorno. See also F. Jameson, *Marxism and Form* (Princeton: Princeton U. Press, 1971), pp. 1-83; also see: "Presentation of Adorno-Benjamin," *New Left Review* 81 (Sept./Oct. 1973), pp. 46-80.

5   On Sholem's view of Brecht's "baleful" and even "disastrous" influence on Benjamin, see his Leo Bäck Memorial Lecture, 1965. The word "baleful" recurs in M. Jay's representation of Adorno's view of Brecht's influence on Benjamin, *op. cit.*, p. 201.

6   On Benjamin see esp.: J. Habermas, "Consciousness-Raising or Redemptive Criticism – The Contemporaneity of Walter Benjamin," *New German Critique* 17 (Spring 1979); B. Witte, *Walter Benjamin: Der Intellektuelle als Kritiker* (Stuttgart: Metzler, 1976). See also: R. Tiedemann, *Studien zur Philosophie Walter Benjamins* (Frankfurt: Suhrkamp, 1965); P. Unger, *Walter Benjamin als Rezensent* (Frankfurt: Lang, 1978); H. Arendt, "Introduction" to Benjamin, *Illuminations*, pp. 1-55; P. Gruchot, "Konstruktive Sabotage: Walter Benjamin und der bürgerliche Intellektuelle," *Alternative* 10:56/57 (Oct./Dec., 1967).

7   W. Benjamin, "Some Reflections on Kafka," in *Illuminations*, p. 141.

8   M. Jay, *op. cit.*, p. 339.

9   W. Benjamin, "Epistemo-Critical Prologue," in *The Origin of German Tragic Drama* (London: NLB, 1977), pp. 27-53; "Theses on the Philosophy of History," in *Illuminations*, pp. 253-264; and "On Language as Such and On the Language of Man," in *Reflections* (New York: Harcourt, Brace, Jovanovich, 1978), pp. 314-332.

10 The various schools of modernistic criticism referred to include the so-called "Yale School" of de Man, Bloom *et. al.* as well as their French sources – Derrida and Foucault. For an introduction, see F. Jameson, *The Prison-House of Language* (Princeton: Princeton U. Press, 1972) and H. Bloom, P. de Man, *et. al.*, *Deconstruction and Criticism* (New York: Seabury, 1979).

11 B. Witte, *Walter Benjamin: Der Intellektuelle als Kritiker*, p. xi.

12 W. Benjamin, cited in Habermas, *loc. cit.*, p. 36. See also the lengthy citation to the same effect from Benjamin's essay on Goethe's *Elective Affinities* in H. Arendt's "Introduction" to *Illuminations*, pp. 4-5.

13 Habermas, *loc. cit.*, p. 37.

14 On Benjamin's notion of the critic as intellectual, see esp. B. Witte, *op. cit.*; P. Gruchot, *loc. cit.*, and P. Unger, *op. cit.* Each of these scholars uses the notion as the primary organizing concept of his interpretation of Benjamin.

15 H. Friedrich, *The Structure of Modern Poetry* (Evanston, Ill.: Northwestern u. Press, 1974).

16 M. Raymond, *From Baudelaire to Surrealism* (New York: Wittenborn, 1950).

17 W. Benjamin, "Surrealism: The Last Snapshot of the European Intelligentsia," reprinted in *Reflections*, pp. 177-192.

18 *Ibid.*, p. 185.

19 W. Benjamin, "The Work of Art in the Age of Mechanical Reproduction," in *Illuminations*, pp. 223-224.

20 W. Benjamin, "The Author as Producer," in *Understanding Bertolt Brecht*, p. 89.

21 S. Kracauer, "Kult der Zerstreuung," *Das Ornament der Masse.*

22 See above, Ch. 4 note 55.
23 W. Benjamin, "The Work of Art...," pp. 223-225.
24 *Ibid.*, p. 224.
25 S. Buck-Morss, *op. cit.*, p. 22, cites a Benjamin letter to M. Rychner written in 1931 which professed this belief.
26 B. Witte, "Benjamin and Lukacs: Historical Notes on the Relationship Between their Political and Aesthetic Theories," *New German Critique* 5 (Spring 1972).
27 Habermas, *loc. cit.*, p. 56.
28 W. Benjamin, "Gebrauchslyrik? Aber nicht so!" reprinted in *Gesammelte Schriften* III:1, pp. 183-184.
29 W. Benjamin, "Krisis des Romans. Zu Döblins 'Berlin Alexanderplatz,'" in *ibid.*, pp. 230-236.
30 W. Benjamin, "Gebrauchslyrik? ...," p. 184.
31 See above, Ch. 3 and see W. Haas's autobiography, *Die literarische Welt* (Munich: List, 1960).
32 W. Benjamin, "Linke Melancholie," *Gesammelte Schriften* III:1, pp. 280-282.
33 W. Benjamin, "The Author as Producer," *loc. cit.*, p. 91.
34 *Ibid.*, p. 93.
35 W. Benjamin, "Politisierung der Intelligenz," in S. Kracauer, *Die Angestellten*, p. 122.
36 B. Witte, "Krise und Kritik," *loc. cit.*, p. 23-24.
37 W. Benjamin, "Politisierung...," *loc. cit.*, p. 122.
38 W. Benjamin, "The Author as Producer," *loc. cit.*, p. 101.
39 *Ibid.*, p. 98.
40 See Ch. 3, esp. notes 56-57.
41 This has been stressed especially by Western interpreters of Brecht with regard to such later masterworks as *The Caucasian Chalk Circle, The Good Woman of Szechuan* and *Galileo*. See, e.g., F. Ewen, *Bertolt Brecht: His Life, His Art, His Times* (New York: Citadel, 1967); M. Esslin, *Brecht: The Man and his Work* (Garden City: Anchor, 1971); and J. Willett, *The Theater of Bertolt Brecht* (Norfolk, Conn: New Directions, 1959).
42 Döblin's alienation from Brecht and Piscator in the final moments of the Republic is connected with this Brechtian choice of Communism. He commented with his usual acidity on the new line Brecht had taken in a review of the Leipzig performance of Brecht's *Mahagonny* (March 1930); "The author is in fact a romantic of the old school, and real workers or even Marxists would laugh themselves sick over his play and his wild west fantasy...But what can the poor fellow do, he and all the other poor Henrys of the bourgeoisie? They need intellectual perspectives and if they have none of their own they steal what they can and thus place themselves in the proletarian forest, bawl along to the Internationale, and save themselves any personal reflection." *Alfred Döblin 1878-1978, Eine Ausstellung des Deut-*

schen Literaturarchivs im Schiller-Nationalmuseum Marbach am Neckar,
10. Juni bis 31. Dezember 1978 (Munich: Kösel Vlg., 1978), p. 287.

43 See esp. Adorno, *Negative Dialectics* (New York: Seabury, 1979).